D0848974

# THE MIND IN NATURE

## C. B. MARTIN

EMERITUS PROFESSOR OF PHILOSOPHY
THE UNIVERSITY OF CALGARY

# The Mind in Nature

C. B. MARTIN

EMERITUS PROFESSOR OF PHILOSOPHY
THE UNIVERSITY OF CALGARY

CLARENDON PRESS · OXFORD

# OXFORD
UNIVERSITY PRESS

Great Clarendon Street, Oxford OX2 6DP

Oxford University Press is a department of the University of Oxford.
It furthers the University's objective of excellence in research, scholarship,
and education by publishing worldwide in

Oxford New York

Auckland Cape Town Dar es Salaam Hong Kong Karachi
Kuala Lumpur Madrid Melbourne Mexico City Nairobi
New Delhi Shanghai Taipei Toronto

With offices in

Argentina Austria Brazil Chile Czech Republic France Greece
Guatemala Hungary Italy Japan Poland Portugal Singapore
South Korea Switzerland Thailand Turkey Ukraine Vietnam

Oxford is a registered trade mark of Oxford University Press
in the UK and in certain other countries

Published in the United States
by Oxford University Press Inc., New York

British Library Cataloguing in Publication Data
Data available

Library of Congress Cataloging in Publication Data
Data available

Typeset by Laserwords Private Limited, Chennai, India
Printed in Great Britain
on acid-free paper by
Biddles Ltd., King's Lynn, Norfolk

ISBN 978–0–19–923410–3

1 3 5 7 9 10 8 6 4 2

For Olga Borysuk Martin, the love of my life and my best friend, for her patience and support for a myopic author

# Acknowledgments

To my colleagues and students on three continents and over fifty years' teaching and learning.

To John Locke and C. D. Broad for their inspiration, and to Wittgenstein, with the proviso that whatever he said needed, for truth's sake, to be negated, turned upside down and inside out.

Portions of Chapter 2 originally appeared as 'Dispositions and Conditionals' (*The Philosophical Quarterly* 44: 1–8). Parts of Chapter 3 are borrowed from 'On Lewis and Then Some' (*Logic et Analyse* 169–70: 43–8). Much of Chapter 6 appeared as 'On the Need for Properties: The Road to Pythagoreanism and Back' (*Synthese* 112: 193–231). A version of Chapter 8 was originally published as 'Proto-Language' (*Australasian Journal of Philosophy* 65: 277–89). I am grateful to these journals and their editors for permission to use this material here.

I have great indebtedness to John Heil for his formidable editorial work when I fell on my face from a stroke, and to Zachary Hoskins for additional high-level editorial assistance.

Kevin Sauvé and Dan Ryder discussed drafts of much of what appears in the volume and were invaluable resources on topics in neuroscience.

Most of all to my wondrous wife, Olga Borysuk Martin for, so often, truths about human emotion, including the too-brief-lived feel of even the negative ones.

# Short Contents

*Preface*                                                                    xv

1  Introduction                                                              1

2  Dispositions and conditionals                                           12

3  Truthmakers and disposition lines: From quark to
   colleague                                                               24

4  Parts and wholes                                                        35

5  Causality                                                               46

6  The road to Pythagoreanism and back                                     54

7  Linguisticism and Pythagoreanism                                        80

8  Protolanguage                                                           93

9  Use, representational use, and content                                 111

10  Emergence, reduction, mental chauvanism                               129

11  Dispositional systems                                                  140

12  Two jokes explained                                                    158

13  Tactile-motor-kinaesthetic perception                                  162

14  Verbal imagery                                                         166

15  Mind in nature: A new view of the mind                                 177

16  Warps and woofs of Einstein                                            194

*References*                                                               199
*Index*                                                                    207
*Index of Names*                                                           216
*Index of Topics*                                                          218

# Contents

*Preface*   xv

## 1. Introduction   1

1.1 Basic ontology   1
1.2 The role of dispositionality   1
1.3 Systemic nonmental use   6
1.4 What makes a system mental?   7
1.5 Perception and imagery   8

## 2. Dispositions and conditionals   12

2.1 Dispositions are not relations   12
2.2 Conditional analyses of dispositions   13
2.3 The inadequacy of the conditional account   15
2.4 *Ceteris paribus* salvation?   16
2.5 Pure chance   18
2.6 Diagnosing the problem   18
2.7 Lewis's response   19
2.8 Counterfactual facts   21

## 3. Truthmakers and disposition lines: From quark to colleague   24

3.1 Truthmaking   24
3.2 Truth and possible worlds   25
3.3 On David Lewis   26
3.4 Polemics: Against possible worlds as truthmakers   26
3.5 More polemics: Against the possible world account of propositions   28
3.6 An alternative to possible worlds   29
3.7 How to suffer a contradiction   33

**4. Parts and wholes**                                          35

   4.1 'Top-down' and 'bottom-up' causation             35
   4.2 The compositional model                           36
   4.3 Composition and identity                          38
   4.4 Roots of the compositional model                  39
   4.5 Physics and the manifest image                    40
   4.6 From physics to ontology                          42

**5. Causality**                                                46

   5.1 Inadequacies of the two-event model               46
   5.2 Disposition lines and fundamental physics         47
   5.3 Causation as mutual manifestation                 48
   5.4 Gradualism again                                  51
   5.5 From nonmental to mental                          52

**6. The road to Pythagoreanism and back**                      54

   6.1 Dispositionality more basic than causality       54
   6.2 Dispositional depth and breadth                   56
   6.3 Non-existent and prohibitive dispositions         58
   6.4 Nonmental dispositions                            59
   6.5 Properties as purely dispositional                61
   6.6 Dispositionality and qualitativity                63
   6.7 Surprising identities                             67
   6.8 Dispositions and quantum theory                   69
   6.9 Indeterminacy and disposition flutters           72
   6.10 Pythagoreanism                                   73
   6.11 Back from the brink                              76
   6.12 Neurological Pythagoreanism                      78

**7. Linguisticism and Pythagoreanism**                         80

   7.1 The linguisticization of properties               80
   7.2 Tropes and universals                             81
   7.3 Classification and composition                    83
   7.4 Capacities and dispositions                       84
   7.5 Forms of infinity                                 88
   7.6 Distinguishing dispositionalities                 89
   7.7 The reciprocity of manifestations                 89
   7.8 Dispositionality of manifestations                91

## 8. Protolanguage                                              93

  8.1 Prelinguistic semantics                          93
  8.2 Linguistic–nonlinguistic parallels               94
  8.3 Truth and falsehood                               98
  8.4 Representational use                              99
  8.5 Bennett on iconic and noniconic vehicles of
      meaning                        101
  8.6 Social and private                                103
  8.7 Higher–order procedures                           104
  8.8 Further parallels                                 106
  8.9 Walking the walk—prior to talking the talk        109

## 9. Use, representational use, and content                     111

  9.1 Mental and nonmental use                          111
  9.2 Representational use in nonmental systems         116
  9.3 The abstract model                                117
  9.4 The working model                                 119
  9.5 The vegetative mind                               123

## 10. Emergence, reduction, mental chauvinism                   129

  10.1 Emergence                                        129
  10.2 Reduction                                        132
  10.3 Qualities and function                           134
  10.4 Vegetative control centers                       136
  10.5 Mental chauvinism                                138

## 11. Dispositional systems                                     140

  11.1 Dispositions: A recapitulation                   140
  11.2 Acquiring a further disposition                  141
  11.3 Perception as dispositional                      143
  11.4 Nonmental systems                                146
  11.5 Fodor's challenge                                148
  11.6 Rules and dispositions                           153
  11.7 A disposition for addition                       155
  11.8 Readiness for algorithmic computation            156

**12. Two jokes explained**                                    158

   12.1 Experiences and the private world problem          158
   12.2 The analogical way of thinking about other minds     159
   12.3 Introspective errors                                 160

**13. Tactile-motor-kinaesthetic perception**                  162

   13.1 Hallucination, illusion, and after-images           162
   13.2 Tactile-motor-kinaesthetic perceiving                163
   13.3 Feeling and feeling back                            164

**14. Verbal imagery**                                          166

   14.1 Kinds of imagery                                     166
   14.2 The physiology of imagery                            168
   14.3 Partial verbal imagery                               170
   14.4 Cue manifestations                                   171
   14.5 Imagery or tacit knowledge?                          173
   14.6 Nonverbal imagery                                    174

**15. Mind in nature: A new view of the mind**                 177

   15.1 From nonmental to mental                             177
   15.2 Dispositions and dispositionality                    181
   15.3 Propositions                                         183
   15.4 Bounds of sense                                      184
   15.5 Introspective privilege                              188
   15.6 Sensate materials                                    189
   15.7 Using sensate materials                              191

**16. Warps and woofs of Einstein**                            194

   16.1 Objects                                             194
   16.2 The argument                                        195
   16.3 The rule                                            196

*References*                                                   199
*Index*                                                        207
*Index of Names*                                               216
*Index of Topics*                                              218

# Preface

*The Mind in Nature* has three foci. First, and most importantly, I defend a *basic ontology*. The ontology includes a realism of dispositions—'causal powers'—and a rejection of attempts to reduce dispositions to conditionals. I respond to criticisms, especially to three objections raised by David Lewis. I take the first steps toward a disposition-based account of causality, and defend a truthmaker principle: 'true' and 'false' designate relations between truth or falsity *bearers* and truth or falsity *makers*. Appeal to propositions is carefully avoided.

My account of dispositions and causality is intended to apply even to unstructured elementary particles, or superstrings (which themselves have many properties), or whatever turns out to be the ultimate basis for the world around us. This account could help with the problem of relating general relativity and quantum physics, a topic to which I turn in Chapter 16.

Wholes, I argue, are nothing over and above the organization of their parts in *all* of their interrelations and inter-reactions with one another and with whatever might exist externally to them.

A sensible ontology equips us to tackle problems in the philosophy of mind, especially problems concerning the status of intentionality and the nature of conscious states, that have long eluded solution.

A second focus centres around the 'vegetative mind.' I discuss, in some detail, *nonconscious*, *nonmental* systems within our bodies. I leave it to the reader to use this material against those who, in characterizing the conscious mind, do so in terms of functions that occur quite naturally in *non*conscious systems. Some will see the implications for mainstream philosophy of mind. Others might need to have them pointed out, perhaps by daring students.

Vegetative systems are wonderful! The hypothalamus includes detailed maps of the inner core (the organs) and of the entire surface of the skin. The hypothalamus deploys representations of spatially and temporally distal states of the environment within the body but external to the hypothalamus. These function as anticipatory for the future and as retention for the past. The hypothalamus can represent another representation, sending a copy of a 'map' indicating where an input is to be expected to come from and its output to go, all of this to the motor system. In so functioning, the hypothalamus makes use of negative and positive feedback and feedforward.

The book's third focus is on conscious systems. The conscious system is marked by the inner life of percept and percept-like dreamings and imaginings. Those who emphasize behaviour fail to notice that behaviour is relevant to the mental only if is accompanied by *sensory* feedback: the sensate and percept again. There is a fight to get experience counted.

In Chapter 12, 'Two jokes explained,' the skeptical use of experience is examined. In Chapter 13, 'Tactile-motor-kinaesthetic perception,' I argue that this is in fact perception against some philosophers and psychologists who would deny it.

# I

# Introduction

## 1.1 BASIC ONTOLOGY

In the pages that follow, I offer an argument in support of a realism of properties and against an operationalist account and a tendency (more frequent and not regularly noticed) toward Pythagoreanism that may spring from the solely quantitative emphasis common in interpretations of scientific theory.

In Chapter 4, I provide a compositional model for parts and wholes that involves no reference to supervenience embellishments. This affords a background for a discussion of reduction and emergence. I argue against conditional reductions of dispositions, thus opening the way for a realist conception of dispositionality. I provide, as well, an account of dispositionalities and qualities that explains the necessities between them. This has been a worry since it was first called to our attention by Locke.

The model I provide is put forward against the need for abstract entities or the numerically-identical-universal-entity-fully-in-each-of-many-spatially-temporally-distinct-instance-entities (D. M. Armstrong), or possible, that is, alternative-to-ours worlds (David Lewis) and in favor of reference only to the nonabstract actual world in dealing with counterfactuals and negative existentials.

Space—time is a bearer of properties; it is not itself borne as a property. Thus it makes no sense in ontology or modern physics to think of space—time as empty and propertyless. Obviously, space—time fulfills the conditions of a substratum.

## 1.2 THE ROLE OF DISPOSITIONALITY

A particular disposition exists or it does not. You could say of any *unmanifesting* disposition that it straight-out exists, even if it is not, at that time or at any other time, manifesting any manifestation. It is the *unmanifested* manifestation, not the disposition itself, that is the would-be-if or would-have-been-if, if anything is. There can be a disposition *A* for the manifestation of acquiring a *further* disposition *B* and, of course, disposition *B* need not itself have any manifestation, but disposition *B* can still be the unfulfilled terminus of that for which *A* has a specific directedness. This is what is 'propositional' about even unmanifested dispositions. Arguments against conditional analyses of dispositions and the states of counterfactuals will be provided in Chapter 2.

In elementary particle, field, or superstring theory, a fundamental particle, field segment, or string will *not* have structure but *will* have multiple intrinsic properties. Even an unstructured quark has many actual readinesses for many nonactual manifestations. This must be so because some manifestations exclude other manifestations from happening at the same time. The readiness of a quark for certain kinds of manifestings with certain kinds of interrelations and interreactivities of quarks and leptons constituting a golden-horned unicorn could fully exist (namely the particular readiness of the quark) even though nothing like a golden-horned unicorn ever existed. The quark actually *has* the readiness for it—it is *ready to go*.

Getting the cart in the right position *behind* the horse, we can begin to see that just as dispositions can exist without their manifestations, so a disposition could exist without the manifestation that would be the relevant 'cause–effect.' Yet a 'cause–effect' cannot exist without the relevant dispositions for which it is a set of manifestations. This suggests that dispositions and manifestations are basic to, and can explain, 'cause–effect' (see Chapter 5).

It is self-defeating to try to explain dispositionality in terms of structural states because structural states are themselves dispositional; the search for a purely qualitative, nondispositional property, structural or nonstructural, is doomed to failure.

Here are three important ways of categorizing properties with their qualities and dispositions:

(1) *Interconnectedness* of the qualities and dispositionalities of properties in which
   (a) simpler properties are constitutive of a more complex property, e.g. four-sided plus equal-sided are constitutive of squareness;

    (b) distinct properties related (at least at first appearance) contingently and nomologically, e.g. freezing of water and expansion of water;

    (c) distinct properties related necessarily, e.g. equilateral and equiangular.

(2) *Reciprocity* between the dispositionalities of the properties of different things or parts of things with their reciprocal disposition partners for a mutual manifestation that is their common product, e.g. the soluble salt and the solvent water for salt in solution in the water.

The reciprocities of these dispositionalities for their mutual manifestations are many, deep and complex. The important point is that for a specific mutual manifestation, any particular dispositional state is itself only one among many other dispositional states that together form reciprocal disposition partners for their particular mutual manifestation.

(3) *Correlativeness* of disposition-manifestation takes four forms:

    (a) The correlativity lies in a dispositionality to be for certain manifestations *rather* than others and to be a particular manifestation it has to be *from* a particular dispositional state. For something to be a dispositional state it must be *for* different alternative typifying mutual manifestations with different alternative reciprocal disposition partners. Any partner is co-equal with the others for their mutual manifestation. Nature comes in package deals.

    (b) In coming to a new account of cause–effect, one should put the matter in the active voice in terms of the manifestings of the manifestations of the disposition in its reciprocatings with its reciprocal disposition partners as active partnerings with mutual manifestings. *That* is cause–effect redesigned and improved. It shows the contemporaneity of cause–effect. Further discussion will be provided in Chapter 5.

A particular dispositional state with its particular set of disposition partners *for* a particular set of manifestations with *different* sets of disposition partners (that may be infinite) will *not* be for or may even be *prohibitive* against manifesting an infinite number of manifestations. This is the basic ontology for the range of directedness and selectedness of dispositionality and for setting the *limits* of the infinities of directiveness and selectiveness of dispositions. This is the case whether the entities or states are psychological or nonpsychological, or even whether they are structural and systemic or nonstructural and nonsystemic (e.g. elementary particles or elementary aspects of fields or strings or whatever might be judged 'elementary' if and when physics itself becomes determinate in what it decides).

(c) When a dispositional state is structural or systemic, a manifestation is what it is only as *from* a deep enough and broad enough disposition base array, and a disposition base array is what it is only as for certain kinds of manifestation with certain kinds of alternative conditions or disposition partners. A manifestation is the tip of a disposition iceberg.

(d) Dispositionalities *must* outrun manifestations, for dispositionalities can be for *alternative* mutual manifestations whose alternative disposition partners mutually exclude the concurrence of those mutual manifestations. A piece of gold is capable of being melted at a certain temperature and capable of being dissolved in *aqua regia*, but both together cannot be manifested even though the directedness and selectedness of the disposition *for* the unmanifested manifestations are fully actual despite the nonactuality of those manifestations together.

This directedness and selectiveness even to what is absent or non-existent (as with a substance that is soluble in a solvent that does not exist in nature and only a shortage of funds blocks its manufacture) is intrinsic to the dispositionality of the properties of all entities, nonmental as well as mental, submicroscopic as well as macroscopic. This 'what for' of dispositionality has a parallel directed selectivity to the 'what *about*' of the semantic (see Martin and Pfeifer 1986).

It should help to see that even in the simplest form of directedness or readiness, through the dispositionality of the simplest *non*mental property of the simplest *non*psychological entity, the directedness can be internalist and narrow. Projectability to any-of-a-kind-that-may-come-along that is F-like is satisfied *within* the entity itself by its dispositional states and obviously does not require that the dispositional states *themselves* have anything F-like as their 'typical cause.' Indeed, nothing F-like may even exist. This directedness or readiness is intrinsic to nonmental as well as mental dispositions, and clearly it is 'narrow,' that is, it goes from inside-to-outside (Martin in Armstrong, Martin, and Place 1996: 188).

It would be outlandish to go against nature *itself* and to deprive the directedness of mental dispositions of such a *natural* narrow (inside-to-outside) function. An externalist account is also readily available for the directedness of a dispositional state toward an *individual* rather than just to anything similar in kind. For a dispositional state of *y* to be for individual *x* and not just anything of the same kind, the individual *x* must be in a causal network in which it is the *only* thing of the kind *x* that can serve as a manifestation condition or reciprocal disposition partner with the dispositional state of *y* for its manifestation. A directedness to an individual *x* is dependent upon a direct or a proximate causal hookup to a particular *x*.[1]

There is a sense in which the dispositionality, even of any property of a quark, is for more than could ever be manifested, because on any occasion some forms of manifestation conditions or reciprocal disposition partners are lacking and can even *exclude* one another. The totality of this infinity of *alternative* manifestations is unachievable, and this is a necessary fact of nature. Although the *actual* dispositionality is infinite in its directedness, it is likely that the infinite manifestations *for* which it is disposed have realizations that are partial and finite in number. This will be discussed in Chapter 3.

Dispositions or capacities, with their reciprocal disposition partners (an explanation of this terminology is included in Chapter 3) exist embodying programs for, *not* for, and even prohibitive against an infinity of mutual manifestations under a limited scope. This account of dispositions as directive, selective readinesses with the correlativeness of disposition and manifestation is such that the *manifestation* 'carries' the richness of the disposition base it is *from* or *of*.

It is *natural* that so little can carry so much. As a manifestation of a particular disposition base, its nature is determined by what it is *from*, namely that disposition base with infinite richness or readinesses not just for future manifestations, but more importantly, being at the time of its manifestation disposed for an infinity of actual or nonactual *alternative* mutual manifestations with *alternative* conditions.

This is all within the scope of the limits set by what it is *not* disposed for and what it is disposed to *prohibit*, that is, the actual readinesses with alternative reciprocal disposition partners for prohibitive

---

[1] Cf. Daniel Dennett's (1981) case of a thermostat and its furnace.

manifestations. *Every* disposition is, in this way, a holistic web, but not just an amorphous spread of potency. The readiness of something's disposition for all of this may fully exist although its disposition partners and mutual manifestations do not. As such, dispositions are not relations. A disposition can exist although its manifestation, or even its reciprocal disposition partners, do not. Salt in a world lacking $H_2O$ would have many of its readinesses unfulfilled. Among the non-actual reciprocal disposition partners for which it would have actual readinesses would be ones that would be simple and very different or complex with a very different mix from those in our world. There could be a realist model for what we need for modality in this.

How far the richness of such a model, the domain of which covers the nonactual as well as the actual, can go towards explaining modalities (*contra* Saul Kripke) needs further examination. It has been shown (also *contra* Kripke) to be adequate for explaining our capacity for infinite rule following in logic and mathematics (see Martin and Heil 1998 and Chapter 11, below).

What appears to be peculiar to the mental case is the capacity to be directed to an *individual x* rather than any other that may be qualitatively similar even when that individual is not in the immediate environment. One needs an account of how such an 'indirect' but still 'unique' directedness is achieved. In §1.4 I sketch an account of this in terms of the need for something for representational use for what is absent or nonexistent. The natural material for such use is imagery that is itself *independent* of stimuli from the immediate physical environment.


## 1.3 SYSTEMIC NONMENTAL USE

Although there is richness even in simple nonmental dispositionality, we find a far greater degree of richness in the *uses* of input and output of complex, nonmental dispositional systems such as vegetative autonomic systems within our own bodies.

The ongoing attempt to clarify and elaborate such very basic concepts as dispositionality and use is of help in discovering a remarkable number of parallel functions in vegetative nonconscious autonomic systems and the conscious systems of the cerebral cortex that had been mistakenly thought to be unique to the conscious cortex.

If directedness and selectiveness (even to what is absent or nonexistent) and integrative, regulatory, adjustive, adaptive (individual-specific and not just species-general), combinatorial, feedforward reactivenesses to (uses of) input are found in vegetative, nonmental integrative control centres such as the hypothalamus and *nucleus tractus solitarii* (that are far more 'clever' than most computers thus far envisioned), then it would be a mistake to ask for all this over *again* at the mental cortex level as if it had not *already* been found. Mother Nature, in her nonmental bounty, provides all this 'for free' to the mind. It can only add confusion to ask twice over for what is already given.

Appreciating this should give us a clearer vision for finding what *further* is needed for directedness and selectiveness to count as mental and for the use of input to constitute *mental* agency. What functions are *unique* to the conscious cortex? An answer to that question will be attempted later in this volume. Meanwhile, some of these answers can be provided in general terms without all of the background work that will be done later.

## 1.4 WHAT MAKES A SYSTEM MENTAL?

The following are functions that seem not to be found in vegetative systems and are apparently unique to the conscious cortex:

(1) The system's continuous capacity in wakefulness and some dreaming, for self-cueing or self-assessments of its own capacity states *without* trial or *preparation for performance* (vegetative systems are power-driven for *performance*). *These cue manifestations* (as opposed to typifying manifestations) *are essential for the economy required for higher cognitive function.*

(2) The capacity for centrally caused 'internal' signals (dreaming, hallucinating, imaging) *qualitatively similar* to 'external' signals (perceptions) produced by external stimuli from the immediate physical environment. Internal signals are primarily for use *within* the central system that produced them and not primarily for use within efferent-afferent feedback loops with the sensory receptors. This is essential for the use of internally caused input (imagery), independent of stimuli from the immediate environment, needed for reflective thinking.

A detailed characterization of these functions, making use of research in neuropsychology and developmental psychology will (with a minimum of gestures to the innate) help to provide a gradualist model for mental and cognitive development.

There is sometimes a comic drive to the verbal from academics. Developmental psychologists occasionally stress how the very young infant is attracted to the mother's voice, and so they suggest an 'innate bias' to vocalizations! But the sound of the mother's voice is one of the most *familiar* sensory inputs, because the infant has heard that sound for some months while in the womb.

Beliefs and desires are not to be thought of as primitives wearing intensionalistic halos, but are to be understood to involve dispositional state arrays, the nature of which is to be explained in terms of what such arrays are dispositions *for*: namely, those typifying appropriate *manifestations* that are the various modes of use of various forms of sensory input, sensory feedback, and sensory-like imagery. If behaviour is manifested, it must be *via sensory* feedback. What would make us knowing must first make us *sensate*. Representationalism gets the order as well as the contents wrong.

## 1.5 PERCEPTION AND IMAGERY

At the start of any discussion of imagery as perception-like, it is necessary to see what a strange thing even *normal* perception is. We can (a) be aware of our perceivings and unaware of what we are perceiving, or (b) be unaware of our perceivings and aware of what we are perceiving, or (c) be unaware of our perceivings and unaware of what we are perceiving. Perceptions can be partial (e.g. a dominance of processing in the motion area of the primary visual cortex over the form and colour areas) and they can be fleeting and kaleidoscopic.

We have 'visual detection without sensory awareness' with peripheral vision. We have 'nonpropositional perception.' An infant in the womb hears noises without hearing *that* something is the case, and, often enough, so do adults. Our visual field is often kaleidoscopic. Just *try* to keep track of the number of different colours that you see at any given time.

We rely on peripheral vision without being aware of it, for example, to keep us from the edge of the cliff without thinking. This is parallel to a particular kind of perception-like use of nonvivid and partial imagery to keep an emotion felt without thinking. The case of using fully vivid and focused vision in scrutinizing a face or complex scene would be another parallel to a kind of perception-like vivid imagery used in the 'sounding' of a symphony you are composing in your head. A detailed account of introspection will exhibit its credentials as a way of succeeding and also as a way of failing to know.

We should see these uses of imagistic fragments as we should see the using of *anything*, whether word, object, or sensation, as the manifestation tip of a disposition iceberg for alternative use-manifestations of alternative imagistic or other input. It is this disposition-base, ready for its reciprocal disposition partners, that gives the actual using its richness and specificity.

In Chapter 9, I sketch an account of how a system could be directive and selective for an *individual* (rather than any other that may be qualitatively similar) when it is not in the immediate environment. The account will make essential use of imagery.

Neuropsychologists and neurophysiologists—including Lawrence Weiskrantz, Daniel Reisberg, Anthony Marcel, Rodolfo Llinás, Eduardo Bisiach, and Aristopolous Georgopolous—have called attention to the role of centrally caused internal signals (in dreaming, working imaging, memory-reliving imaging, and partial hallucinatory illusion and full hallucination) by means of observations through properly cautious and circumspect employment of revolutionary improvements in brain scanning and measurement techniques. We are ready to see the central importance of the existence of *unbehaved* purposive activities and begin the task of characterizing their use and the neurological basis of the inner life of the mind.

Following through from the depiction of the role of dreaming as central for a neurological modeling of the conscious brain by Llinás and Paré (1992), we can direct our attention to cases of lucid dreaming and also to the relatively vivid hypnagogic imagery (occurring *before* sleep) and hypnopompic imagery (occurring *after* waking), and to the much less vivid but more common partial, fragmentary, and fleeting imagery that is idiosyncratically 'rule-governed' and meaningful in its use by the agent (Bisiach 1988). Our use of this multimodal imagery can be *nonlinguistic* and *prelinguistic* or linguistic. As in *verbal* imagery, it is the use of auditory and tactile motor-kinaesthetic sensory-like imagery, similar to perceiving of utterings by oneself or others. Use of imagery is inventive, voluntary, unbehaved, unshared, and not necessarily meant as preparation for communication. It is a form of inner activity, even in its nonlinguistic form, that can be *independent* of stimuli from the immediate physical environment. With that recognition, we can begin to see the crucial importance for early and continuing development of not just motor activity itself, but also the procedural, mostly unshared and not behaved but rule-governed projective *uses* of imagery in all sense modalities—visual, tactile, motor-kinaesthetic, auditory, gustatory, and olfactory.

The voluntary, creative, and rule-governed uses of auditory imagery in composing a musical composition in your head or the multimodal imagistic projectivities involved in going over in your head different textures, aromas, and tastes of ingredients never put together before in the creation of a new recipe should be central cases rather than the mere occurrence of static or noncontrolled episodic imagery.

Neurophysiologists and neuropsychologists are breaking through residual quasi-behaviourist barriers, leaving many psychologists and philosophers behind. Private, unshared and not behaviourally enacted uses of percept, imagery, and dream are the very life of the mind and the *medium* of conscious mature thought, essential for any model of early mental development. If, for instance, imagery and dreaming are qualitatively similar to perceiving—so that you can mistake a stick in your path for a snake as you cannot mistake a tulip for a rainbow or a hippopotamus, then *just* as there can be hearing or seeing without hearing or seeing *as* or *that* something 'external,' so can there also be dreaming in various modalities without dreaming *as* or *that* something, and there can even be wakeful imagery that is not imagery *of* or *that* something external. The remarkable amount of REM in an infant in the womb and in the newly born can be indicative of multimodal dreaming. This might be a good way of internally strengthening and initiating neural connections. Sensory-*like* deprivation (no dreaming or imagery), especially in the young, could be as destructive and inhibitory of development as is sensory deprivation itself.

This is ignored through the almost exclusive emphasis on 'de-learning' as the function of dreaming by Crick and Micheson (1983). They also ignore the usefulness of novel or even occasionally bizarre dream imagery or, indeed, wakeful daydream imagery of combinations of elements such that they set up connectivities for neuronal readinesses available for some unexpected conscious use. The brain is built for possible waste rather than a pared-down tidiness. The creative individual in any discipline should be aware of the more than occasional surprising usefulness of the wilder moments of the mind.

This emphasis on the inner life will be used to develop a physicalist, although not 'materialist,' account of the qualities of consciousness. Studies in neurophysiology and neuropsychology and even recent physics show some promising support for this general kind of model. The model should have considerable explanatory power.

# 2

# Dispositionals and Conditionals

## 2.1 DISPOSITIONS ARE NOT RELATIONS

A thing's dispositions can change. Dispositions have duration. A piece of glass can be fragile for an hour and cease to be fragile for an hour, the result of a change in temperature. Neither a disposition nor a change of disposition need manifest itself. The glass need not actually break during the hour that it is fragile.

Dispositions are actual, although their manifestations can fail to be. It is an elementary confusion to think of unmanifesting dispositions as unactualized *possibilia*, although that might serve to characterize unmanifested manifestations. As such, a disposition cannot be a relation to a manifestation.

If a piece of glass breaks, something has happened to it. If a piece of glass ceases to be fragile, something has happened to it. Saying that the glass broke is saying what actually happened to the glass in terms of how it is actually different from what it was. This actual change to the piece of glass could have come about in ways that are familiar to us or in ways that are only conceivable to us—by the impact of a stone or by the order of some divine agent. The divine agent orders, 'Let it break'; break it does, and no mistake. Is it quite the same when we say that the piece of glass ceases to be fragile? The glass ceases to be fragile at a particular time. Does this tell us what actually happened to the glass in terms of how it is actually different from what it was? Is

§§2.1–2.6 are taken from Martin (1994). Replies to critics begin in §2.7.The main idea of this chapter (set out in §2.1) originated at the University of Adelaide in 1957, was elaborated on at the University of Sydney in 1967, and, coaxed by friends, was cleaned up and published in 1994. I wish to thank J. J. C. Smart, D. M. Armstrong, and Wal Suchting for their critical comments, and George Molnar for his positive and subtle help and encouragement. Prior, Pargetter and Jackson (1982) consider a case put forward by A. D. Smith (1977) that differs importantly from the cases developed here, and the critique of Prior, Pargetter, and Jackson is irrelevant to my cases.

this an actual change to the piece of glass that could have come about in ways that are familiar to us or in ways that are only conceivable to us—by heating the glass or by order of some divine agent? The divine agent orders, 'Let it cease to be fragile'; cease to be fragile it becomes, and no mistake. *Why* is this odd?

The divine agent says: 'I shall make the glass cease to be fragile, but whenever anything happens to it that would make it break if it were fragile, I shall, with my foreknowledge of the future, *make* it fragile again. In this way, it will break whenever anything happens that breaks fragile glass, because it will *become* fragile on those occasions. At all other times, I shall make it cease to be fragile.' If I take the divine agent seriously, then, when I crate the piece of glass and attach the label reading, 'Fragile, handle with care,' I could cross out the word 'fragile' but retain the phrase 'handle with care.' This is absurd of me, but is the divine agent necessarily being absurd? Right after the words from on high are spoken, the glass melts. I throw a stone at it, and just before the impact the glass cools and solidifies and the stone breaks the glass. Then the glass melts again. How is this absurd? If it is not, then *how* is the dispositional state rendered by any conditional account?

## 2.2 CONDITIONAL ANALYSES OF DISPOSITIONS

Statements ascribing dispositions or powers are *somehow* linked to (strict or strong) conditional statements. Attempts have been made to provide reductive analyses of powers in terms of such stronger-than-material-conditionals, that is, to claim that the ascription to an object of a power or disposition is logically equivalent to one or more suitably glossed and qualified conditional statements about events involving the object.

The argument of this chapter will be, first, that the claimed equivalence does not hold if the conditional statement is formulated in a certain way, as demonstrated by two intuitive cases; and second, that this conclusion can be evaded by reformulating the conditional, but only at the cost of making the reformulation trivial.

Let it be claimed that

(a) The wire is *live*.

and

(b) If the wire is touched by a conductor, then electrical current flows from the wire to the conductor.

are so related that (a) is necessarily true if and only if (b) is true.

Consider now the following case. The wire referred to in (a) is connected to a machine—an *electro-fink*—that can provide itself with reliable information as to exactly when a wire connected to it is touched by a conductor. When such contact occurs, the electro-fink reacts (instantly, let us suppose) by making the wire live for the duration of the contact. In the absence of contact, the wire is dead. For example, at $t_1$ the wire is untouched by any conductor, at $t_2$ a conductor touches it, and at $t_3$ it is untouched again. The wire is dead at $t_1$, live at $t_2$, and dead again at $t_3$. In sum, the electro-fink ensures that the wire is live when and only when a conductor touches it.

First, consider a time when the wire is untouched by a conductor, $t_1$. *Ex hypothesi* the wire is not live at $t_1$, but the conditional (b) is true of the wire at $t_1$. In other words, it is true that if this wire is touched by a conductor at $t_1$, then electrical current flows from the wire to the conductor at $t_1$; but because the wire is not in fact being touched by a conductor at $t_1$, the wire is not live at $t_1$—thanks to the work of the electro-fink. Consequently, *the conditional is not logically sufficient for the power ascription of which it is meant to be the analysans.* (This point is brought out even more forcefully by considering the case in which the wire is never touched and consequently is always dead, yet the conditional in its counterfactual form is true: if the wire *were* to be touched, it *would* give off electricity!)

Second, consider a transition from a time when the wire is dead to a time when the wire is live (say, from $t_1$ to $t_2$). In the (unanalysed) language of causal powers, we can express the fact of this transition by saying that the wire acquires the power, or that it *becomes live*. The spirit of the conditional analysis would seem to require that our idea of an object's acquiring, or losing, a power be explicated as a conditionally structured predicate coming to apply, or ceasing to apply, to an object. This move, which works in general, breaks down in the present case: Although the wire becomes live at $t_2$, there is no conditionally structured predicate of the relevant sort that applies to it at $t_2$ that did not apply to it at $t_1$. That the wire has undergone a change in the transition from $t_1$ to $t_2$ seems sayable, yet the conditional analysis makes this unsayable.

We turn a switch on our electro-fink so as to make it operate on a reverse cycle, so the wire is dead when and only when a conductor touches it. At all other times it is live. At a time $t_4$, when the wire is untouched, the wire is live *ex hypothesi*, but the conditional is false of the wire at $t_4$: it is not the case that if a conductor touches the wire at $t_4$, then electrical current flows from the wire to the conductor. But because the wire is in fact not touched at $t_4$, it is live at $t_4$, thanks to the work of the electro-fink. Hence *the conditional is not logically necessary for the power ascription of which it is meant to be the analysans.* (The permanently untouched wire is always live, yet the conditional for it is false!) Because the machine is operating in its reverse cycle, the conditional analysis that in the transition from a time when the wire is untouched to a time when it is touched, the wire undergoes a change, viz. the change from being live to being dead, is likewise unsayable.

## 2.3 THE INADEQUACY OF THE CONDITIONAL ACCOUNT

Objects are capable of acquiring and losing (some) powers. A substance that is not malleable can become malleable, an object that is elastic can lose its elasticity, and so on. The conditional that is offered as the logical equivalent of the power ascription states that the activating conditions for the manifestation of a power are sufficient for the occurrence of the manifestation. According to the conditional analysis 'The wire is live,' if the wire is touched, then it gives off electricity. What ultimately defeats this analysis is the acknowledged possibility of objects gaining or losing powers. If it makes sense to say that the object $a$ has the power $P$ at one time and not at another (and it certainly makes sense to say this of some objects and some powers), then it should make sense to say both that $a$ has $P$ when and only when the activating conditions for the manifestation of $P$ obtain, and that $a$ lacks $P$ when and only when the activating conditions for the manifestation of $P$ obtain. Also, the correlation signified by 'when and only when' should be *determined* rather than *merely accidental*. The cases of the two cycles of the electro-fink are meant to illustrate just this possibility. These cases show the following:

(1) If the activating conditions for the manifestation of $P$ are also caus-ally necessary and sufficient for $a$'s having $P$, then the conditional

will be true of *a* while the ascription of *P* to *a* will be false, whenever those activating conditions do not obtain.

(2) If the activating conditions for the manifestation of *P* are also causally necessary and sufficient for *a*'s lacking *P*, then the ascription of *P* to *a* will be true and the conditional false of *a* whenever those activating conditions do not obtain.

At this point, it might be felt that all that this shows is that the electro-fink cases should not be admitted and that it is simply question-begging to suggest them as admissible cases. But, as M. C. Bradley once observed, 'All good philosophical arguments are either *ad hominem* or question-begging.' The point is that these cases are not *simply* question-begging. The change from live to dead is not revealed by visible changes in the wire. Take the case of a block of ice hitched up to a *moleculo-fink*. The block of ice is fragile, but if anything strikes it, the moleculo-fink instantaneously makes the ice nonfragile; that is, it melts the ice.

So if someone is starved for imagery, let that person consider cases in which the acquiring and losing of a power are typically associated with easily observable changes in the object.

## 2.4 *CETERIS PARIBUS* SALVATION?

The objection that the conditional *analysans* considered above is too simple might arise as a result of this argument against the reduction of powers. Nobody believes, or ought to believe, that manifestations of powers follow upon the single event mentioned in the antecedent of the conditional independently of the circumstances. Conditionals that give the sense of power ascriptions are always understood to carry a saving clause (the *full* details of which are *never* known). One should therefore say that (a) is logically equivalent, not to (b), but to

(b') If the wire is touched by a conductor *and other things are equal*, then electrical current flows from the wire to the conductor.[1]

The criticism of the claimed equivalence of (a) and (b) no longer applies to the claim that (a) is equivalent to (b'). Performances of the electro-fink are included *among* the other things that are required by

---

[1] The need for a saving clause was noted by Goodman (1965: 39).

the conditional analysis to remain equal. The wire that is dead at *t*, although electrical current would flow from it if it were touched at *t*, is not alive but *dead* on this amended conditional analysis. To be *live* at *t*, current would have to flow from the wire in the absence of any change in the relevant circumstances, apart from the touching of the wire by a conductor. This condition is not met in the first case described above. Again, the wire that is live at *t*, although current would not flow from it if it were touched at *t*, is *live* on the amended conditional analysis, not dead. To be dead at *t*, it would have to be the case that current does not flow from the wire if it is touched at *t and* no other relevant change occurs. This condition is not met in the second case described above. Hence, these cases fail to refute the claim that (a) and (b′) are equivalent.

To assess this objection, we should ask, 'What is it about the performances of our electro-fink that justifies including them among the circumstances *relevant* to the occurrence of this power's manifestation?' Perhaps the best way of approaching this question is to imagine that there are some other devices that *bring about the same effects* as the electro-fink. They too will have to be counted among the relevant 'other things.' To secure the equivalence of (a) and (b′), this set has to be the set of *all* such events. The principle of inclusion in the set is similarity of the effects produced by each of the member events. Similarity in what respect? The answer is that each of these events brings it about that it is not the case that the wire is live at a certain time. That is the *respect* in which events included in the set covered by the *ceteris paribus* clause resemble one another in their effects. An *understanding* of the principle of inclusion in the set is required for an understanding of the saving clause, which in turn has to be understood for (b′) to be taken as giving the sense of (a).

It is now possible to state what the objection establishes and what it fails to establish. We are required to understand (b′) in such a way that the clause 'other things are equal' covers the workings of the electro-fink as well as anything else that produces similar effects. So understood, however, (b′) cannot be employed in a reductive analysis of power ascriptions. What (b′) says (according to the way we must interpret it to secure its equivalence to (a)) is 'if the wire is touched by a conductor and *nothing happens to make it false that the wire is live*, and yet other things are equal, then electrical current flows from the wire to the conductor.'

What the objection shows is that there is a conditional equivalent to (a), viz. (b′), but one cannot *reduce* (a) to (b′), because (b′) has to be construed so as to require the intelligibility of (a) prior to any reduction. Without understanding (a), we do not know what to do with the *ceteris paribus* clause. By contrast, (b) does not have to be so construed. But (a) and (b) are not equivalent.

In conclusion, there can be no conditional that is both logically equivalent to a categorical power ascription *and* capable of supporting the elimination of power or dispositional predicates. If the reductive account of powers requires that there be such a condition—as many philosophers have thought it does—then that account is false.

## 2.5 PURE CHANCE

The clumsiness of counterfactuals as linguistic devices for indicating causal factors can be shown by considering how a strong conditional account would be given of an event E such that nothing whatsoever was causally operative for its happening. This would be a case of *pure* chance.

In such an account of pure chance, no necessary condition would be true for the happening of E. Everything of the strong counterfactual conditional form 'If C had not been the case, then E would not have been the case' would be false. This will hold whether C is the happening of something or the *non*-happening of something. As such, a causeless, *pure* chance event becomes, according to the strong conditional account, something that would have happened no matter what else had happened: the non-preventable, strongest natural necessity in the world! This is anti-intuitive.

## 2.6 DIAGNOSING THE PROBLEM

Rendering dispositional claims in terms of counterfactual claims depends on (a) providing an account of what needs to be the case for a counterfactual claim to be true, appropriate, or correct, and then (b) showing that the account is sufficient for dispositions. According to the argument presented here, there is no hope for the success of (b). This contention can be understood better by examining the obstacles to (a). It may help to ask some very simple questions.

How can *anything*—any property or state of affairs, any regularity or whatever actuality you like—be enough to make a counterfactual true, appropriate, or correct? How can what *is* bear upon what would-have-been-but-was-not-if-something-else-had-been-that-also-was-not? It would have to be *shown* how any honest first-order spatiotemporal occupant or regularities thereof could reach such realms of nonbeing. (David Lewis saw this far more clearly than most and suggested *many* first-order worlds to do the job; see Chapter 7.) For the rest, there might be covert refuge in second-order counterfactual *facts*. This is an appeal to the penumbral contrary-to-the-facts-fact-of-the-matter, that is, to pure counterfactuality halos.

On *this* basis, claims to *dispositionalities* as penumbral second-order nonlocalized *facts* ('Rylean dispositions') about something are no less mystery-mongering than are claims to counterfactualities.

If counterfactualities and dispositionalities (or counterfactual facts and dispositional facts) fail to suffice, and if, as we have seen, counterfactuality or strong conditionality cannot explain dispositions, then there is *no* place to turn except to actual first-order dispositions or powers. How could anything else be made to order by nature to do the job?

'Causal' counterfactuals have a place, of course, but only as clumsy and inexact linguistic gestures to dispositions, and they should be kept in that place.

## 2.7 LEWIS'S RESPONSE

In 'Finkish dispositions' (1997), David Lewis considers various emendations that are needed to make a conditional account of dispositions safe from finkishness. He settles for the following 'Reformed Conditional Analysis':

> (RCA) Something *x* is disposed at time *t* to give response *r* to stimulus *s* if, for some intrinsic property *b* that *x* has at *t*, for some time $t'$ after *t*, if *x* were to undergo stimulus *s* at time *t* and retain property *b* until $t'$, s and *x*'s having of *b* would jointly be an *x*-complete cause of *x*'s giving response *y*.

I shall not repeat here the subtle and powerful arguments against Lewis in George Molnar's 'Are dispositions reducible?' (1999; see also Molnar 2003: ch. 4). Lewis makes the '*x*-complete cause' relevant only to properties intrinsic to $x$ and independent of conditions extrinsic to $x$—that is, independent of *most* of what I call $b$'s *reciprocal disposition partners* for $y$ as their mutual manifestation.

We can identify three forms of dispositionality, as illustrated by the examples below.

(i) Being explosive, where the explosion manifestation destroys the explosiveness.

(ii) Being soluble in water, where the dissolution manifestation loses the solubility in the solution, but the solubility is recoverable by evaporation of that solution.

(iii) Most importantly, being stable, which can persist before, during, and after its manifestation.

Lewis ignores (iii) and so fails to express an intrinsic and continuing inhibitor of a continuing intrinsic disposition.[2] The following is an example of an intrinsic continuant inhibitor of an intrinsic disposition.[3] Most cells are intrinsically suicidal. They are disposed to self-destruct, but substances that the suicidal cell ingests from neighboring cells cause an intrinsic state disposed to inhibit the disposition for suicide. This continues until the power of the inhibitory state weakens in proportion to the suicidal power and the cell self-destructs. Most cancer cells are not suicidal. This case does not fit with Lewis's proposed (RCA). It is necessary to distinguish degrees of strength and changes of strength of dispositions from degrees of *being* of dispositions. The former makes sense, the latter does not.

The problem remains, namely, by virtue of *what* in the world is a statement of a counterfactual made true? Lewis knows well enough that the counterfactual conditional needs an ontological grounding greater than a lack of irregularity in the specified conditions. Lewis and I would agree that the disposition might obtain although the specified conditions for the disposition's manifestations do not occur at any place or time. This precludes any law-type gloss's being offered without reference to other worlds. Lewis provides an objective *relation* between our world and alternative worlds. Quine and Armstrong demand a manifestation somewhere, sometime. (Is just one enough?) The question is, 'What is it about something in *our* world that

---

[2] This has the advantage of being intrinsic and internal to what has the disposition.
[3] Alexander Bird (1998) tries to make the antidote an intrinsic continuant state of the entity itself.

makes the strength of the conditional true such that it is true *even* when the antecedent and the consequent of the conditional are false and what they mention might never exist?' Think, for instance, of a particular non-existent complex substance and its non-existent solvent. The *elements* of the substance and solvent exist, but not their combination.

The strength of the strong conditional remains in (RCA). It is not 'will' or 'could,' but instead '*would* jointly be an *x*-complete cause.' It is that part of (RCA) that suggests a *would*-ish readiness in or reciprocal partners as partnerings for particular manifestings. Consequently, (RCA) includes the problem it was meant to solve.

## 2.8 COUNTERFACTUAL FACTS

As part of the frustration of attempting a philosophical clarification of the counterfactual, one could paraphrase Mark Twain: 'It is no more use to anyone than a yaller dawg.' Let me explain.

(A) One must, as C. D. Broad urged, look at what happens *instead*—that is, what happens to the entities involved with claims of the form 'If *x* had not happened, then ___, including *y*, *would* have happened' and 'If *x* had happened, then ___, including *y would not* have happened.' What fills the blanks? A vacuum? Is there a hole that you can fill or a place to remove or change however you like? The nearest neighbor may look like the nearest point or instant—namely, it *cannot* work.

We must look backward *and* forward from the supposed difference to how much and what is different in these counterfactual, contra-causal cases. In many counter-to-the-facts suppositions, there is the notion that those properties an entity has that are intrinsic (and perhaps even essential) might remain the same, but they come to have different causal laws apply to them. This should be challenged. If what the entity could do and could not do because of what it *is* are substantively different in accordance with different causal laws, then the *entity* has changed. Causal laws are summaries of what entities are capable and incapable of. The phrase 'could be or have been otherwise' conceals and consequently cannot be used to clarify confusion (Chapter 5).

So we are supposing differences that are cosmic if the web of interrelations and interconnectivities of nuclear physics is correct.

All of this applies to Lewis's neighboring alternative worlds and 'minor miracle' accounts of counterfactuals as well as the pure chance supposition for the counter-to-the-facts abridgement of the causal laws.

(B) Pure chance has an interesting turn that is obvious, yet little noticed. As we have seen (§2.5), in pure chance, the counterfactuals, sufficient and necessary, are false. The sufficient counterfactual of the form 'If $x$ had happened (when it did not), then $y$ would have happened (when it did not)' is false, no matter what embellishments are added. As such, there was not anything capable of *making* it happen. The necessary counterfactual of the form 'If $x$ had not happened (when it did), then $y$ would not have happened' is false. As such, there was not anything capable of *preventing* $y$ from happening. This makes $y$ happening the strongest force of nature. It happens no matter what!

The moral is Lockean. Locke claimed that we little realize how much our notions of kinds of entity concern their powers. A further trouble, as Locke and Russell knew so well, is that philosophers can be led to confusion by 'the harmony of well-turned periods' and 'surface grammar.'

Some years ago, I realized that if things could have been otherwise causally, then a *very* special reason must be given to show how they cannot *be* otherwise in different spatiotemporal regions. I know of no such reason that has been given. This is the Mixed Worlds possibility. If allowed, it makes universal laws space–time specific and, I think, ontologically otiose. I want to suggest that laws are otiose in any case. If you accept arguments for a realism of dispositions and their reciprocal disposition partners and grant that dispositions could be fully actual although their partnerings or manifestings might not be, then *what* is the need for universal laws? Again, laws appear to be ontologically otiose. This is made fully apparent through both Armstrong's and Hugh Mellor's allowance of singular causality.

There is a surprising identity in causing and affecting. One must take the *reciprocity* of a reciprocal readiness *partnerings* as their *mutual* manifestings seriously and not ask for the action of a single readiness factor only because there is no such action. Instead, actions are the *reciprocal* partnerings of a web or net of readiness. The movement of a single strand of the web can be considered only as the movement of all the interconnective strands including itself. The notions of distinct, sequential causes and effects are not equipped for expressing this model. As such, Einstein's preference for 'local causality' understandably becomes unsatisfiable.

Again, it is vital to recognize that a disposition is not a relation. Dispositional readinesses are for what might not exist or what might be blocked or spatiotemporally unavailable. A realism concerning dispositions and readiness is for some actual disposition of some actual entity (that exists) to have actual readinesses and various partners (that might not exist) in their partnerings as mutual manifestings (that might not exist). This readiness for what might or might not exist is not related to real possibilia or alternative possible worlds; it is *intrinsic* to *what has it*. A central purpose of this volume is to demonstrate the coherence of this realist view, its superiority to alternative views, and its extraordinary seminality.

# 3

# Truthmaking and Disposition Lines: From Quark to Colleague

## 3.1 TRUTHMAKING

We are capable of *using* (not merely *having*) mental imagery to represent how things might be somewhere else, how things were before or behind, or how things would be after certain courses of action. We are not restricted to uses of *mental* representation; we are also capable of representing *via* symbols and languages for more effective communication. With these mental and linguistic capacities, we can represent the world in limitless ways—we represent how the world was millions of years before our arrival, how it would be millions of years after our departure, how it would be if war ceased to be waged and if there were no ozone layer enveloping the earth or no mosquitoes buzzing around atop it.

Not all the ways the world can be represented are ways the world is, so a particular species of creature found it necessary to employ the following convention to distinguish representations from misrepresentations. Representations that indicate the way the world actually is they called 'true,' and representations that failed to do so they called 'false.'

Truth is a relation between two things—a representation (the truth *bearer*) and the world or some part of it (the truth*maker*). The Truthmaker Principle is intended to capture this fact. It is not meant to suggest that things in the world actually make truths as fire makes heat; it is not the 'make' of the sort in which they (in and of themselves)

An early version of the material in §§3.1–3.5 was presented at the Chapel Hill Philosophy Colloquium, October 1999, in response to David Lewis's 'Truthmaking and difference making' (Lewis 2001). A later version appeared as Martin (2000).

cause things called 'truths' to come into existence. A world in which there were no representations (i.e. no truth bearers) would be a world in which there were no truths.

## 3.2 TRUTH AND POSSIBLE WORLDS

Present-day philosophers make much use of the notion of 'possible worlds.' There seem to be two rather different motivations for the invocation of other worlds. As we shall see, however, both are closely connected with the Truthmaker Principle.

The first sort of motivation finds its source in the recognition that certain true statements—conditionals and counterfactuals, modal claims, and mathematical claims—need truthmakers that the actual world seems unable to provide. Consider, for example, the counterfactual claim, 'had he hit the ball three feet further, he would have broken the stained-glass window.' If this claim is true, what part of reality makes it true? The possible worlds theorist replies that of the total set of possible worlds, that set of worlds in which the antecedent and the consequent of our counterfactual are both true is close—more similar in details—than those in which the antecedent is true (he hits the ball three feet further) but the consequent false (the stained-glass window does not break). It is the set of possible worlds similar to the actual world that grounds the counterfactual. In this way, possible worlds are called upon to play the role of truthmakers for a certain group of truth claims.

This is not the only purpose for which philosophers have employed possible worlds, however. The worlds are also moonlighting in discussions of 'propositions.' Propositions, we are told, are 'sets of possible worlds' or, perhaps, 'functions from possible worlds into truth values.' This is, at least superficially, very unusual talk, yet the motivation also finds its source in issues of truth and truthmaking. I have already suggested that truth is a relation between a representation (truth bearer) and some feature of the world (truthmaker). Some philosophers take this to be a two-step process; a representation expresses a proposition, and it is that proposition that is made true (or false) by the way the world is. On this view, propositions are the primary truth bearers. But what are these propositions? 'Well,' we are informed, 'they are sets of possible worlds.' Thus, the second purpose for which sets of possible worlds are invoked is to play the role of truth bearers.

## 3.3 ON DAVID LEWIS

In the following discussion, I shall argue against the use of possible worlds both as truthmakers and as truth bearers. The target of my arguments will be the possible worlds theorizing of David Lewis, although I think any possible worlds account will have to deal with them. I have chosen Lewis as the focus of the discussion for a number of reasons. First, Lewis puts possible worlds to both of the purposes discussed above—and with admirable skill. Second, Lewis is among the few ontologically candid advocates of possible worlds as truthmakers. To claim the truthmaker for a counterfactual, for example, a set of possible worlds, but to deny that these worlds really exist seems pointless. Is there, then, a truthmaker or not? We can trust Lewis's realism, so I suggest that instead of 'possible worlds,' we should speak of 'alternative (to ours) worlds.'

Some philosophers might only be interested in advocating the use of sets of possible worlds in discussions of propositions. For them, arguments against possible worlds as truthmakers will be irrelevant. But my criticism of Lewis's use of the possible worlds account of propositions (the second job they are given) will still apply.

## 3.4 POLEMICS: AGAINST POSSIBLE WORLDS AS TRUTHMAKERS

First, let us see that in the alternative worlds view, working from our world to alternative worlds is an epistemically based priority and not an ontologically based priority. There is no ontological priority of any alternative world over any other, including ours. Our world is just one among multiple alternative real worlds, having no ontological priority as *the* world to which all other worlds are alternatives. Using the notion of 'minor miracle' for the nearest neighbor world to deal with some counterfactuals, as done occasionally by Lewis, I came to the following teasing thought. It would seem churlish to think that ours is safe from serving counterfactuals from some other worlds with the needed minor miracles in our own world. We must remember that it is no easy matter to describe alternative worlds in which things similar to those in our world obey different causal laws. It seems easy until, as I have argued, we try to work out the details. Furthermore, if so many alternative worlds having laws similar to those of our own world are good enough to serve our counterfactual needs with minor miracles, then we should almost be expected to serve with minor miracles in our world. Then, perhaps, the supposed indeterminacies and other mysterious happenings in quantum physics could be a place to look for such miracles!

First I shall discuss an isolatable problem. I shall do this in terms of Lewis's own view of possible worlds rather than the alternatives he lists because his view is clearer, more ontologically honest, and more candid than the others.

Lewis has professed agnosticism about whether there are indiscernible possible worlds. Then he moved to a form of denial of indiscernible worlds. Discernability is achieved by distinct objects. I shall argue why he should have accepted indiscernible worlds and obviate the need for distinctive objects for distinct worlds. Scrubbed clean of verificationist overtones, 'discernible' is just 'difference-making.'

(1) Alternative (possible) worlds each have their own unshared-with-other-worlds space-times. That should be enough to allow numerical difference between those worlds, even if they are qualitatively and relationally similar, just as spatial–temporal difference is enough to make a difference between qualitative and relational similarities *within* a world.

(2) Max Black's 'Identity and indiscernibility' (Black 1952) includes an example of a two-sphere universe. The spheres have exactly similar properties and relations. There is a way of expressing the difference between there being only one sphere and there being more than one. It is done by thinking of there being a part of a sphere that is more than any sphere's diameter's distance from some other part of a sphere. If that thought is applicable, then there is more than one sphere. If it is not applicable, then there is only one sphere. It is differences of space–times that differentiate each possible (alternative) world from all others.

The qualitative and relational similarities between worlds are differentiated by each world's unique and unshared space–time.

## 3.5 MORE POLEMICS: AGAINST THE POSSIBLE WORLD ACCOUNT OF PROPOSITIONS

Truths require truthmakers. This simple idea, to which I have long subscribed, requires care in its spelling out. Thus, the truthmaker principle Lewis ascribes to me is not mine (Lewis 2001). Lewis suggests (and so does John Bigelow in an unpublished paper) that I hold that 'the proposition that a donkey talks is true if a donkey talks.' This would be to claim 'If there exists a talking donkey then there exists a proposition that is representative of there being a talking donkey.'

I accept nothing like 'If $x$, then there is a proposition representative of $x$,' or 'If $x$, then the proposition that $x$ is true.' I do accept that there exist things (or spatio-temporal segments) and their properties, absences, and relations—and their dispositions. I think these can exist without truths about them. Truth requires truth bearers and truthmakers as correlatives. For truth we need a truth bearer that is in use by an individual or within the individual's capacity for use as projective to and selective for what or how something exists that *does* exist (the truthmaker).[1] The basic notion is not 'representation,' but that of 'representational *use*' (see Chapter 9).

The form 'The proposition that a donkey talks is true if a donkey talks' suggests that if a talking donkey exists, then a proposition exists that is representative and projective of their being a talking donkey. These propositions are supposed to be entities that exist even when they are not expressed or, for that matter, when they are inexpressible. These are truth bearers and, as such, must be projective of what would *make* them true or false. How can propositions *as* sets of possible (alternative) worlds play this projective-representative role? I can understand how they could be truth*makers*, but not how they could be truth *bearers*.

Lewis has an account of propositions as sets of possible worlds, but I fail to understand how sets of possible worlds play the projective-selective role of truth bearers. He allows that propositions can be unexpressable and unthinkable. How do these unexpressable and unthinkable sets fill any kind of projective, selective, representational

---

[1] John Heil and I worked out how this could be done for mathematical rules for infinities. See Martin and Heil 1998, and Chapter 12.

role? Truth bearers are representative of what makes them true. The job is to give an account of representation that is naturalistic and in no need of abstract entities. To do this adequately is to find the sources in basic nature that can provide a slide from quark to colleague.

Lewis's notion of the need for a distinctive object for a distinctive world rests on at least a temporary refuge of the identity of indiscernibles for alternative real worlds. As mentioned previously, scrubbing the term 'indiscernible' clean of its verificationist overtones, it just means 'difference-making.' *That* is accomplished by the alternative worlds each having their own, unshared with other worlds, space–times. That is enough to allow numerical difference for qualitative similarities *between* those worlds, as spatial-temporal difference is enough to make a difference between qualitative similarities *within* a world. Counterparts do not share the same space–times. Through his example of a universe consisting of two spheres, Max Black's elegant paper shows how all qualitative and relational properties are had by *each* of the spheres.

## 3.6 AN ALTERNATIVE TO POSSIBLE WORLDS

There must, I think, be a gradualist model from this simple projection to nonlinguistic and linguistic capacities for rule-governed intentional representative activities in the head and behaviour. This will be a model going from the many directional readinesses of the quark, most of which will never be manifested, to the capacities and dispositions for many representations of some English speaker, most of which also will never be manifested.

I shall present a continuum of cases. It will be the individual's choice as to what point in the continuum is enough for a case of full-bodied representation or perhaps representational use. First, some metaphysics is necessary.

An actual disposition or number of readinesses exists, here and now, and is projective for endless manifestations with an infinity of present or absent, actual or nonactual alternative disposition partners. We can think of this projectivity as constituting a complex line—or, perhaps better, a 'web' or 'net,' what I have called a Power Net (Martin 1992). Dispositions differ just in case their disposition lines differ. A disposition line is what the disposition is for, what it is not for, and what it is prohibitive against with alternative actual or nonactual reciprocal disposition partners. In this way, a disposition line encompasses a bounded infinity of readinesses. These readinesses are all actual, although non-existent disposition partners and non-existent manifestations are not. Disposition lines can weaken or strengthen or cease to exist. At any definite freeze-dried moment, there are specific disposition lines having their actual readinesses for an infinity of mutual manifestations with an infinity of actual and nonactual reciprocal disposition-line partners, both intrinsic and extrinsic.

An object possessing a disposition can lose that disposition. This is different from the disposition's being retained but its manifestation's being blocked or inhibited by something intrinsic or extrinsic to the object. There is a parallel distinction between cases in which a disposition line is complicated or 'kinky' (and thus difficult to see as a pattern) and those in which dispositions are in flux and different disposition lines are in play at different times. These cases are different from those in which different dispositions can share disposition lines up to a given point, then diverge.

Dispositionality provides a basis for a naturalistic realism in logic and mathematics. Let there be anything, even just a quark or two. These have actual dispositions with their disposition lines for different manifestations with an infinity of other elementary particles with alternative interrelations and interactivities that are arrangements such that those particles would constitute a chimera, or the very same particles, differently organized, would constitute intelligent, rule-following agents. The readinesses of the original quark are all actual, although not all of the reciprocal disposition partners and manifestations are. The directedness to the infinity of reciprocal disposition partners for, against, or neutral with regard to an infinity of manifestations, with an infinity of different disposition lines, are actual in the quark itself. Therein lies the mathematical reality of infinities—not just in a grain of sand, but in whatever is an elementary particle or aspect of a superstring.

Dispositionality with its disposition-line readinesses for a bounded infinity would seem to satisfy the 'and so on' of recursive functions. Knowing a line, one could move from one place (with a specific set of reciprocal disposition partners) to any other place (with a different set of partners, actual or nonactual) along the line. This suggests that recursion is built into nature at the simplest, most basic level. We can be grateful that such lines of directedness can exist without our having to know them or be mistake-free in our attempts to know them.

It is also possible to see how dispositionality could ground entailment and mathematical necessity. Different disposition lines can have overlapping segments. There is no guarantee that an agent who possesses dispositions with such lines recognizes or appreciates the overlapping. Even so, an agent might anticipate a whole range of overlappings involving different disposition lines and, with great good fortune, come to a detailed awareness of much of this. That awareness, of course, need not take the explicit form of the technical notion of disposition lines. Failure to see a lack of overlap or a point of conflict between disposition lines is a common experience.

A given disposition can have a disposition line for the manifestation (with relevant reciprocal disposition partners) of the acquiring of new dispositions with new disposition lines. The actual seminality of the disposition here is what grounds a naturalistic account of the objectivity of mathematics and logic and also accounts for the sense of real discovery and failure of discovery. From the self-identity of distinct disposition lines flow the necessities of their overlappings (or points of conflict).

The only thing that such a sturdy naturalism for mathematics (and much else, including modalities) cannot account for is the all-times-and-places utterly null universe. Since our own individual existence (and much else) falsifies the universe's being empty, we can live with this false countercase. If that is a reason for peopling the universe (as Lewis, of course, never does) with nonspatial, nontemporal abstract entities and universals, it is not good enough. Physics itself helps here. Space–time cannot exist in a totally empty world—it needs to have (as substance would) properties (see Martin and Heil 1998 for the full epistemic model for this).

After living the relationships between indefinitely many worlds, of which ours is only one, in order to explain necessity, contingency, otherwise-ness, and fictions, it may feel difficult and odd even to attempt to do it all just within *our* actual world. I mean to show how it *can* be done.

There is a need to explain the intuitive notions of would- and could-have-been-otherwise in terms of the actual.

For any dispositional state, there are *actual* readinesses with an indefinite number of alternative reciprocal disposition partners for an indefinite number of alternative mutual manifestations. One implication of this view is that the counterfactual is exposed as an awkward linguistic gesture toward these multiple readinesses. It should not be read as an assertion of what *would* have happened instead of what *did* happen. That is a reference to mere *possibilia*. Keeping only to the actual, there are the varieties of *actual* readinesses for a variety of mutual actual or nonactual manifestations with a variety of present or absent, actual or nonactual, reciprocal disposition partners. The *readinesses* have to be fully *actually* determinately *for* mutual manifestations with the reciprocal dispositions. Of course, manifestations with particular partners can exclude other manifestations with *other* reciprocal partners.

There are actual readinesses for the manifestations of *acquiring* new and further readinesses. This creativity is of great importance. A single quark has actual dispositional readinesses for an indefinite number of mutual manifestations, actual or nonactual, with an indefinite number of alternative disposition partners in the form of its interrelated and interreactive sibling quarks and cousin leptons. Some of these would even take the form of beings with various capacities for representational use.

The initial single quark actually has the readinesses for kinds of entanglement (mutual manifestations) with an indefinite number of actual or nonactual property groupings forming kinds of representational entities in kinds of interrelationships. This richness of (perhaps infinite) readinesses that are actual in the quark (or aspect of a field or string or . . . ) forms truth bearers *for* the relevant truthmaker presences or absences.

The slide from single quark to particle conglomerates of the humanoid type invites us with many places to get off as enough for representational use. I shall not try to describe the continuum and getting-off places here in detail. Very roughly, there are quark-lepton arrangements (systems) in the body under rough 'evolutionary' development that have mappings of their immediate physical environments—*in* the body but outside the central system involved. These mappings allow for spatial and temporal (memory and anticipatory) targets for placing origins of input and determining endpoints of output. There is competition among inputs so that a seemingly stronger input (through central system processing) might fail to win. Thus, if there have been a number of inputs messaging 'cold' in the inner core, then with the retention of these in the central system (perhaps primarily centered in the hypothalamus), a stronger input from an area of the surface of the skin could lose out to a weaker input from the inner core. This is all under the control of negative and positive feedback and, additionally, feedforward, anticipatory, and corrective. It takes many months to mature in the human body. It can function in a permanent vegetative state, so it is not a conscious system. Are its inputs given representational use? Or do you want consciousness? Or do you perhaps want to stay on the slide until the emergence of linguistic representation? You decide where you get truth bearers, but the world easily can do and has done without them and so without truth, yet with a plenitude of being.

Almost all of the discussion here is applicable to the nonstructural ultimate constituents of nature, whatever they turn out to be—particles, fields, superstring energy loops, and so on. These have no separable or mix of parts, but they do have qualitative dispositional properties.

Most noteworthy is that by virtue of their dispositional nature, they have alternative directional, selective readinesses for alternative mutual manifestings—partnerings with alternative disposition partners external to themselves. All of this, in the most fundamental workings of nature, is in answer to Fodor's stirring and basic question, 'How does *anything* get outside itself?' This is the log-breaking move made *before* dealing with mental entities and does not need to be made *again* with them.

This does not give us the account of *mental* for-ness and about-ness, but a breakthrough has been made that is seminal for such an account. The next move is to work out the details of systemic for-ness and, after that, to sort out the for-ness of feedback and feedforward with spatial and temporal projectivities. Finally, we can think about what is left that is special with thinking and feeling about-ness and perceiving capacities of ourselves.

A crucial step has been made. An ontology has been formed on the way to a connectivist physics and a receptor-based neuroscience.

## 3.7 HOW TO SUFFER A CONTRADICTION

Differing disposition lines can have some similar contexts (reciprocal disposition partners). Consider dispositions underlying a capacity for adding numbers. Being given the same sequence of numbers, $D_1$ might be for adding one and $D_2$ might be for adding two. Corresponding to dispositions $D_1$ and $D_2$, are disposition lines $DL_1$ and $DL_2$. Each of these manifestations excludes another from occurring. I do not mean to say there could not be a split-personality or split-brain case with one personality, the writing personality, being very different from the speaking personality. But without a further split, each personality cannot 'travel along' (manifest) the different $DL_1$ and $DL_2$ of $D_1$ and $D_2$. (For more on rule-following, see Chapter 11 and Martin and Heil 1998.)

One disposition can, in a normal case, be dominant over another. You could be disposed to add one and simultaneously disposed to add two, but add one rather than two. There is nothing inconsistent about having both a capacity to stand up and a capacity to sit down. But the manifestation of one of these capacities here and now excludes the here and now manifestation of the other.

There *is* something inconsistent in cases in which an agent is set for following $DL_1$ of $D_1$ and has a momentary lapse into $DL_2$ of $D_2$. When this occurs, the agent might be either aware after the event or unaware; either has the potential for embarrassment.

I can illustrate the point by mentioning a case in which a colleague of mine apparently held inconsistent dispositions for the projections of solidity and nonsolidity of the North Pole. A natural explanation for this is that belief that the North Pole is solid ($D_1$ with $DL_1$) and belief that the North Pole is not solid ($D_2$ with $DL_2$) have different reciprocal disposition partners $DP_1$ and $DP_2$. $DP_1$ manifesting $D_1$ with $DL_1$ is in the context of considering geographical facts (false, in this case) about the North Pole. $DP_2$ for manifesting $D_2$ with $DL_2$ is in the context of considering the trip of the atomic submarine, *Nautilus*, which sailed *under* the North Pole.

My colleague had not brought himself to awareness of the conflict at that point along the disposition line for the manifestation of projecting the North Pole as solid land and that point along the different disposition line for the manifestation of projecting the North Pole (via the voyage of the *Nautilus*) as not solid land.

# 4

# Parts and Wholes

## 4.1 'TOP-DOWN' AND 'BOTTOM-UP' CAUSATION

It must be evident, even to the ontologically timid, that where the simpler parts, properties, and relations go, so must go the complex wholes, but, of course, where the complex whole goes, so go the simpler parts. It appears, however, that there has been confusion about the relationships of constituents of a system to the system, or of constituents of a whole to the whole. My contention is that there is no causal work for the whole that is not done by the parts, provided the complex role of the parts is fully appreciated.

John Searle has very clearly expressed a position that imports levels of being and causality between constituents and wholes and between macro- and microlevels:

> There is nothing mysterious about such bottom-up causation; it is quite common in the physical world. . . . The solidity of the piston is causally supervenient on its molecular structure, but this does not make solidity epiphenomenal; and similarly, the causal supervenience of my present back pain on micro events in my brain does not make the pain epiphenomenal.

> My conclusion is that once you recognize the existence of bottom-up, micro forms of causation, the notion of supervenience no longer does any work in philosophy. The formal features of the relation are already present in the causal sufficiency of the micro–macro forms of causation.

> (Searle 1992: 125–6).

The question to be asked is a simple one: How do things that are identical with constituents of a whole have effects on the whole that *includes* themselves? It is no better to speak of top-down causality. There the question would arise, how does a whole thing that is constituted of its constituents cause something concerning what it is constituted by? The constituents that are being affected by the whole must be part of the cause upon themselves. Added to this is the obvious problem of apparent 'overdetermination' occurring at each and every level. That is what is 'mysterious about such bottom-up causation' or top-down causation and what is *not* 'a straightforward matter.' There appears to be a mystical invocation of levels of being.

The sense that properties of complex objects are mysterious, that they are emergent additions of being, stems from a failure to consider *all* of the constituents with *all* of their interrelations and interreactivities, actual *and* potential, with one another and whatever may be external to them as well as the varying degrees of stability of all of these, allowing, of course, for some degrees of addition, subtraction, alteration, configuration, or even qualitative modification within whatever rough limits are applicable as limits for being that kind of whole.

## 4.2 THE COMPOSITIONAL MODEL

The compositional model needs elaboration. It is best to avoid the weasel word 'supervenience' and get straight to the ontology of whole and parts.

It is a truism that the whole counts for more than the summation of individual parts taken in their separateness. As constituents of the whole, they *are not* individually separate. It is not as if the brick of the building's foundation has *only* the weight of the bricks immediately above it or presses *only* with its own weight on the earth below it. The interrelatednesses and interreactivenesses of parts as *reciprocal partners* bring a congeries of dispositions into *mutual manifestation*; those parts that could not be manifested if they existed separately and without such interrelatednesses. An obvious example is a particular part coming to be at the apex, corner, or fulcrum in its interrelatings with other parts. These interrelatednesses, interreactivenesses, *and* the dispositionalities among the parts themselves and whatever might exist externally to them for which they might be reciprocal disposition partners—*all* of these concerning the parts—make up the whole *without* remainder.

To give the parts a less impoverished description is only to give them their due as interactive parts. When this is done, having levels of being and speaking of the whole (or *system*) as having supervenient and emergent properties and causality between parts and wholes no longer remains plausible. Whatever emergence there might be, can and should be found at the particle level. Between differing concatenations of particles, it might even be *expected* that special concatenations of particles are productive and explanatory regarding the mutual manifestation of some irreducible properties not contained in the original concatenation. Causality need not be a pipeline or nature a bore, and novelty need not be an unexplained mystique.

This compositional view of the nature of things will explain why a swarm of spatially separated, fast-moving bees is perceived as a solid quiescent entity, and how a red-hot poker (or even a cold one) is much like that, and it will explain how glass is a liquid, mercury a solid, and whales are mammals. That is, it will open our eyes to interrelatingnesses to which we have been blind. The interrelatingnesses that we have seen and by which we made our classifications can be as real as ever in many cases. They show the *differences* between the swarms of bees and the red-hot poker, glass and cold molasses, mercury and wood, and whales and cows. Even after learning the deeper and non-apparent interrelatingnesses, we still can choose to classify by the interrelatingnesses that are least arcane and most apparent outside the academy and learned societies. In turn, they can have their base and constitution in a congeries of interrelatingnesses at a sub-atomic depth. That is, they do not just *free-float*, *pace* some philosophers of biology and some sociologists.

Thinking of a whole as something over and above all of its constitutents (with all of their interrelations, interreactions, and dispositionalities), requires thinking of the 'over-and aboveness' of the whole as a causal factor apart from anything concerning the causal operativenesses of any or even all of the constituents. Among its effects, we must suppose there will be effects on the constitutents as well as effects on other things that cannot be traced to the causal operativenesses of any or even all of the constituents. That is what commonly is meant by 'top-down causality.' 'Bottom-up causality' also applies a notion of over-and-aboveness of the effect of the whole in addition to *all* of the effects of the constitutents on one another and whatever is external to them (with all of the effects of acquiring further dispositions).

This dubious invocation of levels of being with duplicated causes and effects at each level is tempting only because compositionalist accounts tend to be grossly inadequate. Any supposed over-and-aboveness of wholes to their constitutents, however, becomes totally incomprehensible when the roles of the constituents are given their fair due in a well-developed compositional model. What are ordinarily called 'collections,' 'wholes,' or 'objects' can be added to, subtracted from, have substitutions made, or be changed in their properties (heated or cooled, for example) with linguistic propriety. Attributing such things to a whole or an object is not inconsistent with attributing identity. We must *avoid* a use of the term 'identity' that implies that any entity over time must be said to lack continuing identity simply because it has changed properties or has lost, added, or had substituted some parts.


## 4.3 COMPOSITION AND IDENTITY

The old example of the statue not being just the ultimate constituents of clay is grossly misleading. The sculpture *is* just the clay constituents with a certain conformation of shape and size within rough limits of allowable deformation, loss, addition, or change of properties of the constituents with the further condition of having an intention-al formative action of an agent or agents who themselves have a compositional account.

To make sense of what kind of compositional account will work for what kind of whole or object, we must first decide the spatial-temporal bounds, properties, and relations of what we are designating as a whole or an object; we must also decide what capacities for affecting and being affected by *other* actual and possible things and what degrees of allow-able loss, gain, or substitution of parts and alterations of their properties there can be. Then, and only then, can we begin to plot the spatial-temporal bounds of the constituents with their allowable range of interrelations and interreactions, and capacities or dispositions of these, with one another and with whatever might be external to them with allowable degrees of stability, loss, gain, substitution, and alteration concerning the properties of the constituents for the relevant whole or object to be rendered without remainder in terms of those constituents.

When suitably formulated, the compositional model expresses the thought that (a) there are no levels of being (or, rather, there is only one level of ultimate constituents), although there are levels of description and explanation; and (b) the constituents in all of their interrelatednesses, interreactivities, and dispositions for these with one another *and* with whatever might be external, in all of their varying degrees of stability, do fully constitute and together *are* the whole (admitting some additions, subtractions, and alterations of properties and configuration suitable for being that kind of whole). Nothing less than this will do as a compositional model.

This is to think that, if the properties and relations of entities that we are considering are complex, then the entities must have simpler constituents, and their properties and relations must be simpler. The *ultimate* constituents are best left to theoretical physics to detect, although the completeness and correctness of the description given to them might be suspect.

This general way of talking about the properties of ultimate constituents (elementary particles, aspects of fields, or superstrings, etc.) is not affected by doubts about our present or even future capacity to develop a complete and true physics. The claim is that *whatever* (known or unknown) properties the ultimate constituents of nature have, they are no more purely qualitative and non-dispositional and in 'pure act' than any of the more macroscopic and structural properties. (I take it as obvious that any structural property involves dispositionality and, therefore, cannot be used to 'explain' dispositionality.) The properties of even supposedly elementary and nonstructural particles themselves must be capable (at any time or space–time segment) of more than they manifest. This is sometimes expressed (not so happily, on the present view) as possible-world lines.

Any account of properties and dispositions whose concepts exclude application to the domain of elementary particles, fields, or strings, etc., would be grossly deficient. Perhaps it would be useful to see (*without* any scientific theory of their nature) why it is rationally inescapable to believe in their existence.

## 4.4 ROOTS OF THE COMPOSITIONAL MODEL

Reasonable belief in the existence of what Locke called 'insensible corpuscles' in the seventeenth century, and unobservable 'atoms' before that, never depended on a well worked-out or even badly worked-out scientific theory or technology for the detection of their nature.

(1) *First stage.* We grasp the notion of composition in which a whole of a particular kind is supposed to be composed of, completely

constituted by, and no more than parts of different kinds *in* various relations. The individual parts of a chair are not chairs, the individual parts of a tree are not trees, and the individual parts of a curry are not curries.

(2)  *Second stage.* We recognize that things get larger by addition of parts and get smaller by loss of parts and not by inflation and deflation.

(3)  *Third Stage.* With this knowledge, we note that a tree gets larger and a ring, once worn for a long time, gets smaller *imperceptively*. That is, no matter how closely we observe the tree or the ring, we cannot observe an increase by an addition of parts or a decrease by a loss of parts.

Spurning an explanation in terms of expansion as with a balloon, the thought of increase in size by the addition of unobservable parts of different kinds in various relations so as to constitute the tree is an understandable thought and a reasonable belief, and we do not have to think of observable entities or observable parts of entities as *plena*.

All of this is accomplished with no theory of the nature of these unobservable parts of things. That much, and it is a great deal, is not threatened by the doubts raised by Cartwright, or even by van Fraassen, about how much we can know about what Locke called 'the finer interstices of nature.'


## 4.5 PHYSICS AND THE MANIFEST IMAGE

The bearing of developments in theoretical physics on our views of things taken at the level of 'ordinary' observation of and language about the macroscopic world is made graphic by the discordances between what Wilfrid Sellars called the 'scientific image' and the 'manifest image' of ordinary things and their properties, the colors, for instance (Sellars 1962).

My first encounter with that kind of discordance occurred when, at the age of nine, I attended a public lecture by a physicist. The physicist said that the objects we see, such as a table, were composed of parts called 'particles' that were much too small for us to see or feel. These particles had far more space between them than the space they occupied. He went on, to my further astonishment, to say that these part-particles making up the objects were of many kinds and were moving, constantly, at very great speeds. I thought the physicist mad and, on the instant, resolved never to attend a university where such nonsense was taught.

Then the physicist went on to say it was as if we could not get close enough to be almost within the swarm of particles without very different and sharper sense. Observing an ordinary object, a table, for instance, is rather like observing a swarm of bees from a great distance. The swarm can appear as a solid object until you move closer. I was persuaded by this clumsy analogy, and the excitement of the thought set me, on the instant, to resolve to attend a university where such matters were discussed.

I had, as did others in the audience, a view of the solidity of things as some kind of *plenum*. That was why what the physicist said was so shocking at first. I gave up this view of solidity *qua plenum* from that moment.

When I was a student at Cambridge, the dispute between Eddington and Stebbing about the solidity of a table was much discussed. Eddington claimed that theoretical physics refuted our ordinary view of the solidity of a table. Stebbing disagreed, arguing that our ordinary view was inviolate because 'If I drop a piece of paper on the table, it doesn't pass through it.' I thought that Stebbing had missed the whole point, which was that the ordinary implications that people make of 'solidity' as implying a *plenum* turned out to be *false*. True enough, there are other ordinary implications of 'solidity,' such as that paper will not just pass through the 'solid' desk, that remain true. I would claim that, often enough, the false implications and the true implications are wrapped together in how we think of the solidity of things. That explains the shock (as Stebbing cannot explain) my younger self and others in the audience received by what the physicist said.

Faced with some of the more mind-boggling theories of modern physics, our most basic concepts are up for at least enough bending and twisting to allow intelligent consideration of what is being proposed.

It should be emphasized that even in terms of the most anti-intuitive among seriously considered hypotheses of physics, there is something like a relative retention of edges of boundedness. That is, there would be relative degrees of density of populations of particles (or aspects of fields) and relative degrees of stability of that density of such populations (or field-aspects). This provides an analogue at the level of elementary particles (or field-aspects) for the sizes and shapes and the edges, continuance, and movements of macroscopic things and, therefore, a further reinforcement of a realist compositional model for the relationship between the macroscopic and the submicroscopic.

None of this ought to suggest that the philosopher should react with dumb faith to the latest and changing revelations from theoretical physics, or with an arrogant disbelief or a 'That's what they say *now*' cynicism. It should instead incline philosophers to a greater alertness to alternative ways the world might be.

## 4.6 FROM PHYSICS TO ONTOLOGY

Ontology sets out an even more abstract model of how the world is than theoretical physics, a model that has *placeholders* for scientific results and *excluders* for tempting confusions. Ontology and theoretical science can help one another along, we hope, with minimal harm. The compositionalism recommended here need not be equated with Scientism. The methodology of actual science has very naturally led to an incomplete and partial account of the 'finer interstices' and constituents of nature.

If objects belong to classes in virtue of similarities or resemblances they bear to one another, they resemble one another in virtue of their properties. Objects do not resemble one another *tout court*, but in some way or respect. You could think of these ways or respects as *properties*.

Consider two balls, one red and the other blue. Do these objects resemble one another? Yes, both are spherical. Do they differ? Again, yes, they are differently colored. It is natural to suppose that being spherical, being red, and being blue are properties possessed by the balls. Differently put: there is something about one ball in virtue of which it is true to say of it 'the ball is spherical,' and something about the ball—something else about the very same ball—in virtue of which it is true to say of it 'the ball is red.' These somethings about the ball are its properties; each endows the ball with a distinctive qualitative character and a distinctive range of powers or dispositionalities.

Objects resemble or fail to resemble one another in particular ways or respects. These ways or respects are properties. Two balls can be similar with respect to their shapes. The balls' shapes are similar, not with respect to anything, but similar *tout court*. Properties are the bases of similarities; properties account for similarities among objects.

The balls, we say, while differing in color, have *the same* shape; they *share* a property. What is the significance of the italicized expressions in the previous sentence? Philosophers who regard properties as universals are inclined to read 'the same' in such sentences as 'the selfsame' or 'one and the same.' There is some one thing that the balls literally have in common or share: their shape. But, if the balls occupy distinct, non-overlapping regions of space, then their sharing a property cannot be like two subway riders sharing a seat, or under-graduates sharing a pizza. Rather, the sharing must be *sui generis*. Each ball is or encompasses a distinct instance of the universal sphericity. Universals differ from particulars precisely in this amazing capacity to be 'fully in' each particular.

I follow Locke in regarding properties as particulars. Two distinct, spatially non-overlapping spherical objects possess distinct, though similar, properties, both of which answer to the general term 'spheric-ity.' What sense, then, can we make of talk of distinct objects *sharing* a property or possessing *the same* property? Two people can share a dislike for anchovies or Reggae, and two bankers can arrive at work wearing the same tie. In neither case do we have anything like identity or selfsameness, nor anything that would tempt us to imagine that aversions and ties are not, like everything else, entirely particular. Sameness in such cases need not be anything more than resemblance. For that matter, identical twins are twins; and objects with identical shapes need not be objects that stand in a unique relation of instantiation to a single universal entity.

On this view, one ball's sphericity is entirely distinct from the sphericity of another ball. To be sure, the sphericity of the first ball might be exactly similar to the sphericity of the second. But the sphericity of the first ball is a (particular) way the first ball is and the sphericity of the second ball is a (particular) way the second ball is.

Properties, then, can be real without being universals. Properties so construed are *tropes* (Descartes's, Locke's, and Spinoza's 'modes'), rather than universals, although I want to distance myself from the idea, promoted by many friends of tropes, that objects are nothing more than 'bundles' of tropes (see, for instance, Williams 1953; Campbell 1981, 1990; Simons 1994; Bacon 1995; Robb 2005.). The bundle theory treats properties inappositely as *parts* of objects. Objects can have parts, but an object's properties are not its parts, they are particular ways the object is. A tomato's redness and sphericity are not parts of the tomato in the way the tomato's skin, seeds, and stem are parts of it. The tomato is not made up of its properties in the way it is made up of its parts.

It is important to distinguish bundle theories, according to which objects are *made up* of properties, from a view according to which objects are regarded as regions of space–time that possess properties. I favor the old idea of substratum: the haver of properties not itself had as a property (Martin 1980). Space–time might itself be *the* bearer of properties, not itself borne as a property (see Chapter 16). It makes no sense in ontology or modern physics to think of space–time as empty and propertyless. Space–time nicely fulfils the conditions of a substratum. I regard this latter view as, at the very least, an open possibility, providing only that the properties in question are nontransferable, nonexchangeable between entities or space–time regions.

Properties, then, are particulars: tropes, not universals. Properties are had by substances, they do not make up substances. Properties are nontransferable. The redness or sphericity of this tomato cannot migrate to another tomato. This, in fact, is a consequence of the idea that properties are particular ways things are. The identity of a property—its being the property it is—is bound up with the identity of its possessor.

Philosophers commonly distinguish dispositional and categorical properties. Dispositional properties are taken to endow their possessors with particular dispositions or powers; categorical properties are thought to endow objects with nondispositional qualities. Some philosophers have denied the existence of categorical properties, arguing that every property is purely dispositional (see, for instance, Mellor 1974; and Shoemaker 1980). Others deny dispositional properties (Armstrong 1968: 85–8). Still others have regarded dispositional properties with suspicion, treating them as dependent on or grounded in categorical properties (see Prior *et al.* 1982; and Jackson 1996).

In contrast to this, I take properties to have a dual nature: in virtue of possessing a property, an object possesses *both* a particular dispositionality *and* a particular qualitative character. The overall dispositionality and qualitative character of an object depends on properties its parts possess and relations these bear to one another. A ball's sphericity, for instance, gives it (in concert with the ball's other properties) a distinctive appearance and disposes it in particular ways (it will roll, for instance, and reflect light in a certain pattern). I shall have much more to say on this topic in Chapter 6.

# 5

# Causality

## 5.1 INADEQUACIES OF THE TWO-EVENT MODEL

It might be a gross error to try to make causes and effects distinct temporal events—the one earlier than the other. Doing so results in a problem of timing. Lacking a temporal gap between cause and effect events suggests that two mathematical point-instants serve as one another's closest neighbours, which simply cannot make mathematical sense. A spatial point has no size. A temporal instant is supposed to have no duration and, as one mathematician warns us, no nearest neighbour. That is, there cannot be closest neighbours concerning point-instants, yet there cannot be a temporal gap either. There also cannot be simultaneity because the cause is supposed to happen at a different time from the effect as *part* of their distinctness. It will help a great deal to move to the active voice for partnerings and manifestings.

The two-event cause-and-effect view is easily avoided and replaced by the view of mutual manifestation of reciprocal disposition partners, suggesting a natural contemporaneity. This is not surprising in the least because the reciprocal dispositional *partnering* and their mutually *manifesting* are *identical*. No time gap or spatial gap is needed—not one happening before another. It is not a matter of two events, but of one and the same event—a reciprocal dispositional partnering as a *mutual* manifesting. This surprising identity of what we had dimly thought of as the two-event cause and effect loses its surprise in the clear light of day.

This identity of partnering–manifesting becomes clear at the atomic level of bindings for molecular formings. The dispositional partners of key and lock, in their hardnesses, shapes, kinetic and resistance forces, etc., *are* the manifestings of the locking, jamming, or unlocking. The more closely a cause-and-effect is examined, the more natural the replacement view—of seeing the event of partnering as an activity identical with the event of mutual manifesting—becomes.

## 5.2 DISPOSITION LINES AND FUNDAMENTAL PHYSICS

The model being developed here is not limited to particle-objects-in-space—time; it also fits well for explanations in terms of warps and woofs *of* space—time as infinitesimal energy-loops or superstrings (Chapter 16). I have insisted that space—time *has* properties, yet it is not itself had as a property or even a set of properties, and it could not exist without properties. A propertied space—time is a one-object universe and space—time satisfies the correct definitions of 'substratum' (Martin 1980).

I have suggested that dispositions be thought of as holistic nets: 'power nets.' A disposition endows its possessor with endless readinesses that could be represented as lines, 'readiness lines.' Manifestations are intersections of these readiness lines. Stating identity conditions for the identity of readiness lines poses a problem.[1] To *describe* a particular readiness line $L$, one has to assume the nature of other readiness lines $L_1, \ldots, L_n$, actual or nonactual, for which $L$ has readiness so that the reciprocal (including $L$'s) partnering, actual or nonactual, serves as their mutually manifesting $M$, which is actual or nonactual. The *for-nesses* of $L$ are actual whether $L_1, \ldots, L_n$ are actual or not.

It does not matter how short $L$ is, spatially or temporally. A superstring loop in physics is supposed to be so short that the number of superstrings in a single atom is greater than the total number of atoms in the universe. However short a readiness-line or superstring is, it is *for* an indefinite number of reciprocal readiness line partners $L_1, \ldots, L_n$ (energy loops), actual and nonactual, for mutual reciprocatings $R_1, \ldots, R_n$ or actual or nonactual mutual manifestings $M_1, \ldots, M_n$.

---

[1] Of course, all of God's children have identity conditions. I have not seen a detailed and full set of identity conditions for any spatiotemporal entity (chair, rock, suit jacket, cricket ball, etc.). Abstract entities (in the sense of being non-spatiotemporal) seem to be the only candidates for specific and full identity specifications, so it is understandable that detailing identity conditions for things in the world is, as Locke says, endless. The demand for them is the ploy of the mad logician.

As to all of this in 11 or 26 dimensions, I know of nothing that would be incompatible with the partnerings for manifestings model of readiness lines, although I begin to see a way to parse the appearance of more than dimensions in terms of only our four dimensions in this account.

## 5.3 CAUSATION AS MUTUAL MANIFESTATION

My suggestion is that dispositionality provides all we need for an understanding of causal phenomena. The Humean, events-as-causes-and-effects model is at best misleading. It conflates everyday and scientific procedures—our taking steps to ensure particular out-comes—with the ontology of causation.

With this in mind, it is worth restating what a realism about dispositionalities does and does not include. Both our everyday and theoretical talk are rife with dispositional language. When we say a piece of glass is fragile, for example, we mean that it is disposed to exhibit a kind of shattering behaviour when suitably struck.

So, we have dispositions and their manifestations. The distinction between these is crucial. When we attribute a disposition to an object, we do not claim the object is currently displaying its propensity for the kind of behavior in question. The having of the disposition and the displaying or *manifestation* of the disposition are two very different things. A particular rubber band has an elastic disposition, although it might not currently be exhibiting (i.e. manifesting) its stretching propensity. Indeed, an object can have a disposition without *ever* manifesting that disposition. We can think of a rubber band that never once had the opportunity to display its elasticity, condemned to a limp existence in the bottom of a drawer for life. As such, we must conceptually distinguish between a disposition and a manifestation of that disposition.

What is the ontological significance of all our dispositional talk? One answer is this: none at all. Philosophers defending views of this kind insist that to say a thing has a disposition, say elasticity, is not to claim that it has some ontologically real elastic property. They prefer, instead, to analyze dispositions in terms of conditionals. To say a thing is elastic is merely to make a claim about the thing's behaviour in a set of counterfactual circumstances (for some, possible worlds), not about the thing itself in its actual circumstance.

I have already argued against the conditional account of dispositions. The upshot of rejecting this account is that we must give real ontological status to dispositionality. The picture that emerges is as follows. A particular disposition either exists or it does not. One can say of any *unmanifesting* disposition that it straight-out exists, even if it is not, at the time, manifesting any manifestation. It is the unmanifested *manifestation*, not the disposition itself, that is the would-be-if or would-have-been-if, if anything is. There can be a disposition, *a*, for the manifestation of acquiring a further disposition, *b*, and of course disposition *b* need not itself have any manifestation, but the disposition *b* can still be fully actual.

This is the view I want to urge in the first half of the volume, but there is another competitor to consider: the reductive account. The reductionist agrees that when we attribute a disposition to a thing, we are making a claim about the thing itself in its actual circumstances, not about its behaviour in a set of counterfactual circumstances. Reductionists, however, resist the conclusion that dispositionality is an actual feature of the world. Instead, they insist that statements attributing dispositions can be reduced to statements attributing 'structural' or 'categorical' properties: only the 'categorical' properties have real ontological status. For example, reductionists argue that when we attribute fragility to a glass bottle, we need not suppose that there is some irreducible shatter-propensity about the glass, but simply that it is composed of a particular kind of material structured in a particular way.

The initial appeal of this sort of view is due, no doubt, to certain facts about scientific methodology; in the end, however, all it really does is pass the metaphysical buck. Consider the case of fragility more closely. If we want to understand the fragility of glass, standard scientific practice suggests that we look at its internal structure—that is the parts of which it is composed and the way these parts are organized. Reductionists interpret this practice as explaining away dispositionality; the problem remains, however, for how do we explain the dispositions of the parts to come together in the particular ways they do and their dispositions to interrelate in the particular ways they do? To stay the reductionist course, we could try to explain the dispositions of the parts away by reducing them to still smaller parts and structures, but the problem will only reappear. Eventually, we are going to reach the point of the smallest ultimate constituents of our piece of glass. It is at this point that we can see clearly that the reductionist has only been shifting the problem rather than solving it.

As noted previously, in elementary particle, field, or superstring theory, a fundamental particle, field segment, or string will *not* have structure, but it *will* have multiple intrinsic properties. Quarks are apparently unstructured, but quarks have countless readinesses, countless dispositions for countless (nonactual) manifestations. Some kinds of manifestation exclude others, in the way your standing excludes your (simultaneously) sitting. The readiness of a quark for certain kinds of manifesting with certain kinds of interrelation and interreactivity of quarks and leptons constituting a chimera could exist as a particular readiness of the quark, even though nothing like a chimera ever existed or will ever exist. Even so, the quark has, *actually has*, readinesses for it. The quark is *ready* to go. Dispositionality remains intractable, even down to the ultimate particles of nuclear physics.

Thus, it is misleading to try to explain dispositionality in terms of structural states, as the reductive account does, because such structural states are dispositional themselves, and the search for a purely qualitative, nondispositional property, structural or nonstructural, is unlikely to succeed.

It appears that we must then see dispositionality as a real feature of the world; there is, however, a danger of falling into the opposite error as the one motivating the conditional and reductive accounts. Proponents of such accounts sought to deprive the world of dispositionality, whereas others have tried to make the world *nothing but* dispositionality. That is, they have tried to make objects into nothing over and above their causal powers, removing all qualities from their ontologies. In particular, interpretations of contemporary physics often fall into this error. In Chapter 6, I will discuss this 'Pythagorean' tendency and argue that it ought to be rejected. The view I will urge the reader to accept is one in which the world is seen as constituted by myriad properties that are at once qualitative *and* dispositional.

Up to this point, I have been writing overly simply about dispositionality. I have been talking as if a disposition exists unmanifested until a set of background conditions is met, resulting in manifestation. This picture is misleading, however, because so-called background conditions are every bit as operative as the identified dispositional entity. A more accurate view is one of a huge group of disposition entities or properties which, when they come together, *mutually manifest* the property in question; talk of background conditions ceases, replaced by talk of power nets (Chapter 3).

You should not think of disposition partners jointly *causing* the manifestation. Instead, the coming together of the disposition partners *is* the mutual manifestation; the partnering and the manifestation are identical. This partnering–manifestation identity is seen most clearly with cases such as the following. You have two triangle-shaped slips of paper that, when placed together appropriately, form a square. It is not that the partnering of the triangles *causes* the manifestation of the square, but rather that the partnering *is* the manifestation.

## 5.4 GRADUALISM AGAIN

The richness of the dispositional account is in keeping with the kind of gradualist picture of reality alluded to in Chapters 3 and 4 and presented more fully in chapters to follow. We need to see the world as consisting of properties that are at once dispositional and qualitative. I have begun to fill in what an ontological model that recognized this point would look like. If we accept this general ontological model, certain features thought to typify (and mystify) the mental are present already in the nonmental and even the nonsystemic cases that have been considered.

Dispositionalities *must* outrun manifestations; this should be clear from a number of kinds of case. The first type of case is one in which a disposition exists but is never manifested because it never meets the required disposition partners. The glass bottle that is melted down at the recycling plant without ever shattering is a good example. Here, all the needed partners exist (suitably hard projectiles, agents capable of launching the projectiles, correct temperature, etc.), but they never come together in mutual manifestation.

A second type of case is similar except that not only do the disposition partners never come together, but also one or more of them do not even exist (and may never have existed).

A third type of case making it clear that dispositionality must outrun manifestations arises from the fact that dispositionalities can be for *alternative* mutual manifestations whose alternative disposition partners mutually exclude the concurrence of those mutual manifestations. A piece of gold is capable of being melted at a certain temperature or dissolved in *aqua regia*, but both together cannot be manifested, though the directedness and selectedness of the disposition *for* the unmanifested manifestations are fully actual despite the nonactuality of those manifestations.

The dispositionality of any property—of a quark as much as a glass bottle—is inevitably for more than *could* ever be manifested. On any given occasion some manifestation conditions or reciprocal disposition partners will inevitably be absent or, if present, excluding or inhibiting one another. The totality of this infinity of *alternative* manifestations is unobtainable. This, as we have noted, is a necessary fact of nature.

## 5.5 FROM NONMENTAL TO MENTAL

A central theme in this book is the existence of an important parallel between the hyperdispositionality of nonmental, nonsystemic cases of the kind just discussed and features considered unique to mental intentionality. Symbols and propositional attitudes are puzzling to many because they can be about (can be directed at and selective for) things that are not present or do not even exist. I can hope my friend will visit today, desire to ride a unicorn, or believe that I am being stalked by the Abominable Snowman. As we have seen, however, this directedness and selectiveness, even to what is absent or nonexistent (as with a substance that is soluble in a solvent that does not exist in nature and whose manufacture is blocked only by a shortage of funds), is intrinsic to the dispositionality of the properties of *all* entities, nonmental as well as mental, submicroscopic as well as macroscopic. This 'what for' of dispositionality has a parallel directed selectivity to the 'what *about*' of the semantic.

Another important parallel to be drawn is between the outrunning of manifestations by dispositionalities and various modal concerns. I noted that dispositionalities must outstrip manifestations by far. It is *natural* that so little can carry so much. As a manifestation of a particular disposition base, its nature is determined by what it is *from*, namely, *that* disposition base with infinite richness of readinesses, *not* just for future manifestations, but more importantly, at the *time* of its manifestation, it is disposed for an infinity of *alternative* manifestations under *alternative* conditions within the scope of the limits set by what it is *not* disposed for and what it is disposed to *prohibit* among its actual and nonactual reciprocal dispositional partners. A disposition could be thought of in this way as a holistic web. Among the nonactual reciprocal disposition partners for which it would have actual readinesses would be ones that would be simple and very different or complex with a very different mix from those in our world. In this, there could be a realist model for what we need for modality.

We have seen that the projectability to any-of-a-kind-*K*-that-may-come-along is satisfied *within* the entity itself by its dispositional states and does not require that the dispositional states *themselves* have anything *K*-like as their 'typical cause.' There is an important parallel between this nonmental dispositionality and the generality of mental intentionality. I can have beliefs or desires about mammals generally, but what about cases of mental directedness to *individuals*?

We have seen already that an 'externalist' account is readily available for the directedness of a dispositional state toward an individual rather than just to anything similar in kind. For a dispositional state of *y* to be for individual *x* and not just anything of the same kind, the *individual* *x* must be in a causal network such that it is the *only* thing of the kind *x* that can serve as a manifestation condition or reciprocal disposition partner with the dispositional state of *y* for its manifestation.

What does appear to be special to the mental case, however, is the capacity to be directed to an *individual x* rather than any other that may be qualitatively similar, even when that individual is not in the immediate environment. One needs an account of how such an 'indirect' but still 'unique' directedness is achieved. My suggestion for such an account appears in Chapter 10, which concerns the need for something for representational use for what is absent or nonexistent. The natural material for such use is imagery that is itself *independent* of stimuli from the immediate physical environment.

# 6

# The Road to Pythagoreanism and Back

## 6.1 DISPOSITIONALITY MORE BASIC
## THAN CAUSALITY

Dispositionality is ubiquitous. It is a mistake to try to explain dispositionality in general in terms of structural states. This is so, as we have seen, partly because it is just explaining more complex dispositional states (solubility) in terms of simpler sets of dispositional states (molecular structures) and partly because some entities (elementary particles) that do not have structural states have dispositional states.

Properties of elementary particles or spatiotemporal segments of fields are not structural states, yet such properties are not in pure act: they are not manifesting at each moment or temporal stage *all* of which they are capable. The particles have dispositions, not *all* of which they are *always* manifesting, and, in the nature of the case, *qua* elementary particles, their dispositionality is not explained in terms of the properties of their constituents.

You should not ask, 'Is there causality at the *quanta* level?,' but you should ask the ontologically more *basic* question, 'Are the dispositionalities of properties of *quanta* in pure act (no potency) always manifesting everything of which they are *capable*, or are these capable of far more than on any particular occasion they actually manifest?' The answer to the second question is clearly 'The latter disjunct.' In this way, we have placed what *can* be and *can't* be manifested and how that can *change*, all of what anyone could want from causality, in the dispositionality of the *quanta*. Only the properties of mathematical entities are in pure act and, of course, the entities of physics (*contra* Quine) are not numbers.

Much of this chapter appeared as Martin (1997).

Putting the cart firmly *behind* the horse, one can see how misleading it is to try to explain dispositionality in terms of 'structural states.' First, because structural states themselves are loaded with dispositionality. Second, because properties of elementary particles or spatiotemporal segments of fields are not structural states. These properties are not in pure act, that is, manifesting at each moment or temporal stage all of which they are capable. They have dispositions and, in the *nature* of the case, their dispositionality is not explained in terms of their constituents.

Dispositions spend most of their time waiting, 'ready to go' for mutual manifestations with reciprocal disposition partners that are never present or may not even exist. The best image of 'waiting' dispositions is that of a lock with its 'fit' there *ready* for being turned by what might never exist or of a key with its 'fit' *ready* to turn what might never exist.

The dispositionalities of the 'finer interstices' even at the particle level are like locks with *or* without keys and keys with *or* without locks. It becomes obvious that dispositionalities are prior to and more basic and far more numerous than their mutual manifestations, which is cause and effect. Disposition and manifestation are the basic categories by means of which cause and effect are to be explained. A manifestation of a dispositional state should be seen in *depth* as the tip of a disposition iceberg at the *time*, rather than looking to a temporal spread of apparent manifestations perhaps for epistemic purposes.

Care must be taken in describing even an ordinary case of the manifestation of a causal disposition. The dissolution of salt in water might fail to be a manifestation of the salt's solubility in water *even* if the salt is soluble in water and the salt comes to be in dissolution in the water, because something could have brought about the dissolution before the water had its chance to team up with the salt to *do* the job.

In giving an account of something in terms of a disposition for a specific manifestation, care must also be taken not to obfuscate for the sake of a gestural tidiness the need for a rich (and difficult to adumbrate) variety of alternative mutual manifestations with alternative reciprocal disposition partners of the disposition. Quine's brusque account of believing 'The disposition to assent' only prompts the question, 'Assent *sincerely*?' To express this, one needs the central concept of the correlativity of disposition and manifestation.

A dispositional state or, what I shall call a *disposition base array*, derives its character from the pattern and complex variety of *alternative*

manifestations (under a complex range of *kinds* of manifesting condition, kinds of *reciprocal disposition partner*) *to* or *for* which it is directed.
Manifestations themselves are such only as *from* the depths of the
relevant disposition-bases.

It is best to replace cause and effect by the more basic and useful
concepts of reciprocal disposition partners for mutual manifestations.


## 6.2 DISPOSITIONAL DEPTH AND BREADTH

(1) *Dispositional depth.* An infatuated lover thinks he hears his lover
say, 'I believe she will come,' and he instantly leaps to agree, saying,
'Oh yes, I think she will come.' The lover coolly replies, 'I said I
*didn't* think she would come,' and the infatuated lover sputters (*all* of
this, of course, with sincerity), 'Oh yes, yes, I mean, I meant she *won't*
come.' We could say that the manifestation does not come from a
deep enough, strong enough disposition base.

(2) *Dispositional breadth.* A child is being taught the 10-times table
and is told that $10 \times 2 = 20$. The child is bright and of a strong,
determined nature and instantly learns at least to say, '$10 \times 2 = 20$'
under many conditions. The child has the *saying* of it from a deep
disposition base. But it lacks breadth. The child does not know *any*
arithmetic. The child resembles another child who, when asked what
$2 + 2$ makes, replies, 'I don't even know what $2$ makes.' With
the first child, we could say the disposition base has *depth* but lacks
*breadth*.

It will help to consider a nonmental case. How are we to think best
about the *soundness*, in the sense of being made to last, of the bridge's
standing up when a truck crosses it? Is it *just* that the bridge bears the
stress, without deformation, of the truck's crossing it? Or is it instead
that what is needed are many different kinds of event interrelated to
the one in question in which the bridge, over time, in many ways
bears stress without deformation? That cannot be so. We know that
the *one* occasion of bearing the stress is not enough simply in itself,
and yet we also know that it does not *need* those other stress-resistant
events actually to occur for the bearing the stress on the one occasion
to be that of doing so *soundly* in the sense required. It should be
*something about* the bridge on the occasion, and that should not be
the Rylean disposition halo of the counter-to-the-facts fact about the
bridge.

We are able to think of the bridge's standing up soundly on that occasion as a manifestation of the soundness of the bridge as embodied in the stability of its substructures (with nothing built in for untimely deterioration or breakage, etc.) *rather* than divine interference or the purely accidental proppings up of a happenchance wind-carried piece of gravel, or the like. The soundness of the bridge can, then, in terms of its actual disposition base, quite understandably be there in *full* for a fraction of a second if a hydrogen bomb vaporizes the bridge. More might be needed *epistemically*, but that is irrelevant.

Michael Dummett (1979) advances an ill-chosen example of a capacity, 'good at learning foreign languages.' This is a poor case because it is tied to performance. The case should be 'capable of learning foreign languages easily,' which could be said of those who never, in fact, get around to learning a foreign language but whose facility with their first and only language suggests, rightly or wrongly, the further capacity for acquiring foreign languages.

If attention is focused *only* on the manifestation (whether the case is mental or nonmental) or even on a number of manifestations, to provide the richness of directedness and selectiveness that has occurred, then attention is focused in the wrong place, where we *know* we cannot find what we are looking for.

This is reinforced by the unfortunate disjunction, 'dispositional or occurrent,' applied to propositional attitudes: believing, having a thought, desiring, intending. The disjunction suggests that in the *occurrence* of the sounding of a word, making an inscription, visualizing, having the 'Aha!' experience, or saying in one's head, 'Oh, dear me, yes' (fill in the occurrence any way you like), *somehow* the whole relevant aboutingness is *there*. Whatever *occurs*, however, is consistent with a different aboutingness or 'expressive potential' being possible, or even none at all.

'Everybody knows that!' Yes, but its implications must be faced and an explanation given. If it is not and cannot be *there*, then one should not make a problem or a mystery of not *finding* it there! Then where *is* it? On the particular occasion what else *is* there? It has been shown to be in the depth and breadth of the actual disposition base from which the manifestation comes, whether the case is nonmental or mental, and in the correlativity of manifestation *from* and disposition *for*. The richness consists in the actual disposition being *for* an indefinite number of (but not just *any*) alternative manifestations with alternative reciprocal disposition partners, and its specificity consists in what the disposition is *not* for or could even prohibit.

## 6.3 NON-EXISTENT AND PROHIBITIVE DISPOSITIONS

Any disposition or readiness potential, mental or *non*mental, simple or complex, is *for* an infinity, within limits, of *alternative* manifestations with an infinity, within limits, of *alternative* reciprocal disposition partners actual and *non*actual, present and absent, and even never-existing. The limits of directedness are set by the still greater infinity of manifestations the disposition is *not for* as well as the manifestations it *prohibits*. This is the ontology of the specificity of dispositionality.

A difference must be drawn between

(A)  *not* having a disposition for manifesting *x*, and
(B)  *having* a disposition for *prohibiting x*.

The distinction is essential to understanding the constraints and limits of infinities. This difference is one between

(A′)  a state's or entity's simply not having a disposition for a particular kind of manifestation, although there is nothing about the state or entity that would require alteration for its addition, and

(B′)  a state's having a disposition that is prohibitive against a particular kind of manifestation such that it would require *alteration* for the addition of the disposition that is prohibited. An example would be a square peg disposed to prohibit fitting into a round hole as a round peg would.

Seeing the richness of correlativity between manifestation and disposition, we can understand how a thought could be an indivisible unity though only partially expressed. The manifestation fragment gets its fullness of import by being *of* a deep enough, broad enough, relevant disposition base array that is for an infinity of alternative manifestations with alternative disposition partners—an infinity within limits.

It can be seen just how the 'occurrent or dispositional belief' is a clumsy and superficial disjunction. What is occurrent is some manifestation fragment that can have the specificity and richness of its import only by being *from* the richnesses of the disposition base array of which it is the manifestation.

## 6.4 NONMENTAL DISPOSITIONS

Causal dispositions are directive and selective—that is, they are dispositions *for* and *to* some kinds of manifestation rather than others—and so they are, whether physical or mental, in their very *nature* directive, projective, discriminatory readinesses *for* and *to* what is external to themselves.

The disposition can be *for* what may never exist—the fit of a particular lock for a non-existent key, or a substance soluble in a solvent that does not exist in nature and whose manufacture is simply too expensive and so never gets made. And finally, there may be some fundamental particles irreducibly different in kind from one another that are disposed for reactions to one another but eternally fail to manifest such reactions because of cosmic space–time separateness.

A nonmental dispositional state needs, just as much as a mental state, to be characterized in terms of that to which the state is directed, which may or may not be present or even exist.

Just as a belief needs *content*, namely, what would follow the 'that' in 'belief that . . . ,' so a disposition needs a *what-for*, namely, what would follow the 'for' in 'disposition for . . . ,' for instance, 'disposition *for* dissolving in $H_2O$ (and not *aqua regia* or XYZ).'

A nonmental (as well as mental) dispositional state can be directive in a way that is indeterminate in reference to a particular individual or in a way that is determinate (to a *particular* individual) in reference.

A particular hen has or does not have a set of dispositions and capacities for laying an egg (not any *particular* egg), and furthermore, the hen might have a set of dispositions and capacities for laying a *particular* egg provided by the causal context (e.g. the *one* egg that has actually begun to form). 'Externalism' (and 'broad content') unarguably could enter where the directedness is to a *particular* entity, uniquely provided in the physical context, rather than to just *anything* that happens to be of a particular kind.

Holding a belief or having *understanding* (or kindness, for that matter) can be 'holistically' and 'fully,' at a particular time, *in* the head, without magic, as *soundness* can be *in* the bridge at a particular time, namely as an actual disposition state array that might or might not have actual manifestations at the time, or ever.

The correlativeness of a disposition-manifestation is such that for something to be a particular kind of manifestation, it must come *from* a relevant deep enough, broad enough disposition base, and for something to be a disposition base it must be *for* alternative typifying manifestations. Nature comes in package deals. One should see that the dispositionality *for* a range of manifestations will also *not* be for or even be *prohibitive* against manifesting an infinite number of other manifestations. This is the basic ontology for setting the limits of the infinities of directivenesses and selectivenesses, whether the entities or states are psychological or nonpsychological, and even whether they are systemic or, as in the case of elementary particles, nonsystemic.

Dispositions or readiness potentials exist embodying programs for, *not* for, and even prohibitive *against* an infinity of manifestations under a limited scope as described above. This account of the dispositional as directive, selective, readinesses with the correlativeness of disposition and manifestation is such that the manifestation 'carries' the richness of the disposition base it is *from* or *of*. It is natural that so little can carry so much. In this way, every disposition is a holistic web.

Through the concepts of 'reciprocal disposition partner' and 'mutual manifestation,' a way can be seen to bridge the 'narrow-content'/'broad-content' gap. The physical environment and the individual human mind should be considered to be *reciprocal* disposition partners for the *mutual* manifestation of perception. The reaching out comes from *both* sides of the partnership in their mutual manifestation.

The externalist and the internalist both miss the point. Readiness for the mutual manifestation of perception is found in *each* disposition partner, whether state of a perceiver *or* state of the environment, even if the other does not exist! Both are needed for the actualization of the perception that is their *mutual* manifestation.

It is clear that forms of readinesses with their directedness and selectiveness are gifts of nonpsychological nature and should *not* be asked for all over again at the psychological level. It is, of course, another matter to say what more is needed to make the directedness and selectiveness *mental*.

Given a realist view of dispositions as fully actual even without the actuality of their manifestations or their reciprocal disposition partners, a purely dispositional account of properties has a degree of plausibility. This plausibility is enhanced by the impossibility of characterizing any property as purely qualitative, that is, as existing without any implications of dispositionality. I shall argue, however, that, in the end, it is equally implausible to characterize any property as *purely* dispositional.

## 6.5 PROPERTIES AS PURELY DISPOSITIONAL

Sydney Shoemaker (1980), James Fetzer (1981), and Hugh Mellor (1974, 1991) have been recent proponents of the claim that a property is identical with its causal powers. Take the following passage from Shoemaker, for instance:

> Suppose, however, that all of their causal powers and potentialities, all of their dispositions to influence other things or be influenced by other things, were exactly the same. Then, I suggest, they would share all of their properties in the narrow sense, all of the 'intrinsic' properties. Likewise, when I say that the loss by my pencil of the property of being fifty miles south of a burning barn, or the property of being such that Gerald Ford is President, is not a real change, the cash value of this is that the acquisition or loss of these so-called properties does not in itself make any difference to the causal powers of a thing. This suggests a view about what intrinsic properties, properties in the narrow sense, are. According to this view, what constitutes the identity of such a property, what makes it the particular property it is, is its potential for contributing to the causal powers of the things that have it. . . . If we could indicate all of the ways in which the having of this property could contribute to the causal powers of things, we would have said all there is to say about the intrinsic nature of this property. (Shoemaker 1980: 332)

My initial response to any such account is to state it fairly but baldly and let its absurdity show through.

The image of a property as *only* a capacity for the production of other capacities for the production . . . , etc., is absurd, even if—indeed, *especially* if—you are a realist about capacities. Whether you take this response as just question-begging or as revealing a *reductio ad absurdum*, my opponent cannot plead misrepresentation.

A more measured response to Shoemaker's purely dispositional account of properties, requires us to reflect on a more general point. A lack of candor has characterized the formulation of some of the great reductive ontologies: phenomenalism, behaviorism, and operationalism, for instance. The vocabulary used in presenting these theories discouraged a clear view of their ontological commitments. I am not trying to push defenders of these views into giving translation or logical entailment accounts. I am perfectly happy if they scrub up their vocabulary, then add 'etc.' When that is done, the doctrines will at least be ready for consideration.

(a) *Phenomenalism* got away with:

For 'There is an F in the next room': 'It would tend to look F-ish to me if *my sensory capacities were in good working order and I were to go into the next room and look in the direction of F, etc.*'

The italicized part of the sentence is not expressed in terms of the basic terms of the ontology. When the candid attempt is made to do so, to scrub the vocabulary clean, its anti-intuitiveness becomes apparent.

(b) *Behaviorism* got away with:

For 'I am having mental imagery of *Greensleeves* as played by Glenn Gould': 'I would behave as if *hearing* Glenn Gould play *Greensleeves*, or by saying *sincerely*, if I *thought* the occasion called for it, that it was as if Glenn Gould were playing *Greensleeves*, etc.'

Again, the italicized part of the sentence is not expressed according to the ontology. 'Hearing,' 'sincerity,' and 'thought' are not behaviourist terms. When the attempt is made to scrub the vocabulary clean, the anti-intuitiveness of this view likewise becomes apparent.

The very same holds true of the Shoemaker–Mellor–Fetzer view that all that is intrinsic to properties is exhausted in their dispositionalities.

(c) *Pure Dispositionalism* gets away with:

For '*x* and *y* are equal in length': '*x* and *y* are disposed to *fit* or *not fit* into the same *containers* in the same way, ignoring their *width and weight*, etc.'

The story is no different than it is for phenomenalism and behaviourism. The need is to couch all of the vocabulary in terms of dispositionalities and only dispositionalities.

Let us demand maximum candor here. If properties are treated only as capacities–dispositions, let us have that clear from the outset. Explicitness is necessary in all ontological domains, but particularly in the domain of the mental because of the ambiguity of terms such as 'behaviour,' in which *sensory* (therefore, sentient) feedback might be implicit. When stated explicitly, the Shoemaker–Mellor–Fetzer view is revealed to have the anti-intuitiveness of a reduction of all the properties of whatever the dispositions are for (namely, the manifestations) to just further dispositions themselves. What, on this view, is introspected as the very quality of the *feel* of the feeling of a kind of pain? Indeed, what, on this view, is the account of the (non-number) quality of the length as directional spread seen or felt of a form of extension?

Your knowledge of the existence of physical *x* or mental *y* has to involve the causal dispositions of *x* and *y* to affect your belief that *x* or that *y*. Those dispositions are specifically operative on that occasion for that belief. This, however, does not establish (*contra* Shoemaker) that the content of what you know or believe is nothing more than the collection of causal dispositions or functions that make you or would make you believe *x* or *y*.

Dispositionalists believe that all that appears to be qualitatively intrinsic to things reduces to capacities–dispositions for the formation of other capacities–dispositions for the formation of other capacities–dispositions for the formation of. . . . And, of course, the manifestations of any disposition can only be further dispositions for. . . . This image appears absurd even if one is a realist about capacities–dispositions. It is a promissory note that may be actual enough, but if it is for only *another* promissory note that is. . . , it is entirely *too* promissory.

## 6.6 DISPOSITIONALITY AND QUALITATIVITY

When we try to state or to think through what justifies, warrants, or makes true a counterfactual or causal dispositional statement, it seems absurd to attempt to find it in something purely dispositional and nonqualitative, and *equally* absurd to find it in something purely qualitative and nondispositional. The purely qualitative is as much a 'logical fiction,' in Hume's phrase, as is the purely dispositional. The truth is obvious: in this matter, *nothing* is pure.

The only way to express this Limit View of real properties that does not amount to treating real properties as compounds of purely qualitative and purely dispositional properties is to show how the attempt to abstract these as distinct elements is unrealizable in reality and only approachable as *limits* for different ways of being of the *same* unitary property such that they may be necessarily or contingently covariant. This will hold for *all* real properties, encompassing even the most ultimate properties of elementary particles or fields.

We have seen that it is useful to replace talk of cause and effect with talk of disposition and manifestation (under triggering and manifestation conditions). Whatever resistance there may be to speaking of a causality at the quantum level, it should be obvious that *quanta are not potency-free, in pure act, or at all times manifesting all of which they are capable* under every sort of manifestation-condition. The dream of either a purely qualitative, nondispositional account or a purely dispositional account of properties is philosophical fantasy. On the one hand, no property is in 'pure act,' free of all unfulfilled potency unless it is a property of God or, perhaps, the number 2. On the other hand, no property is *only* its capacity for the production of further capacities for. . . . This ontological fact is more evident than is any hypothesized lawlike regularity that seems not to occur at the level of quanta, nor, for that matter, at the macroscopic level.

My suggestion is that properties of entities constitutive of any state of affairs must be qualitative as well as dispositional, dispositional as well as qualitative. Dispositionality and qualitativity are correlative (Locke), complementary, inseparable, and covariant when they are displayed in their intrinsic and irreducible form at the level of the finer interstices of nature. I contend that they have a surprising identity. In this regard, properties resemble duck–rabbit pictures, in which the duck picture and the rabbit picture are surprisingly identical.

What I have called (perhaps misleadingly) the Limit View (Martin 1993: 519; see also my contribution to Armstrong *et al* 1996) treats any intrinsic property not as a two-part compound of the purely qualitative and nondispositional and of the purely nonqualitative and dispositional, but as a two-sided dispositional–qualitative coin. These cannot be abstracted as fully distinct and separable elements, but must be considered unrealizable limits for different ways of being the selfsame unitary property. Supervenience is not to the point. The dispositional and the qualitative are equally basic and irreducible; there is no direction for one being basic in a property and the other being 'supervenient.' The dream of a purely nondispositional categorical property is as much a philosophical fantasy as the purely noncategorical dispositional property.

The Limit View has maximum flexibility in expressing both necessary (if any) and contingent (if any) relations between categoricality and dispositionality of properties. This is an important and largely unexplored area of ontology. If an idea is expressed only in terms of quantities, then the system of relations of quantities is natural material for the necessities accruing to the mathematicization of nature.

This was the place, namely, among 'the finer interstices of nature' and 'the insensible corpuscles,' at which Locke suggested that the real necessities between the primary quantities resided, although he thought we would be largely ignorant of them. Locke believed the molecular theory of heat provided an approximation to such hidden necessities. Necessities will have to be earned, but so will contingencies. The Limit View is specially suited for the statement of either or a judicious *mixture*. For antimodalists, it can suit nonmodal talk as well.

The preliminary characterization above in terms of 'different *ways* of being,' however, is still too suggestive a mixture. It is even more than necessary covariance (as exhibited by equiangular and equilateral). For any intrinsic and irreducible property, what is qualitative and what is dispositional are one and the same property considered as what that property exhibits of its nature and what that property is directive and selective for as its manifestations. These cannot be prised apart into the purely qualitative and the purely dispositional. What is exhibited in the qualitative informs and determines what is the for-ness of the dispositional, and the for-ness of the dispositional informs and determines what is exhibited in the qualitative. There is no direction of priority or dependence. There is no reduction of one to the other.

The only way this can be expressed is by affirming that the qualitative and dispositional are identical with one another and with the unitary intrinsic property itself. This is perhaps a surprising identity, but frequently it happens that different representations turn out (to one's surprise) to be of the selfsame entity.

This claimed identity might be easier to see once you understand clearly that it is not a matter of one aspect being nonrelational (the qualitative) and the other aspect being relational (the dispositional). Dispositionality is *not* a relation between what is dispositional and what is its manifestation. A disposition can fully exist and be 'ready to go' with the total nonexistence of the manifestation and reciprocal disposition partners needed for the manifestation. Their absence or nonexistence does not affect the readiness of the dispositional state. The state would not have to alter to yield the manifestation.

What is qualitative and what is dispositional for any property is less like a two-sided coin or a Janus-faced figure than it is like an ambiguous drawing. A particular drawing, remaining unitary and unchanged, can be seen or considered one way as a drawing of a goblet and, differently considered, as a drawing of two faces staring at one another. The goblet and the faces are not distinguishable parts, components, or even aspects of the drawing, although you could easily consider the one without considering, or even knowing of, the other. The goblet drawing is surprisingly identical with the two-faces drawing. The duck drawing and the rabbit drawing are likewise surprisingly identical.

It might be thought, however, that something could exist in a qualitative state but in no dispositional state. You might be able to imagine something that is totally inert and unchanging. That is different from being without any dispositionality, however. A thing or property that is intrinsically incapable of affecting or being affected by anything else, actual or possible, is not merely a case of inertness—it amounts to a *no-thing*.

Getting clear about the nature of properties, determines the scope of the empirical question of what properties in particular there are or might be, including their qualitativity as well as their dispositionality, in either the physical domain (which includes 'theoretical entities') or the psychological domain.

According to a realist theory of dispositions, the notion of a distinct, purely dispositional property existing on its own is an important and powerful notion, however anti-intuitive it might appear at first. Correct or incorrect, the notion has an honorable lineage and ought to be discussed in terms of some of its past and current forms.

Historically, the supposition of the purely dispositional can arise from operationalism cum functionalism that can, in turn, arise from a verificationism that makes an infinitude of possible forms of neural and bodily activity (verification-operations)—that need not be actualized—basic.

*Weak verificationism* is the view that no statements of any finite set of verifications/falsifications or confirmings/disconfirmings entail the truth or falsity of what is confirmed/disconfirmed. *Strong verificationism* is the view that some finite set of verifications/confirmings entails the truth or falsity of what is confirmed/disconfirmed. Strong verificationism is evidently *too* strong.

It is ironic that *weak* verificationism is *itself* verification-transcendent. Any possible set of statements about confirming-happenings is consistent with the *falsity* of a statement about the existence of what is being confirmed. Whatever verification is effected, it is transcendently projective beyond any finite amount of verification-exemplifications.

This incompleteness is underscored by the fact that, typically, the performance of a set of one kind of verification *excludes* the possibility of the performance of some other kinds of verification. Recourse to falsification or disconfirmation changes nothing.

Gestures to the 'Ideal Observer' are of no help here. Verification of the ideality of an 'Ideal Observer' must be incomplete as well. Weak verificationism has the seeds of a verification-transcendent projectivism within it!

Reductivist ontologies that tend to emanate from weak verificationism—operationalism, phenomenalism, behaviorism—inherit the same verification-transcendent project to the limitless and numerically indefinite would-have-been-ifs that take precedence over and against any possible finite set of *actual* confirmings in the form of operations, observings, or behavings.

A focus on the incompleteness of verification or falsification and the recourse to the rough linguistic gesture toward an indefinite number of dispositionals and counterfactuals is a focus toward the purely dispositional (*mostly* unmanifested) and away from the purely categorical.

## 6.7 SURPRISING IDENTITIES

You might initially balk at the suggestion that the dispositional and the qualitative are in fact identical. If $x = y$, it might be supposed that we ought to know it immediately. But this supposition is a mistake. Examples of *surprising* identities abound (especially in discussions of identity and reference) from the Morning Star/Evening Star and the man with the martini to Simon Blackburn's 'the bleeding foot is mine!' The example I want to explore here is the well-known duck/rabbit (Fig. 6.1). We can recognize a number of parallels between this perceptually ambiguous identity case and a conceptually ambiguous identity case, as well as between the foibles of perceptual eyes and conceptual 'eyes.'

The parallels to be established are between the perceptual surprising identity in the duck/rabbit picture and the conceptual surprising identity in the quality/disposition case. In each case, duality lies only in the eyes of the perceiver or the 'eyes' of the conceiver, for the

**FIG. 6.1.** Duck/Rabbit

seeing one rather than the other as a duck and then as a rabbit is, of course, not identical.

(1)   Some can only see the duck.

(1′)  Some can only 'see' the quality in its pure act, with no potency—e.g. D. M. Armstrong. (St Thomas would apply pure act only to God.)

(2)   Some can only see the rabbit.

(2′)  Some can only 'see' the dispositionality—e.g. Hugh Mellor.

(3)   Some can see nothing about the picture.

(3′)  Some can 'see' nothing about properties—e.g. Quine's linguisticism.

(4)   Some can alternatively see the duck or the rabbit in the picture.

(4′)  Some can alternatively 'see' the quality or the dispositionality of the property.

(5)   Some can see both the duck and the rabbit *at once*, each filling the picture. (Try seeing the eye as looking directly at you to help with this effect.)

(5′)  Some can 'see' both the quality and the dispositionality at once, each filling the property. (Try reading pertinent passages in this book several times to help with this effect.)

(6)   It is false to suppose that we see part of the picture as purely and solely rabbit and a different part as purely and solely duck, because the parts are not exclusive of one another—they fully overlap.

(6′)  It is false to suppose that we 'see' an aspect of the property as a purely and solely nondispositional quality (the Thomistic pure act holding only of qualities of God) and another aspect of the property as purely and solely nonqualitative dispositionality, because the aspects are not exclusive of one another—they fully overlap.

(7) The duck drawing and the rabbit drawing are the selfsame unitary drawing. That explains, as nothing else can, the fact that they 'fully overlap.'

(7′) The quality property and the dispositional property are the identical unitary property. That explains, as nothing else can, the fact that they 'fully overlap.'

It becomes obvious that the epistemic and the ontological conditions (as in the case of everything) are very different for identity and nonidentity. Examples abound in mathematics and logic for mistaking one for the other. Descartes knew this rather well; Locke knew it better.[1]

An argument that identity (of quality and disposition, for instance) is the best explanation for necessary covariance appears to be threatened by cases of distinct properties—being equiangular and being equilateral, for instance—having such covariance.

Three straight lines or edges at their three points of connection form a three-sided plane figure with three angles. Consider an equiangular, equilateral triangle. Disproportional increases or decreases of the lengths of the sides are matched by increases or decreases of the amounts of the degrees of the angles. *Proportional* increases or decreases of the lengths of the sides are not matched by proportional increases or decreases of the amounts of the degrees of the angles, however. There is consequently a *lack* of covariance between the sizes of the sides and the sizes of the angles of equiangular, equilateral triangles.

## 6.8 DISPOSITIONS AND QUANTUM THEORY

Instead of measuring operations or observations, we can speak of measures. Quantum theory has commonly been interpreted as encoding measurement predictions and the irreducible indeterminacy of quantum 'states of affairs' understood as irreducible probabilities (less than unity) stated in measurement predictions. This interpretation imposes an essential mind-dependence of quantum events described in the theory. The choice is whether to interpret the wave function as a physical continuant at all.

Arthur Fine has shown a fascinating vacillation in Schrödinger's interpretation of measurement predictions between referring to and

---

[1] And perhaps Spinoza knew it best of all; see Chapter 16.

not referring to the wave function as a real continuant. Fine describes Schrödinger's laconic letter of July 13, 1935, to Einstein:

Schrödinger then proceeds to set out briefly what he thinks is going on; namely, that the classical physical model has in fact been abandoned but that instead of replacing it with another, one has simply declared all of its determinables to be exactly measurable in principle and in addition prescribed with wise, philosophical expressions that these *measurements* are the only real things, which is, of course, metaphysics. Then in fact it does not trouble us at all that our claims about the *model* are monstrous. (Fine 1986: 76)

In such a mood (very different from the mood in which he attempted interpretations in terms of wavelike models), Schrödinger rejects all attempts to provide a model. He even dismissively describes the model of sparse and intermittent measurement events as the only 'real' posits as 'metaphysical.' This vacillation provides few crumbs for ontologically hungry philosophers, whether realist, antirealist, or something in between.

The introduction of the term 'measurement' is disturbingly ambiguous. Any measurement procedure will involve certain physical movements. Surely, if precisely similar physical movements were brought about by something that was not an intelligent agent, or if the experimenter performed the 'measurement' but no measurement was recorded, perhaps due to a lapse of attention, then, in one sense, no measurement would have been made. The physical outcome of the physical experimental procedure would have occurred, however, although it remained unknown.

The alternative to this interpretation is an interpretation that would include mental dependence through the observer-dependent notion of measurement from the very beginning so that it should be no surprise that mental dependence would be excluded in a final account. It would be no more than clumsy question-begging to use (perhaps without notice) such a mind-dependent interpretation of quantum physics as an authority against forms of realism. Looked at quite literally, if the *physical* result of measurement requires the knowing attentiveness of an observer, that would be a mind-over-matter factor not even specified in the theory, but only evoked in some interpretation of the theory. This ought to remind us of Einstein's reference to the quantum theorists' 'epistemology-soaked orgy.'

The drive to Pythagoreanism and the tendency to deprive properties of their nature can take the form of limiting basic physical descriptions to statistical or probabilistic claims concerning purported states. Einstein stated this doctrine clearly, though with the strongest disapproval:

They [Born, Pauli, Heitler, Bohr, and Margenau] are all firmly convinced that the riddle of the double nature of all corpuscles (corpuscular and undulatory character) has in essence found its final solution in the statistical quantum theory. On the strength of the successes of this theory they consider it proved that a theoretically complete description of a system can, in essence, involve only statistical assertions concerning the measurable quantities of this system. (Einstein 1949: 666)

If what is claimed is taken seriously, and if this is not to be a Pythagoreanism of pure numbers, it is an ontology of pure 'probabilifyingnesses'—probability facts or probability bundles somehow embedded in space–time.

The ontology of such probabilifyingnesses, if it is not Pythagorean, could be expressed as equivalent to primitive dispositionalities, propensities, or potentials. A probabilifyingness is more like a propensity than it is like a specific manifestation-directed disposition. Propensities can admit of degree, so there might be a propensity of a certain degree for both outcome $A$ and (incompatible) outcome $B$.

Consider interpretations that take Schrödinger's wave function as a state that grounds, or is the truthmaker for, measurement predictions and probability statements concerning measurement outcomes, such that its 'theoretically complete description . . . involve[s] only statistical assertions.'

Such an interpretation of quantum theory represents quantum states of affairs as probability-less-than-unity states that ground measurement predictions. In such an interpretation, the full characterization of a state of affairs is just in terms of irreducible probabilities; it excludes any further complement that could not itself be expressed in terms of probabilities. A parallel interpretation in terms of tendencies is that of a full characterization of a state of affairs just in terms of irreducible tendencies or readiness potentials. Perhaps the most difficult feature to mathematize of reciprocal disposition partners would be their respective degrees of availability.

Speaking of probability facts, or even probability bundles or states, is merely an alternative way of speaking of pure, but unspecified and perhaps unknown, tendencies. This becomes most apparent when it is claimed of their ontological status that they are not reducible to and need not have or be based on a ratio of actual relevant occurrences. What other than tendencies could be the ontological ground for such cases of probabilities with non-occurrent frequencies? Opportunities for mathematicization undoubtedly afford this metaphysics an added measure of respectability.

The ontology of this is the positing of non-categorical pure probabilities or probabilifyingnesses or pure dispositions, propensities or 'potentials.' A probabilifyingness is more like a propensity than it is like a specific manifestation-directed disposition. Propensities can admit of degree and so there can be a propensity of a certain degree (probability) for outcome $A$ and also a propensity of a certain degree (probability) for outcome $B$.

Characterizing states of affairs only in terms of irreducible probabilities, then, if it has a non-Pythagorean ontological status, is just equivalent to a characterization in terms of irreducible tendency or propensity properties. The probability (less than 1) or the tendency can be satisfied or actualized for a particular state of affairs in the absence of the outcome the probability is *for* or the propensity is *to*.

## 6.9 INDETERMINACY AND DISPOSITION FLUTTERS

The irreducible disjunctivity in higher-order accounts of irreducible probability rests in the probabilifying 'linking' or 'connecting' as a primitive relation between universals (Armstrong 1983) above pure 'happening' in a way that is far from clear. Disjunctive 'linking,' even if we allow it, does no work for the production of the particular disjunct that actually results. Even a view that admits primitive tendencies or propensities has the similar problem of being irresolubly disjunctive and not taking us up to the very production of the specific result itself.

This is not a naïve complaint about indeterminacy—I am pointing out a metaphysical gap. The gap resembles a nomination procedure for a disjunction of candidates that does not decide among them. Were it to elect one disjunct or candidate, it would decide for one rather than another, and be determinate between them. If there is not such a selection or production of one disjunct rather than another between the candidates, there is no election nor a production of a disjunct at all. The explanation of the success of a candidate or production of a disjunct, short of magic, would be incomplete, and the links in this disjunctive linkage would not take us to the result, but only to a pre-result determination of disjunctivities.

We need an account of disjunctivity that could take us all the way to the result. This is no more than a graphic presentation of what is anti-intuitive in current models of the collapse of the wave function. Perhaps an account in terms of a primitive *disposition flutter* would help.

The disposition flutter is an ontologically primitive oscillator built into the basic and irreducible properties of the elementary particle itself rather than something fixed by hidden conditions outside the particle and its properties. Each flut of the flutter (oscillation) of the dispositions intrinsic to the properties of the particle, however unpredictable, would be an irreducible ontic ground for the manifestation of a determinate result.

Thus conceived, the disposition flutter is intrinsic to irreducible properties of an elementary particle. There would be no need to look to hidden factors extrinsic to the basic properties of the particle itself, just as the rate of 'decay' has sometimes been represented as intrinsic to the nature of an atom and not to be explained by extrinsic and hidden causes or variables.

The intrinsic disposition flutter *itself* is not a mutual manifestation of reciprocal disposition partners, though the particular flut of a disposition flutter could, with its reciprocal partners, *have* a mutual manifestation.

A disposition flutter might occur too quickly to measure, thus appearing to be random or nondeterminate, or the disposition flutter might be intrinsically irregular, giving the impression of nondeterminateness.

If a disposition flutter is intrinsic, it is like other irreducible intrinsic factors for elementary and basic particles or aspects of spatiotemporal segments (if one exchanges particle theory for field theory): their presence and nature is not to be explained in terms of anything else. An account of this kind provides maximum determinacy.

## 6.10 PYTHAGOREANISM

The progression to Pythagoreanism (all is number) goes from the measure of the observably measurable to the quantity of that observed measure as it is used for further quantity assessments of what is unobserved. The dispositionality and qualitativity of any intrinsic property might be analogous to the way shape and size are of extension. In each case, the one cannot exist without the other, although it appears that one could *vary* independently of the other. *Contra* Hume, they are distinct but not separable. And *contra* Hume, there are cases of distinctness that lack separability but which *must* co-vary, for instance, the old example of equiangular and equilateral.

We must logically exclude separability and affirm the necessity of both dispositionality and qualitativity for any property, but then we are free to decide on any given case whether their co-variance is necessary or contingent. The properties that are constitutive of any state of affairs must be qualitative *as well as* dispositional and dispositional *as well as* qualitative. They are correlative (Locke) and inseparable.

It also appears that causal relations between properties involved in causal situations could be necessary or contingent. An example of necessary causal relations between distinct properties is how a square peg does not fit into a round hole in quite the way a round peg does. An apparent example of contingent relations between distinct properties in a causal situation is that obtaining between the freezing and expansion of water.

Examples of contingency of causal situations, following Locke's suggestion, might be only 'seeming' examples. When we get, if we ever do, to what constitutes macroscopic entities, we get down to a specificity of how the work gets done. As we move among the fittings within the 'finer interstices' of the 'insensible corpuscles,' the appearance of contingency could fade. It is there that the measures of quantities are suited to the mathematicizations of nature itself with its accruing necessities. Relations within the most intimate parts of nature also get their expression (and, it is tempting to think, their *full* expression) in terms of algorithms and mathematical formulae.

Let there be a warning: 'This way lies Pythagoreanism.' We must see that physics has tended to be, in Locke's phrase, a 'partial consideration' *qua* the measures of quantities and not let it become a denial and an expungement of the properties for and of which the quantities have a measure. Richard Feynman puts it this way:

If we look at a glass of wine closely enough we will see the entire universe. There are the things of physics: the twisting liquid which evaporates depending on the wind and weather, the reflections in the glass, and our imagination adds the atoms. The glass is a distillation of the earth's rocks, and in its composition we see the secrets of the universe's age, and the evolution of stars. . . . There are the ferments, the enzymes, the substrates, and the products. There in wine is found the great generalizations: all life is fermentation. . . . How vivid is the claret, pressing its existence into the consciousness that watches it! If our small minds, for some convenience, divide this glass of wine, this universe, into parts—physics, biology, geology, astronomy, psychology, and so on—remember that nature does not know it! So let us put it all back together, not forgetting ultimately what it is for. Let it give us one more final pleasure: drink it and forget it all!' (Feynman *et al.* 1963: lec. 3, 10)

Physicists' partial consideration of qualities *qua* only their measures works well enough until perhaps the end of the road of the *reductio ad absurdum* of Pythagoreanism. Then the task must be to state the indispensable qualities for which we have considered only their measures. We must 'put it all back together,' and that will take *more*, much more, as Feynman himself sometimes realized, than to 'drink it and forget it all!'

Properties of things at the macroscopic and molecular levels are complexes of the simpler properties of their constituents in all of their interrelatednesses and interreactivenesses. The tendency toward Pythagoreanism increases as the posited constituents and their changes are further and further removed from direct observation. At the level of the entities of particle physics, the quantities assessed for changes and change potentials are projected from the observable changes of objects and measuring devices and by the direction derived from available mathematical models. These quantities do service for what is required for mathematicizations in terms of which the theory is to be ultimately expressed.

Properties that the quantities of changes and change potentials are of might not be explicitly denied, but they are considered exclusively in terms of their numerical nature. From a Pythagorean point of view, quantities of projected change and change potentials are nested or grouped uniquely as intrinsic to, and typifying of, the numerical nature of some theoretical entity, rather like number-packets of algorithms and mathematical formulae in space–time. What changes and change potentials represent over and above pure quantity can be disregarded in the partial consideration *qua* numbers formed by the mathematicization of projected quantities of changes and change potentials. This non-regard of the properties in terms of which changes occur and change potentials stand can, if it turns into a denial, become

Pythagoreanism or, perhaps, the propertyless there-nesses of the simple atoms of extreme atomism.

We have been led by Quine and by others to think that necessity and contingency are one, that there is no distinction in reality between them. This brings to mind a comic strip in which one character says to the other, 'Marriage is where two people become one.' In the next panel, the second character clearly is considering the statement. In the final panel, the second character asks, 'Which one?'

Quine's answer seemed to be, 'All is contingent.' But then, in 'Whither material objects?' (1976), he took the step from the need of the existence of numbers for physics (the measure of quantities), with an invocation of the Principle of the Identity of Empirically Isomorphic Theories (a fancy term for the verificationism Quine never rejected), to Pythagoreanism—all is number, that is, numbers and their relations—the mathematicization of space and time:

> Carnap was propounding such a *Koordinatensprache* already in 1934 [*Logische Syntax der Sprache*, 11, 40], and not because of constraints on the notion of physical object from the side of physics; for the scheme has also a certain intrinsic appeal. Numbers and other mathematical objects are wanted in physics anyway, so one may as well enjoy their convenience as coordinates for physical objects; and then, having come thus far, one can economize a little by dispensing with the physical objects. . . . As physicalists we have welcomed bodies with open arms. . . . On the other hand the mathematical objects attained the ontological scene only begrudgedly for services rendered. . . . It is ironical, then, that we at length find ourselves constrained to this anti-physical sort of reduction from the side of physics itself. It is this I have wanted to bring out. (Quine 1976: 502)

and

> Physical objects, next, evaporated into space–time regions; but this was the outcome of physics itself. Finally the regions went over into pure sets; still, the set theory itself was there for no other reason than the need for mathematics as an adjunct to physical theory. (Quine 1976: 502–3)

After that, the Quinean answer to the question, 'Which one?' might better be, 'All is *necessary*.'

## 6.11 BACK FROM THE BRINK

The unfettered deontologizing that results in a world of pure number seems as clear a *reductio* as any in philosophy. There are two hoary alternative detours on the road back from the unworldly abstraction of Pythagoreanism. Reversing direction to move back from the Quantities to the Measures and Measure Potentials is just old-fashioned Operationalism all over again. Moving further back to the measurer's possible measure-observations is just Idealism–Phenomenalism–Subjectivism all over again.

Once we recognize that the properties of nature require the qualitative as well as the dispositional, there seems no alternative remaining for the road back from Pythagoreanism but to ask, 'What are the *physical qualia* (that is, qualities)?'

This is not to ask for anything inconsistent with the conservation of energy or the laws of thermodynamics. The question is meant only to indicate that mathematicizations in physical theory are partial characterizations of what is changing and at work. To make explicit the need for qualities is not to add more work by something not measured or measurable. Properties (including both qualitative and dispositional aspects) of elementary particles or segments of fields, whatever these properties might, in the end, turn out to be, are what change and have typical change potentials whose measures are ascribed and given quantities. These properties have been tacitly there all along, as they needed to be.

We must see physics as a partial consideration *qua* projected quantities of changes and change potentials, not as the expungement of properties including their qualities and dispositions for which there are those quantities and change potentials. What the simpler properties among the 'insensible corpuscles' that constitute the macroscopic properties really are (whether sentient or nonsentient) might be a real surprise.

Qualities of shape and size are intrinsic and provide the form and extent of the 'shell' of the entities that have them. These qualities are space-fillings noted by Berkeley, Hume, and Blackburn (1990) in that they are needed as intrinsic to what has size and shape and are the extension limits of these specific properties. They are needed for *what* is changing or different by virtue of which all of the quantities of such changes and differences of ultimate constituents (whether particles, aspects of fields, or superstrings) are assessed.

These needed qualities should not be ontologically questionable secondary qualities that, for many, have come to be thought of in terms of primary qualities, leaving aside the status of the questions of their powers to affect observers.

## 6.12 NEUROLOGICAL PYTHAGOREANISM

When we consider the need for physical *qualia* (that is, qualities), even in the finest interstices of nature, largely unregarded and unknown, among them should belong the *qualia* (qualities) required for the sensing and feeling parts of physical nature. But first things first—let us appreciate the need for physical *qualia* (qualities) in nonsentient nature and make sure we do not leave out any that are needed.

An account of neuronal qualities in terms of a purely directional vector function with its dispositionality for potential alternative trajectories would embody a pure dispositionalism, something like the on-the-go American Sunday driver. Every arrival point is seen only as a point for departure, and the qualitative nature of what is present at any point in the driver's progress is of no interest. The qualitative nature of what occupies the place is spelled out in terms only of its actual and potential trajectories from and to other places. This vectorial approach mathematizes nicely, but one needs a model explicitly incorporating vectors (for directional connectivities) and single cell groups (for the properties of *what* are connecting) with the different research emphases of each made necessary to the other.

It is almost inevitable for functionalist-driven researchers and theorists to place exclusive emphasis on the neuronal interconnections within the neural network. This is the road to Pythagoreanism of the brain. Against this is a useful corrective by P. A. Getting:

Although knowledge of connectivity is essential, network operation depends upon the 'cooperative interaction' (Selverston *et al.* 1983) among multiple network, synaptic, and cellular properties, many of which are inherently nonlinear. No longer can neural networks be viewed as the interconnection of many like elements by simple excitatory or inhibitory synapses. Neurons not only sum synaptic inputs but are endowed with a diverse set of intrinsic properties that allow them to generate complex activity patterns. Likewise, synapses are not just excitatory or inhibitory but possess an equally diverse set of properties. The operation of a neural network must be considered as the parallel action of neurons or classes of neurons, each with potentially different input/output relationships and intrinsic capabilities interconnected by synapses with a host of complex properties' (Getting 1989: 187).

The task is to discover those quality-disposition properties, in both psychological and nonpsychological domains, for which changes and change potentials have been given quantities. At the most basic level of elementary particles, this task needs not only the discipline of physics and what Bertrand Russell called 'a nose for reality,' but also a great deal of luck.

Let me repeat: this is no threat to the laws of thermodynamics. I am not suggesting the addition of 'an excess of work from nowhere,' but instead noting that our task is to make what is intrinsic to the properties by virtue of which the work is done salient and evident to the mind. It is simply taking note of what is needed to make natural properties *whole*. This will not be expressed *only* in terms of further algorithms and other mathematical formulae, however essential these may be for the depiction of the intrinsic character of Locke's 'finer interstices of nature.'

There is, then, a *physical* qualia-qualities problem, leaving aside what problem, if any, arises for *mental* qualia-qualities.

One objective of this and the two previous chapters has been to outline a gradualist account of reality that will emerge more fully in subsequent chapters. One element of that account is the thesis that the world includes properties that are at once dispositional and qualitative. I have begun to fill in what an ontological model that recognized this point would look like. If we accept this general ontological model, certain features thought to typify (and mystify) the mental can, with a little effort, be seen to be present already in the nonmental and even the nonsystemic cases that have been considered.

# 7

# Linguisticism and Pythagoreanism

## 7.1 THE LINGUISTICIZATION OF PROPERTIES

Predicates are linguistic, mind-dependent entities; many properties of objects are neither. Linguisticism is silly, but it is also endemic and largely unnoticed by many practising ontologists. Its suggestion needs expunging from the motto 'To be is to be the value of a variable' (Quine 1948; cf. Martin 1984a), but appears unmistakably in what can be described as a kind of *holus bolus* view (Martin 1980 and 1993) that suggests that it is the object *simpliciter holus bolus* that makes each of many statements about it true or false. When the statements

(a) The passion fruit is round.

and

(b) The passion fruit is purple.

are true of one and the same object, it is something in particular *and* different *about* the object that makes the statement true in each case. The predicates are built to pick these out.

Furthermore, *different* ways (properties) *about* (or of) the *same* object are causally operative in different ways (or inoperative) for different effects. The object is causally operative in some event for particular effects only by virtue of *some* of its properties *rather* than others. It is not operative *holus bolus* for each and every effect. Properties are needed for causality. Without properties, objects are empty and predicates blind (Martin 1980, 1993).

If you compare *objects* in terms of their similarities and dissimilarities, you are necessarily concerned with some respects thought to be 'in common' between them. This has led to the invocation of the numerically identical universal as the common element. The need for universals is removed, however, once you recognize that object detection, discrimination, and even identification is dependent on a more basic detection, discrimination, and identification of things about objects, namely, properties of objects—colours, movements, shapes, loudnesses, tastes, textures, and the temporal pulses, changes, and spatial spread of these.

## 7.2 TROPES AND UNIVERSALS

This requires a *mind-shift* from the philosophers' usual emphasis on exact or inexact similarity between *objects* (that need a *respect* in which they are similar) to exact or inexact similarity between a specific property or *respect* (of an object), which, since already detected or specified, needs no *further* respect in which to be similar or dissimilar. It is a similarity *simpliciter* between one, unique, individual specific property instance and some other property instance, such as a *specific* hue or saturation or brightness.

Such reflections can affect how we think in developmental psychology. An infant or an adult can be selectively attending to a specific property of an object or to exactly similar specific properties of a number of objects without attending to the object or objects themselves. An agent's exercising the natural and basic capacity to detect and come to fix upon some specific property arousing the agent's interest, enables the agent to group exactly similar properties either of different parts of the same object or of different objects. Rather than treating the *object* as prime individual, agents can discriminate between these properties and relations and dissimilar properties and relations as specific individuals (a specific movement or relations of position or a specific hue or shape) and then treat differences and similarities between objects as needing selective attention to further property-respect individuals *about* the prime-individual object. An agent can do these things without the need for further respects.

This account answers one common objection to property-individuals. You are able to detect distinct instantiations of the same universal in the universals account, yet you can do this only by noting a *similarity* between these instantiations. In this account, when the similarity becomes *exact* similarity, it becomes identity. I opt for treating instantiations as individuals.

The natural direction for detecting, discriminating, recognizing, or identifying properties is through the perception of what is demarcated *about* an object through its 'outline' marked and bounded (allowing for occasional 'overlap') by differences and similarities, exact and less-than-exact, from and to what else is within perception *about* the object and its environment. This can be achieved at the most primitive level of detection and also at the higher levels of discriminatory, recognitional, and identificatory responses required for cognitive expertise. Whether you prefer a many-exactly-similar-tropes view or a many-instantiations-of-one-universal view, you will see agents as acquiring cognitive skills reacting to similarities and differences concerning properties *gradually*. If there are many exact similarities, it is natural for us to *group* them.

Noting (1) the physical extent and/or duration of some *one* simple property—universal in a particular instantiation or set of many instantiations, and noting (2) the physical extent and/or duration of some simple trope or set of exactly similar trope, appear to be strikingly similar procedures.

At the ontological level, whichever of these notations one uses (and the tropes versus universals issue might come to no more than that), it is the resemblance or difference between the properties of objects, events, or states of affairs that is basic to the resemblance or difference between objects, events, or states of affairs. Objects are similar to and different from one another *by virtue* of the similarity to and difference from different things *about* (properties *of*) the objects.

This ontological-epistemological model is a corrective to overly object-oriented and misleading accounts of the perceptual and conceptual development of infants in the womb and the very young. An experimental subject might be struck by movements, colours, sounds, and textures more than by enduring objects. Even as adults, we can be as the infant, that is, in total disregard of what *has* the qualities or properties with which we happen to be wholly absorbed. This often is the case with painters, composers, and even more pedestrian sensualists.

The 'respects' are there as spatiotemporal individuals, namely, as individual properties (*not* as universals, but instead as *this* red and *that* exactly similar—yet numerically different—red). They are perfectly objective and in their similarities and differences provide *simpliciter* what is basic to whatever similarities and differences obtain for the object.

The innumerable *interrelatings* between various property instances of things, events, and states have ready-made mind-independent and classification-independent reifications for *alternative* modes of classifying things. The manifold of colours (leaving aside the secondary-quality question) contains interrelatings between these colours that are ready-made for countless modes of classifying the colours, whether or not any such classifying activities ever exist. Any particular kind or universal consists of similar interrelatingness instances between similar property-instances.

If you were to reject the ultimacy of objects and replace them with space—time segments, 'worms,' or fields, there would still be properties—things *about* or things *had* by these segments or fields that would not be those segments or fields themselves or *parts* of them. These properties would be more than mere mathematicized measures. Even concerning such elementary particles, fields, or space—time representations, there is a need for more than quantities and numbers. Every quantity or measure is such only by virtue of there being qualities *for* or *of* which it is the quantity or measure. The alternative is an unacceptably empty desert of Pythagoreanism unsurprisingly endorsed by Quine in 'Whither physical objects?' (Quine 1976).

## 7.3 CLASSIFICATION AND COMPOSITION

The anti-realist notes that there can be alternative ways of classifying nature and falsely concludes that the world is indeterminate and classification-dependent. On the contrary, a completely realist way of representing the manifold variety of nature is available (Martin 1993).

Such factors as the stability and (observable) reproducibility of some varieties rather than others of interrelated properties in nature make some modes of classifying things more 'natural' or 'useful' than others. Factors concerning the evolution of the complex structures of classifying organisms themselves correlate with this. For instance, some interrelatings of properties rather than others produce figure—ground perceptions that provide for greater ease of recognition and interest, which in turn produce conditions for the movement, sustenance, and survival of the organism. An organism must be selective and reject or ignore most of the interreactivities and interrelatednesses that exist in nature. The organism would not survive if it tried to accommodate the endless variety of interrelatednesses in nature in its classifications. Of course, it does not follow either that the unselected interrelatednesses are not just as *real* as the selected ones, or that there are not limits to the scope of interrelatednesses. Square and round pegs do not fit the same way into square holes and round holes. Furthermore, some relationships of properties simply do not obtain, such as those required for the existence of a unicorn, for example.

Believing what is false might be helpful for survival, even, on occasion, necessary to it. There seems no *a priori* limit to place on this (*contra* Davidson), but let us take the more optimistic view that the human organism has one of the best classificatory mechanisms that nature can provide, a mechanism eminently useful for discovering at least something of what is basic in nature. This mechanism includes both perceptual classificatory capacities and extrapolatory (from perception) capacities. The extrapolatory capacity is used to fashion explanations of the more complex and directly observable in terms of the simpler. That is, complex things with their complex properties and complex interrelations as various wholes can be explained by reference to their having a composition or constitution of simple or simpler parts with simple or simpler properties and relations that are not directly observable.

## 7.4 CAPACITIES AND DISPOSITIONS

Before moving ahead, it will be helpful to settle on some terminology. Picking one term to do all the work that my use of the term 'disposition' is supposed to do is asking a lot of any single word. Some explanation will, I hope, show that the choice of words has not been thoughtless.

The difference between capacities and dispositions disappears once you ask, 'Under what conditions (reciprocal disposition partners) would the capacity be *exercised*?' If the answer is 'None,' then that is a null capacity. If the answer is 'No *determinate* conditions,' then the reply is 'Waffle!' If the answer is 'I cannot say exactly,' then the reply is 'Of course—but try for *inexact*, if you can.'

Capacities are capacities *for* (dispositions for) their exercises or fulfillments (mutual manifestations) under certain conditions (reciprocal disposition partners).

Differences in the circumstances of usage of 'capacity,' 'tendency,' and 'proclivity' lie in what is presumed to be the degree of availability or proximity of (spatially or temporally) reciprocal disposition partners or, perhaps, the degree to which there is the *start* of a process toward a result that would need the *loss* of reciprocal disposition partners, or the *introduction* of a reciprocal prohibitive disposition partner, to stop or interfere with the culmination of the mutual manifestation.

'Capacity' can also be used as the most nonspecific indicator of a disposition's reciprocal disposition partners for mutual manifestation.

I will continue to use the terms 'disposition' and 'manifestation' as the basic causal terms.

Expressing the qualitativity and dispositionality of any real property merely as 'a way of thinking of, mode of prediction concerning, way of regarding or looking at, etc.' suggests that it is merely in the eye (or voice) of the beholder. If those who use such deontologizing expressions intend to claim anthropomorphism, then they should make *that* ontology fully explicit. If they do not intend to endorse anthropomorphism, however, they should join in the task of saying clearly *what* in the world the expressions indicate.

Dispositions, I have suggested, come in at least three classes:

(1) Dispositions such as solubility are such that what is soluble when the solubility is manifested, by its going into solution, thereby ceases to be soluble. What is in solution, however, can be recovered from the solution and become soluble again.

(2) Dispositions such as explosiveness are such that what is explosive when the explosiveness is manifested is not recovered from the explosion by its being exploded and does not become explosive again.

(3) Dispositions such as the soundness of a bridge are such that what is sound when the soundness is manifested does not then cease to have soundness by its performing soundly.

I shall mainly be concerned with dispositions in the third group.

All intrinsic properties are dispositional, and dispositionality is fully real and actual. Dispositions can be actual even if their manifestations are not. The properties of elementary particles or spatiotemporal segments of fields are not structural states, yet such properties are not in pure act, that is, manifesting at each moment or temporal stage all of which they are capable. The particles have dispositions, not all of which they are always manifesting, and in the nature of the case *qua* elementary particles, their dispositionality is not explained in terms of the properties of their constituents. I have already (Chapter 2) argued against explaining dispositions in terms of counterfactuals and will not repeat those arguments here.

Trying to account for dispositionality in terms of structural states is misguided, not only because what is structural is *evidently* intrinsically dispositional *itself*, but more importantly because the issue can be more clearly discussed in terms of *non*structural properties. A great advantage of discussing properties at the nonstructural, nonmacroscopic, elementary particle or elementary aspects-of-fields level is that we can thereby avoid some reduction vs. nonreduction debates.

Discussion at a structural or macroscopic level is vitiated by debate concerning whether the properties at the higher level are anything over and above properties at a lower level, with the usual gesturing toward all of the many varieties of supervenience that are at best ontologically toothless. Discussion at an elementary particle level (even with epistemic qualms) stops moves attempting to account for such properties in terms of still other properties at a *lower* level because (if we are epistemically lucky) there *aren't* any!

I devised the following case in the mid-1950s as a counterexample to verificationism and later as a counterexample to many reductive accounts of causal dispositions including Quine's account in *Word and Object* (Quine 1960: 222–6). Quine claims that an unmanifested disposition is explicable in terms of an object having a structure similar to a structure of an object that has manifested the supposed disposition.

My case is one of a cosmic geographical fact concerning the spatiotemporal spread of kinds of elementary particle. It is supposed that there are kinds of elementary particle in some spatiotemporal region of the universe that are different from the kinds of elementary particle of our own region, that the regions are so vastly distant that the many special dispositions they have for intercourse with one another *never* have and never will have their very special manifestations, and that nothing else in the universe, in the nature of the case, is *like* them that does have the manifestations. But the particles have causal dispositions ready to *go*. The dispositional is as real and irreducible as the categorical. (Or, as I would prefer to say, the dispositional is as real and irreducible as the *qualitative*. Talking of the distinction as being between the dispositional and the categorical can suggest that dispositionality is not really categorical, not really 'there' in the object.)

On one occasion when I referred to this case, a devoted Quinean replied, 'And if pigs had wings they would fly.' When I complained that he did not know any better than I did that this was not a *true* case, he responded, 'And if pigs had wings they would fly.' (I did not have the wit on the occasion to point out the somewhat irrelevant truth that if pigs had wings they *still* would not fly.)

Cause and effect itself should be explained in the more basic terms of the mutual manifestation of reciprocal disposition partners. Dispositionality and manifestation are well equipped to deal with elementary particles because even a quark is capable of more than it manifests at any time, given different reciprocal disposition partners. Start with any disposition partner and you find a network—a Power Net. (This should be useful in the characterization of nonlocal causality, if needed, in physics.)

Any disposition is one among many alternative reciprocal disposition partners for some mutual manifestations.

A typical causal situation is Locke's case of the turning with a particular force of a key of a particular shape, size, and hardness, etc., in a lock of a particular shape, size, and hardness, etc., which is showing a particular force of resistance or lack of resistance, etc., to the key for their *mutual* manifestation of an unlocking.

The reciprocity of dispositional states for their mutual manifestations that are their *common* product is deep and complex. This reciprocity should not be expressed in terms of unhelpful distinctions such as power to give *vs.* power to receive, agent *vs.* patient, active *vs.* passive, causal conditions *vs.* standing conditions: what?—standing by?! Instead, *whatever* is causally operative should have its full status as reciprocal or collaborative disposition partner for a mutual manifestation.

The important point remains that the manifestation of *one* dispositional state requires reciprocal disposition partners, *if they exist* and are in the relevant relationship. A match's lighting is a mutual manifestation of the dispositional state of the match that needs to be a reciprocal partner with the cooperation of the reciprocal or collaborative disposition partner of the enfolding oxygen among a great deal else.

This view of the innumerable interconnectednesses and dispositional reciprocities of properties, largely unknown but existent still, contrasts with the simple-minded view that because nature does not lay out The Cause of each event, causality itself is mind-dependent.

A dispositional state is *there* in the most simple or complex physical instances or psychological instances. It is there to provide the relevant richness of alternative manifestations with its multiple alternative reciprocal disposition partners, some of which would be mutually exclusive in their actualization, but *ready to go* for present, distant, non-existent, or even *never*-existent manifestation conditions, that is, reciprocal disposition partners.

With reciprocal disposition partners *each* being for the *mutual* manifestation, *each* must have the directedness and selectivity *for* such a manifestation. If, by misfortune, one or more partners does not in fact *exist*, the reaching out, directedness, and selectivity *for* their manifestation is fully contained in the existent partner.

Water has the directedness of a dispositionality as solvent *for* salt and *not* gold, even without the existence of salt, for the *mutual* manifestation of a coming into a solution of salinity. And salt has a directedness and dispositionality as soluble in water and not *aqua regia*, even without the existence of water, for that same *mutual* manifestation of a coming into a solution of salinity. An existent reciprocal partner entity having the directedness of an existent disposition is needed, but *any* existent reciprocal partner is sufficient and does not need the existence of its other reciprocal partners for the existence of its directedness to what would be *their* mutual manifestation.

## 7.5 FORMS OF INFINITY

(1) The disposition of a particular thermostat is directive and selective to a *particular* furnace to which it is connected at $t_1 P_1$ *for* the alternative *mutual* manifestations of degrees of change in heat *with* alternative reciprocal disposition partners of a cat's tail, falling plaster, the coat sleeve of the butcher, the horn of a unicorn, or . . . altering the set point of the thermostat. This appears to be infinite.

(2) The disposition of a quark is directive and selective *for* the mutual manifestations of a *particular* kind with particular kinds of reciprocal disposition partners of various arrangements of its quark cousins, *wherever* or *whenever* they may be. It has its disposition readiness for them, even if they were to cease to exist. This appears to be infinite.

(3) The disposition of a quark is directive and selective *for* the alternative mutual manifestations of *various* kinds with alternative kinds of reciprocal disposition partners proximate, distant, unreachable, and of kinds that may not even exist. This appears to be infinite.

(4) The disposition of anything is likely not at all places and times, so it will be finite in duration and extension. The infinity of

directedness and selectedness of any disposition, however, is from the here and now to an infinite number (any anywhere, anytime) of reciprocal disposition partners of a particular kind for a particular kind of mutual manifestation or for any number of reciprocal disposition partners (actual and non-actual) of different kinds for different kinds of mutual manifestation. The duration of a disposition helps verification, but that is irrelevant to the ontology.

## 7.6 DISTINGUISHING DISPOSITIONALITIES

There cannot be exactly similar dispositional states in exactly similar reciprocal partnerships for different mutual manifestations. If the dispositional states are *complex*, then, in a way, there can be different dispositional state partners that have similar mutual manifestations. That is, among the different aspects of the mutual manifestations there also could be similar aspects. It is clear that the same dispositional state can have different mutual manifestations with different reciprocal disposition partners. For example, the same water thrown on burning wood or burning oil on water has very different consequences. (I take up this example in greater detail below.)

What we tend to select as *the* dispositional state for a particular kind of mutual manifestation is a reciprocal disposition partner that has the greatest stability and availability to its varying reciprocal disposition partners or, more trivially, that happens to be of the greatest interest to us. What a dispositional state is depends, not only on for which alternative partners it is, but also for which alternative partners it is *not*, and even against which alternative partners it is prohibitive.

## 7.7 THE RECIPROCITY OF MANIFESTATIONS

No dispositional state is bound to its manifestations independently of its possible differing reciprocal disposition partners. The concept of reciprocal disposition partnerhood for mutual manifestation loosens the simplistic linguistic bondage of a specific and unique dispositionality for a specific and unique manifestation. Instead, it allows that the *identical* dispositional state with *different* reciprocal disposition partners can have *different* mutual manifestations. The same dispositional state will vary in the nature of its manifestation as it plays its role as reciprocal disposition partner in varying mutual manifestations with its varying reciprocal disposition partners. The differences can be striking.

Consider the case of burning wood and burning oil mentioned previously.[1] Water thrown on burning wood and the very same water thrown on oil burning on water results in strikingly different mutual manifestations owing to differences between the reciprocal disposition partners in the burning wood and the oil burning on water. In wood fires, water acts as an extinguisher by (a) effectively covering up the microstructure of wood, sealing it from the oxygen needed to advance the combustion through the wood, and (b) generating steam and otherwise absorbing thermal energy required for the combustion to advance through the wood. In the case of an oil fire, water (a) does *not* seal the oil from the air, but rather sinks beneath the oil, while (b) absorbing combustive thermal energy; if the water reaches its boiling point, however, steam will rise quickly through the oil with such kinetic energy that it impels oil particles into the air, thereby dramatically increasing the aggregate exposure of carbohydrates to oxygen, which radically increases the rate of combustion—which can, in turn, increase the quantity of steam generated, thus creating an explosive positive feedback loop. This effect is the opposite of the reduction of carbohydrate exposure to oxygen in the wood case. *The shared disposition is the dousing water's tendency to absorb thermal energy to the point of creating steam.* In one case, the disposition in the reaction of the steam helps for the mutual manifestation to extinguish the fire, whereas in the other it contributes to the mutual manifestation of exacerbating the fire. One disposition manifests itself in two wholly different ways given different reciprocal partners.

Similarly, according to the dispositional nature of the receptor sites in the post-synaptic membrane, the capacity of the synapses from the pre-synaptic membrane can, with the introduction of acetylcholine (ACH), be inhibitory *or* excitatory in its manifestation, whether receptors in the post-synaptic cells are masked or not masked. The capacity state of the synapses from the pre-synaptic membrane remains exactly the same with identical dispositionalities. The only difference lies in the difference in their reciprocal disposition partners (the receptors in the post-synaptic cells) allowing differences in their *mutual* manifestations.

---

[1] I was greatly helped in the expression of the details of this case by Kevin Sauvé.

This becomes particularly obvious in mental cases. A smiling face could be a reciprocal partner for very different and indeed opposite mutual manifestations, depending on which of its alternative reciprocal disposition partners are present and involved. A disposition can have antagonistic reciprocal disposition partners that even extinguish it or block it. And of course a disposition can have, in a particular situation or *forever*, no existing relevant reciprocal disposition partner.

## 7.8 DISPOSITIONALITY OF MANIFESTATIONS

In thinking of how to give an account of dispositions, it could be tempting to treat manifestations as themselves disposition-free or at least not to raise the question of their dispositionality. This would be a gross error. Salt manifesting its solubility in water by the manifestation of dissolving can be such only if the salt in solution is recoverable. Whatever is involved in the manifestation event *itself* is not in pure act, that is, manifesting everything of which it is capable. One cannot hope for disposition-free manifestations.

D. M. Armstrong has provided a counterexample to the notion of causality as the mutual manifestation of reciprocal disposition partners. Armstrong's case of the previous state of a thing causing its own successive state without having any reciprocal disposition partners is a case of an entity that exists in and for itself, absolutely independently of everything else (including electromagnetic and gravity fields of force, etc.). Even so, it is not an example of a total lack of reciprocal disposition partners. A previous state $x$ of a thing $a$ at $t_1$ has innumerable reciprocal dispositional partners in *other* states of $a$ at $t_1$ for the continuance of state $x$ of $a$ at $t_2$. Armstrong would need an object with only a single simple irreducible state—perhaps God.

It becomes obvious that dispositionalities are prior to, more basic, and far more numerous than their mutual manifestations, that is, causes and effects. A particular kind of cause and effect might not exist although the relevant dispositions *do* exist, but a kind of cause and effect cannot exist if the relevant dispositions do not exist. As such, ontological priority and candor require cause and effect to be explained in terms of reciprocal disposition partners in their mutual manifestation and not *vice versa*. Disposition and manifestation are the basic categories by means of which cause and effect are to be explained. A manifestation of a dispositional state should be seen in *depth* as a change that might endure for less than a billionth of a millisecond—not long enough for observation, except indirectly as the observation of traces.

Manifestations and dispositions are correlative. A manifestation is what it is only as *from* a relevantly deep enough and broad enough Disposition Base Array, and a disposition base array is what it is only as *for* kinds of alternative manifestation under alternative kinds of condition.

# 8

# Protolanguage

## 8.1 PRELINGUISTIC SEMANTICS

The adage, 'To be is to be the value of a variable,' *should* cause laughter. In this chapter I attempt to reveal the richness of what is both prior and basic to language. There was life before language in the history of the race and the individual. The development of the preverbal activity of the race and the individual is a progression by degrees from semantic ooze to sophisticated nonlinguistic patterns of interrelated behaviour, both shared and unshared.

The battle over the primacy of language could well have been largely won in showing that prelinguistic and nonlinguistic behaviour can be complex and intentional (Kirk 1967; Bennett 1976; Martin 1984b). In this chapter, I take the battle against the persistent mystique of language still further, arguing that nonlinguistic activity at its most sophisticated and structured levels has a remarkable pattern of parallels to linguistic activity. It is a matter of degree, but when an agent shows enough of this pattern of parallels, this structured network of interrelated procedural activity could be called 'protolanguage.' Bear in mind that the development of linguistic behaviour is also a matter of degree.

We can make a new beginning toward seeing that nonverbal activity itself can have semantic point by remembering that if we have not (by some supposition, assumption, or actual observation) settled on or hypothesized concerning an interpretation of some other linguistic group's complex and interrelated *non*verbal doings in and *with* their physical environment, then there is no alternative nonmagical route to the semantic point of their *sayings*. Our knowledge of, or supposition concerning, another linguistic group's nonverbal doings is basic to, prior to, and *easier* to ascertain than knowledge of the group's sayings.

A version of this chapter appeared as Martin 1987.

Imagine watching a film in a language you do not understand, and you will see what I am driving at.

An example of procedural activity described as protolinguistic might seem over-interpreted only because the example is lacking detail. Any instance of procedural activity must be embedded in a vast complex of interrelated activity of the agent for it to bear the suggested interpretation. Made fully explicit, each case would require a novel-length description or a full-length film.

In this chapter I will provide an intuitive array of examples, set out in enough detail to *suggest* the indefinite range of interrelated activities required for instances of behaviour in the examples to have a degree of determinateness of semantic import.

The word 'protolanguage' includes the word 'language,' but this is not meant to suggest that protolanguage is a kind of language. It is meant to indicate that protolanguage is a structured, rule-governed network of semantic, procedural activity prior and *basic* to linguistic activity, having an almost totally unnoticed and surprising pattern of parallels to language itself. Rules of protolanguage, like rules of language, need not be explicitly known by particular users or, for that matter, by any user at all. But then some of us are not sure that a clear description of what a linguistic rule is has ever been stated or that any clear examples of such rules have been spelled out.

The idea behind this chapter is to make a start in detailing the structure and nature of protolinguistic activity in its individual and social usage. This will lead to a model for explaining a natural developmental flow (also allowing for, incorporating, and making understandable inventive 'leaps') in the semantic evolution of the race and the individual before—and into—language. After first acquiring a language (racially or individually), we do not, indeed could not, abandon the use of protolanguage. The subtle interplay between language and protolanguage and their separate domains of semantic dominance and richness call for investigation.

## 8.2 LINGUISTIC-NONLINGUISTIC PARALLELS

(1)  Word as token—word as type; sentence as token—sentence as type.

(1′) Step as token—step as type; procedure as token—procedure as type.

(2)   The sentence, not the word, is the basic unit. Ryle: 'We *use* words to *make* sentences.'

(2')   The procedure, not the step, is the basic unit. 'We *use* steps to *make* procedures.'

It is no easier to give clear, unproblematic, nonintentional rules for the distinction between step and procedure than it is to give parallel unproblematic, general, nonsemantic rules for the distinction between word and sentence.

There can be greater gaps between phonemes than between words in a sentence, so purely mechanical general rules for word-detection are not possible. The semantic function of how an agent's use of a writing-the-token action or sounding-the-token action must be introduced, and rules for this are not clearly and unproblematically general. If semantics can be kept out of syntax entirely, no one has clearly shown how.

There are, of course, dictionaries that recognize and codify words. There are also recognized steps for procedures. There can be instruction in nonverbal procedures exhibiting discrete and sequential steps. Before there were dictionaries, there was vocabulary instruction. Before there were illustrated manuals, there was instruction in the steps of various procedures—how to set the foot for a noiseless step in various hunting procedures, for example. There can be pronunciation practice of a word and protopronunciation practice of a step to be used (practicing a grip on a golf club). The very same kind of action used as a noiseless step in a stalking procedure could be given a different use as a nonslipping step in a walking across the ice procedure.

You might still think there is a special difficulty in answering the question 'Why isn't *any* step in a procedure to be thought of as a procedure itself?' Almost any procedural steps *would* be used as a procedure, just as almost any word *could* be used as a sentence. In both cases, it depends on how the action is used and grasped by the agent. An action might be used and seen as a procedural unit for its own projected outcome or merely as a part (step) in a more encompassing procedure taken as a unity for some projected outcome. This is parallel to a verbal action's being used and seen as a sentential unit for its own declarative use or just as a part (a word) in an encompassing sentence taken as a unity for its declarative use.

A particular action might have been intended as a one-word sentence or might have been intended as part of a sentence that was interrupted and so remains only an incomplete sentence. Similarly, a particular action might have been used as a one-step procedure or might have been used as part of a procedure that was interrupted and so remains only an incomplete procedure.

(3) Similar words in a sentence could have different semantic use, and different words in a sentence could have similar semantic use.

(3') Similar steps in a procedure could have different operational use, and different steps in a procedure could have similar operational use.

(4) Similar sentences could have different semantic points (express different statements) by virtue of similar words having different semantic uses, and different sentences could have similar semantic points (make the same statement) by virtue of different words having similar semantic uses.

(4') Similar procedures could have different operational points (perform different operations) by virtue of similar steps having different operational uses, and different procedures could have similar operational points (perform similar operations) by virtue of different steps having similar operational uses.

(5) You could ask, 'Which sentence shall we use to express the statement?'

(5') You could ask, 'Which procedure shall we use to perform the operation?'

(6) A speaker has the capacity to make sentences expressing an indefinite number of statements using a finite number of words.

(6') An agent has the capacity to undertake procedures aimed at performing an indefinite number of operations using a finite number of steps.

(7) Satisfaction—the predicate of a sentence is satisfied by something.

(7') Satisfaction—the discernings about the representational activity of an observational procedure are satisfied by something.

The kind of nonlinguistic procedural activity that I am calling 'protolanguage' does not have anything like a full grammatical structure. It is not, after all, language! There is, however, a rough parallel to subject-predicate that can yield a further parallel to the satisfaction of a predicate. A spatiotemporal region and something in it are represented and fixed by, for example, the direction in which you are looking or the position of your hand in touching and the direction of your attention to what is within the region. This works roughly as the 'subject.'

By the selective, comparative, abstractive, contrastive, projective *use* of sensory input, you perform procedurally in discerning representational activity *about* what has been represented in the spatiotemporal region. This 'procedural-discerning-about representational activity' works roughly as the 'predicate.'

An observational discernings-about-representational *parallels* (but, of course, is not the same as) the predicate of a sentence, and an observational *fix* of something *parallels* (but, of course, is not the same as) the subject of a sentence.

I have emphasized nonbehavioural activity, but what could be called 'experientially-loaded behaviour' is commonly and importantly involved. Your own behaviour is experientially-loaded as you have visual, tactile, kinaesthetic sensory feedback concerning that behaviour as you turn your head for a better view, move your hand to get a better feel of the object, or walk closer to observe in more detail, etc.

(8)  A sentence is true only if the predicate is satisfied by something.

(8′)  An observational procedure is veridical only if the discernings about representational activity is satisfied by something.

(9)  What *is* or *is not* (a rock falls down a cliff, but does not hit a boulder) that is represented in a sentence expressing a true statement typically would still have *been* or *not been*, though unrepresented.

(9′)  What *is* or *is not* (the rock falls, etc.) that is represented in a procedure performing a veridical observation-scanning operation typically would still have *been* or *not have been*, though unrepresented.

(10)  *What is required for there to be an unexpressed statement?* There would be someone's real (although unexercised) linguistic capacity to generate a sentence that would have or have had a particular semantic point (expressing the statement), and there is what *is* or *is not* that *would* provide, or would have provided, satisfaction for the predicates if the individual had manifested his capacity to generate such a sentence.

(10′)  *What is required for there to be an unperformed operation?* There would be someone's real (although unexercised) procedural capacity to generate a procedure that would have had a particular procedural point (performing and operation), and there is what *is* or *is not* that *would* provide, or would have provided, satisfaction for procedural projection if the individual had manifested his capacity to generate such a procedure.

(11)   What is required for there to be an unexpressed statement without even the existence of utterances or any individuals capable of language? It would be for there to exist a way of using words simpliciter that could exist though nothing capable of using words existed.

(11′)  What is required for there to be an unperformed operation without even the existence of any individuals capable of complex interrelated procedures? It would be for there to exist a way of using steps simpliciter that could exist though nothing capable of using steps existed.

As there would be a way of (nonexistent) speakers using (nonexistent) word-tokens, there would be a way of (nonexistent) agents using (nonexistent) unicorn horns.

Why not say, instead, that, in such exigencies, what remains is only what *is* or *is not*? For *that* can be, if realism is correct, without language or procedural action, even without beings capable of such action. Truth is a relation between such beings and what is or is not. What is or is not can be without truth, but truth cannot be without what is or is not (see Martin 1984a and Chapter 3, above). Such a stricture would keep faith with the truth that language consists in the capacities and actions of people.

However one goes in this contentious field, whether to luxuriate in universals, propositions, or possible worlds, or to take the sterner stand that less is enough, parallels between the linguistic and the nonlinguistic are evident and striking. That is enough for the purposes of this chapter.

## 8.3 TRUTH AND FALSEHOOD

The most basic kind of sentence is a declarative sentence that represents something truly or falsely. Here, the activity of representation does not serve primarily to affect what is represented.

An agent's representation of observing a rabbit running from a dog is achieved by the agent's procedural *use* of sensory input. This might be done, in a particular instance, by the agent's selectively attending to the movement of a rabbit, contrasting this against a stationary background of trees and mountains (and not attending to passing clouds), and affixing comparative attention to the movement of the dog getting closer to the rabbit.

The status of such a simple case depends on the degree to which it, as a procedure, fits into a complex interrelated network of such procedures for the agent. If the degree of fit is sufficiently sophisticated, then even such a simple case could attain the status of what I have called protolanguage. All this is required for making the scope of veridicality and nonveridicality determinate.

Agents in such observational cases need not be more self-conscious about *what* they are using and *how* they are using it on a given occasion than an ordinary speaker would be in deploying a language.

Different observational procedures can subserve the same observational function by virtue of different steps being given similar operational use. Selectively attending to the movement of the front legs of the rabbit might be a step in an agent's selective ordering and abstracting in the use of sensory input for the procedural representation of visually tracking a rabbit running from a dog. That step could have been replaced by the step of selectively attending to the back legs of the rabbit without altering the operational point of the representation.

## 8.4 REPRESENTATIONAL USE

My account has not been couched in terms of belief states and desire states as intentional primitives. Let me explain why. We have already had occasion to reflect on Locke's observation that 'universality belongs not to things themselves.' Generality, rather, turns on a 'capacity they are put into by the understanding, of signifying or representing many particulars' (Locke 1690, III, iii, 2).

We can paraphrase Locke by stating that nothing particular, no *entity*, is intentional in itself, but it is made so only by its *use*. Beliefs and desires or 'information' states are particular states and so, *in themselves*, are not intentional. Nor does their intentionality result from complex causal interrelationships with other states with perhaps biogenetic explanations concerning their evolution owing to their complex environmental sensitivities. That account does well enough for such nonintentional states as states of the digestive system (see Martin and Pfeifer 1986 and Chapters 9 and 11).

Following Locke, and employing his seminal notion of 'partial considering,' we can say that intentionality comes only from procedural *use* by the agent of the agent's states. Belief or desire states are not apt for such procedural use. They are, instead, *capacity* (and tendency) states for the use of what *can* be used. What can be used are our sensory input and imagery and our *experientially* loaded (through sensory feedback) behaviour.

Rather than attempting to explicate experientially loaded doings in terms of beliefs and desires, it would be more fruitful to consider the explication of belief and desire states in terms of doings and an interrelated complex of doing capacities (and tendencies). The experiential is an intrinsic and essential part or aspect of anything *used* in such a doing (and if the doing is a 'mental' doing, it is the *principal* part).

This active, procedural model for perceptual discernings, is meant to replace the model of perception that either gives *no* role to sensation (replacing it with belief) or gives sensation only the dumb middleman causal role of being an effect of physical stimulation and a cause of belief. In the active model, sensation is the material for procedural use.

Paul Snowdon, in correspondence, has suggested that in the linguistic case only, one reason for going through the activity of saying that it is raining is that it is a way of making a declarative representation that it is raining. The characterization is part of an explanation for procedural use.

In a parallel way, however, I can put myself into the observational position of having a good look at what I *already* know—the familiar contours, colours, textures, etc., of my hand. Part of the reason for engaging in such representational activity is that it is a representation. I like the *look* and *feel* that I know I can alter (by half-closing my eyes, etc.) without altering the hand. I am not doing this to get *new* information or even to reaffirm *old* knowledge. This might be as close as we can hope to get to representation for representation's sake.

I have tried to isolate activity pursued only for the semantic purpose of representing something to be the case. This purity is rare in both linguistic and nonlinguistic domains, but it is possible to achieve as much in the nonlinguistic as in the linguistic case.

## 8.5 BENNETT ON ICONIC AND NONICONIC VEHICLES OF MEANING

In his splendid book *Linguistic Behaviour,* Jonathan Bennett writes:

The human situation differs from the tribal one in another way. To explain it, I need to distinguish three ways in which U might get A to believe that P. (1) He might reveal to A some intention-free evidence for P, i.e. some item which is evidence for P independently of U's intentions in making it available to A. (2) He might employ the credence mechanism to get A to believe P, by some action containing what I call a 'natural pointer' to P, that is, something which naturally tends to induce in the observer some thought closely connected with P; for instance, a pantomime of a snake if P is about a snake. (3) He might employ the credence mechanism by means of an action which did not naturally point to P, e.g. saying 'There is a snake near you' to warn A that there is a snake near him.

(2) and (3) could be described as involving, respectively, 'iconic' and 'noniconic' vehicles of meaning. The 'natural pointer' involved in (2) need not be 'iconic' in the strict sense of involving a resemblance between the action and something to do with P; for the pointer could be an actual object which is involved in P—for example, U might hold up a dish meaning that U wanted A to give it to him. Still, 'iconic' is a handy label, and I shall use it. (Bennett 1976: 148–9)

Useful as it is, Bennett's classification fails to capture the following kind of case. Nonlinguistic modes of mathematical thinking in topological and geometrical ways are achieved by projections from actual *and* imagined, performed *and* unperformed, manipulations and groupings of objects. This is procedural and operational thinking; it can be private or public, shared or not shared.

A carpenter can come to know general characteristics of different kinds of wood—what *kind* of wood is suitable for what *kind* of use—nonlinguistically with constant projections (right or wrong) for new and untried kinds of use. This is procedural and operational thinking; it can be private or public, shared or not shared.

Someone who has mastered *these* modes of procedural, projective thought could, on sighting a particular shape of a part of a distant mountain, *use* that shape in various complex *procedures* of thought, projecting the shape as part of a plan for the possible use of a special wood to be used in a special new fitting relationship in a novel shelter design.

Bennett considers only communicative behavioural forms of representation. This works well for the purposes of his argument. I have been emphasizing forms of representation that are not for, or not primarily for, communication. Shared, communicative uses of language seem to me to have been overstressed. At least 80 percent of our linguistic activity is neither shared nor communicated. It occurs in our silent verbalizations in the head in talking to ourselves, or in notes written only for our own eyes. It is the most common mode of representation for our assessments, claims, wonderings, plans, projects, reflections, and hypothesizings. Such activity deserves full status as linguistic utterance. It is not something 'behind' utterance—it *is* utterance.

The socialization and sharedness of semantic activity, both linguistic and nonlinguistic, has been overemphasized and made wrongly inclusive. (Indeed, the first *linguistic* use of an artificial sign could well have been an agent's heaping of stones as a communicative act intended to remind *himself* at a later time of where something was buried, or an agent's breaking branches to serve as a reminder of the way back to a starting point.) How far a child could go with its own unshared idiolect is a real question that has been botched by bad research.

There are things an infant must begin to do, and continue to do, for *itself*. An infant's sensory discriminatings, comparings and contrastings, its reachings and graspings under sensory control are not all learned from others. An infant's own inventive way of crawling need not have been socially reinforced. Watch a child find its own way with things without sharing this with or getting reinforcement from anyone; a child can retain these skilled procedures, taking pleasure in their success. No doubt, as social beings, children require what might be called 'hugs in general' to reinforce particular sorts of inventive activity to which it was not specially directed.

The 'born Crusoe' is quite another case. Such an isolated agent would have to be nurtured impersonally and most luckily by nature. A Crusoe would have to be by nature (and most improbably so) the very limit case of the autistic. At any rate, the born Crusoe is no model for us; we require not only hugs in general, but also a great many hugs in particular for reinforcement.

## 8.6 SOCIAL AND PRIVATE

We are, of course, social animals, but we are private animals too, with private ways of learning and private ways of performing, some of them basic to the social ways.

Much of our procedural activity that is directed successfully or unsuccessfully toward an outcome, is neither learned from others nor, especially in its many inventive forms, merely a socialized result of interaction with others. This procedural activity is not a shared activity, let alone a conventionally shared activity, and its purpose is not communication.

Many natural procedural ways of behaving that are directed toward a particular outcome (that might or might not be successful), need not be learned from others. These procedures are reinforced by successful outcomes and not necessarily by rewards from others. We are *innately* built so that, to a degree, success is its own reward. We are also, fortunately, *innately* built to bear up, rather than being in every way dependent on social encouragement, *and* built to try repeatedly to overcome failure. The physical environment itself has a role to play in our learning by rewarding our endeavors with success and punishing them with failure.

I have meant to emphasize the important role of an individual's semantic enterprise in which the individual can carry on with what *works*, not needing others to 'catch on' and share before the action has semantic point. No one could think that *immediate* uptake was a requirement. It follows, then, that perfectly good semantic procedures could be used by individuals and be lost for want of, or have a long wait for, effective sharing. Indeed, if semantic procedures required immediate uptake from others for sharing and communicative use, the evolution of both protolanguage and verbal language would be unthinkable.

This discussion of private protolanguage is not meant to touch that philosophical tar baby, the private-language argument in any of its many forms, but only to dissolve what cannot be circumnavigated.

I believe in a mixed economy. We can allow a degree of private entrepreneurial enterprise *and* a degree of socialization in semantic endeavors.

(12) The *semantic* point of a declarative utterance is not to cause a belief in someone else or to 'share' or to communicate; it is, instead,

to go through an utterance-representation procedure that is true or false—to represent successfully (or unsuccessfully) what is.

Frequently, we satisfy that semantic point in our silent or solitary musings or jottings. This is not to deny that an utterance of a declarative sentence might not have many other functions as well as to make its semantic point.

(12′) The *semantic* point of an observational representational procedure is not to do anything to *show* someone else or even get anything *done*, but rather to represent successfully or unsuccessfully what is.

This is not to deny that the performance of a representational procedure might not have many other functions as well as to perform its semantic point.

(13) Communication effected by means of *shared* rule-governed verbal activity in which assent and dissent can figure.

(13′) Communication effected by means of *shared* rule-governed procedural activity in which acceptance and rejection can figure.


## 8.7 HIGHER-ORDER PROCEDURES

People working together in the building of a complex structure could be doing more than birds building a nest. They might be, by employing diverse procedures, cooperatively and inventively testing the feasibility of other procedures for the fit, strength, stability, and beauty of various alternatives. In so doing, they can correct or reject procedural recipes of others and substitute their own. In that kind of complex, interrelated pattern of activity, one person's rejecting an element (perhaps as a *sample* of a kind of building material) that would not be suitable is a proto-parallel to the person's dissenting to an offering-as-suitable procedure. Accepting an element that is suitable is a proto-parallel to the person's assenting to an offering-as-suitable procedure.

(14) Sentences/metasentences.

(14′) Procedures/metaprocedures.

Just as there can be sentences about sentences, so there can be procedures about procedures. A testing procedure, perhaps with a model, for another procedure is a metaprocedure.

(15)  Sentence-meaning/speaker-meaning.

A grasp of the sentence-meaning/speaker-meaning distinction requires that an individual be capable of taking the sentence as an object of attention and assessment and not just what is represented by the sentence. It requires, as well, that the individual should have some conception of an *accepted* or *set* way for the sentence to function (either in some shared, public use or even in the individual's own rule-governed idiolect) as well as of how someone using the sentence *intended* it to function, which might or might not be at variance with the accepted or set way.

(15′)  Procedure-meaning/agent-meaning.

To have the notion of the procedure-meaning/agent-meaning distinction requires that an individual be capable of taking the procedure as an object of attention and assessment and not just the outcome projected by the procedure. It requires, as well, that the individual have some notion of an *accepted* or *set* way for the procedure to function (either in some shared, public use or even in the individual's own rule-governed procedural network) as well as of how someone deploying the procedure *intended* it to function, which might or might not be at variance with the accepted or set way.

An example of an accepted procedure would be a recipe (not in verbal form) developed and practiced by an individual for a particular dish. One day, the individual follows that procedure but, by some mental lapse, takes it to be for quite a different dish. All of the permutations possible in the linguistic case are paralleled in this procedural case.

(16)  You can say what you believe not to be the case, usually in an attempt to deceive someone else concerning what is the case.

In the course of making a declarative utterance concerning what you believe to be false, you can by mistake and against your wishes say what is true. Or, having no beliefs one way or the other, you could utter a sentence constituting a *guess* that by luck is true or by luck is false. Through a slip of the tongue, you could even say what is true whether you believe it or not. This is how we can be led by the nose, as it were, by language.

(16′)  You can perform a procedure projective of a particular outcome you believe will not be the case.

In the course of this, the outcome might be satisfied to your surprise. You might believe, for instance, that turning the key in the lock one final, exasperated time (not because you think it is worth trying, but out of frustration) it will *not* open the lock, yet it *does*. The procedure has the right outcome against your beliefs. Or, having no beliefs one way or the other, you come to a fork in the path and, on a whim, take the left fork. This is a procedure projective of a particular outcome that is satisfied only by luck. You could even, by a slip of the hand, have an outcome satisfied as part of your procedure whether you want it or not.

It is interesting to see how natural it is for us to take credit without guilt for undeserved truths of our linguistic declaratives or undeserved satisfactions of outcomes of our procedures. We are charitable not only to our own unintended linguistic and protolinguistic successes, but even to the unintended successes of others. We are all in on the cheat of this particular inverted form of the principle of charity. This is understandable, even laudable, given our general desire for the satisfaction of the outcome of what we do and the truth of what we say, whatever form, intended or unintended, it might take.

## 8.8 FURTHER PARALLELS

(17)  In some cases of verbal declarative activity (such as saying, 'That, over there, is a big one'), the perceptual perspective of the agent figures as a constituent of the declarative action. It is worse than misleading to call this the 'context' of the assertion. For the verbal declarative action to have the semantic content it has and to be representative of a *particular* state of affairs, the perceptual perspective must be used by the agent as a constituent in the declarative action as much as the bodily movement must figure as a constituent.

(17′)  In some cases of procedural actions (such as getting water ready to douse a *particular* fire, as opposed to having it ready for any fire that might occur), the agent's perceptual perspective is *used* by the agent as a constituent of the procedure. For the procedural action to be representative of a *particular* outcome, the perceptual perspective must be used by the agent as a constituent in the procedural action as much as the bodily movement must be used as a constituent.

(18)  Some sentences can have a strong conditional or counterfactual point.

(18′)  Some observational, investigative procedural activities can have a strong conditional or counterfactual point.

A native man has noticed that when a fish eats things, these things can be found in the stomach of the fish. He has also noticed that fish eat different things at different times. When he catches a fish, he opens it to see what it has been feeding on, so he will know what to use as bait. On one unsuccessful day's fishing, he notices an approaching storm that looks as if it will be spoiling the fishing for a long time. Frustrated, he intends not to return to the fishing hole until the weather changes. He picks up his fishing gear and starts for his cave. He happens to frighten a mink eating a fish. His curiosity overtaking him, he opens up the stomach to see what the fish had eaten and takes out some grasshoppers.

This is a procedural action the projected outcome of which is information about the past. It also has the point of finding out what *would* have helped him to catch fish had he used it as bait. He takes a moment to confirm this by throwing some grasshoppers in the water and watching the fish rise to take them. Miserable that he cannot use the bait that he now knows *would* work, he hurries to the cave to escape the threatening storm. When the storm unexpectedly begins to clear, he gathers his fishing gear and, watchful for the resurgence of the storm, he goes in search of grasshoppers.

(19)  Using language, you can assert that, if causal factors $A$ and $B$ occur, effect $E$ occurs, although you might know that $E$ can occur in the absence of $A$ and $B$ by means of other causes.

A speaker should be able to differentiate between checking on the occurrence of $A$ and $B$ and the nonoccurrence of $E$ versus checking on the adequacy of the causal claim itself.

(19′)  Without language, an individual could have gotten procedurally onto the general causal way of things, as a carpenter can know the many, many causal ways of various kinds of wood, or a master chef can develop causally general (what other kinds are there?) recipes.

Suppose a cook knows that ingredients $A \ldots N$ go to produce $Z$, although the cook knows $Z$ can be produced some other way without

$A \ldots N$, that is, the cook knows another recipe for $Z$. When $A \ldots N$ seem to have been added and yet $Z$ is not produced, the cook has two alternative checking procedures to follow: the cook could check on whether $A \ldots N$ really *were* added and whether $Z$ really was not produced, or the cook could check on the adequacy of the general recipe procedure itself by seeing if the degree of heat was or was not a relevant, though neglected, factor.

(20)  There can be a first-person-singular use of words in a sentence.

(20′)  There can be a first-person-singular function of steps in a procedure. A young person takes a choice morsel belonging to the elder of the tribe. The elder is angry upon seeing that it is gone and looks to each of the young people present. The young people know *everyone* will be punished if the guilty one does not admit it. The others become distressed, and the miscreant steps forward, showing remains of the stolen food in his hand and accepts his punishment.

(21)  Sentence/sentence implicature.

(21′)  Procedure/procedure implicature.

A procedure and its projected outcome are fulfilled, as in New Guinea a gift of pigs might *actually* be made by one tribe to another, but the accepted procedural implicature (that the recipient tribe should at a later date itself give back at least as many pigs) is not performed.

(22)  Question.

(22′)  A *quest* is a procedure that is structurally *directed* to achieve the projected outcome of finding out something not fully known.

(23)  Order.

(23′)  A proto-order is a procedure followed for the projected outcome of making someone do something partly by the person's knowing that was the *point* of your procedure—for example, pushing someone to get the person to go the rest of the way.

(24)  Lying.

(24′)  Hiding, seriously or as a joke, can be deceptive, but not a lie. As Brian McLaughlin pointed out to me in correspondence, for you to lie to me about $p$, (a) you must intentionally represent (by some action) yourself to me as believing that $p$, (b) you must take yourself to be thereby misrepresenting your belief to me, and (c) you must attempt intentionally to conceal the fact mentioned in (b) from me.

You hear a wild goose calling from the meadow. You believe that the wild goose will fly to a particular pond. You are known in the tribe as a great hunter. Others in the tribe take direction and guidance from your example in matters of hunting. On hearing the wild goose calls, you make sure the other hunters can see where you are going, then start running in the direction that leads to only one hunting spot, namely, the meadow. You let the other hunters run past you toward the meadow. When they are out of sight, you change direction, go to the pond, kill the wild goose, and eat the prized meat on the spot.

(25) Promise.
(25') A protopromise is doing something to get people to think they could depend on you to do something else.

An animal is about to break into a cave with several people in it. There is little time to spare. Only one person can go to try to kill the animal because the others are needed in the cave. It is a matter of which one will go. You stand, gather your weapons, and put on your leather armor. You do all this in the *sight* of the others to declare that you will kill the animal and to make them *depend* on your going because the duration of your preparation excludes anyone else's doing it. If you then do not carry this action to fruition, you break your proto-promise.

(26) Homophonic and nonhomophonic sentence translation.
(26') Homophonic and nonhomophonic procedure translation.

In watching a silent film, you can recognize a procedure followed as step-by-step the same procedure that you have followed, or you see a procedure followed as step-by-step a different procedure from the one you have followed, but you take it to be a different procedure to perform the *same* operation.

## 8.9 WALKING THE WALK—PRIOR TO TALKING THE TALK

I have tried to make salient a *pattern* of parallels between linguistic activity and nonlinguistic procedural activity. To a surprising degree, racially and individually, we *live* it before we *talk* it. The more clearly we see this, the more natural the easement from the nonlinguistic to the linguistic becomes.

Even strikingly simple cases begin to occur to me. It would be a *natural* extension of the reaching procedure for it to be made and used in pointing because the natural reaching procedure already has the point of directionality to something not within immediate grasp. That could help explain the universality of the pointing gesture.

Not all of the universal grammatical niceties studied by linguists would have such tidy explanations. How *much* and *what* and *how* of innate structures (still largely a posit of *a priori* gesturing) we need for the transition from our semantically sophisticated procedural activity to language gets a different look through the protolanguage model, but it is too soon for answers.

# 9

# Use, Representational Use, and Content

## 9.1 MENTAL AND NONMENTAL USE

Unlike dispositional directedness-selectivity (a disposition is *for* this *rather* than that), use is only *almost* everywhere. Use is limited to the systemic. Use is intrinsic to *systems* of dispositional states and admits of all kinds of complexity. The thermoregulatory system, in its vegetative and totally nonpsychological functioning, is such a nonpsychological physiological system. An individual in a persistent vegetative state is still capable of uses of input through the function of the brainstem. Indeed, these uses may be far more complex and intelligence-like than the machines of artificial intelligence. This use of input is use in a straightforward and nonmetaphorical sense even though it occurs in a system that appears to be nonmental.

Philosophers have tended to look for forms of directedness or use that are exclusively mental, altogether excluding use in nonmental domains, or, more grotesquely, have limited their investigations to the linguistic. Such a procedure all but guarantees that mental directedness will appear deeply mysterious, a phenomenon inexplicable by any natural means.

I have argued that directedness and selectivity or readinesses are found in the dispositionality of any natural property. Now I shall argue that these are found along with *use* in any dispositional *system* whatever: psychological *or* nonpsychological. This does not entail panpsychism, however (*contra* Place; see his contribution to Armstrong *et al.* 1996).

To a first approximation, I mean by 'use' regulatory, adjustive, combinatorial, spatially, and temporally projective reactiveness to input and formativenesses of output. Use is possible only with the systemic. Use is required for complex functions, whether psychological or vegetative-autonomic, and even for much that is inorganic as well. I want to insist that this nonmetaphorical sense of 'use' is straightforwardly applicable in nonlinguistic and nonmental cases. The aim is to make clear just what more is needed and what is not needed for conscious, voluntary intentional use.

Before providing definitions of 'use,' 'representational use,' and 'content,' a few basic functions should be described.

(1) *Feedback*. Part of the output is fed back to the input component of the system.

(2) *Negative feedback* is feedback that keeps input and output in equilibrium or homeostasis.

(3) *Positive feedback* is feedback that tends to amplify and strengthen output and long-term potentiation.

(4) *Feedforward*. In contrast to a feedback controller that requires continuous monitoring of output while a control output is being emitted, a feedforward control does not depend upon such continuous monitoring. This enables the system to apply anticipatory output without, at the time of signaling, having to depend on feedback input concerning immediate effects on the controlled system (Sinclair and Challis 1993).

With these preliminaries behind us, I shall attempt definitions of the terms 'use,' 'representation,' and 'content' in a way that permits their nonmetaphorical application in nonlinguistic, as well as linguistic, and nonmental, as well as mental (conscious and voluntary), contexts. This is required so that their inclusion in an account of the linguistic and the mental will not be merely presumptive and circular.

Properties of all entities, linguistic or nonlinguistic, mental or nonmental (even the fundamental particles), have dispositionality. Dispositionality is directive and selective: a disposition is *for* some manifestations (involving entities, states, situations, events, or relations *other* than itself) *rather* than others. This directedness and selectiveness is not to be considered sufficient for something to be a representation, otherwise *every* entity would be a representation. Instead, representations, linguistic or nonlinguistic, mental or nonmental, come to represent only when they are so *used*. Indeed, the fundamental notion is not that of *representation* but of *representational use*. A representation has *no* life of its own apart from its usages and capacities for usages. This principle applies even to the most sophisticated cases of linguistic representation.

(5) *Use.* Use occurs in a system's reactivities *to* input and reactivities *for* the production and continuance or alteration of projective output.

(6) *Material of use.* The intrinsic properties of *input* received and processed, and the intrinsic properties of the *output* formed and continued or altered.

It is necessary to make a distinction between two ways in which material could be said to be in use:

(a) The material could be in the form of a *substance*, such as blood, that is used in the cardiovascular system in a manipulative and directive way.

(b) The material could be in the form of a *stimulus* whose signals are received within a systemic region that has capacities for use in the form of integrative, adaptive, projective (to other systems that are hierarchically ordered within the organism) responses and reactivities that, as in the case of some autonomic as well as cerebral systems, might be individual-specific and not merely species-general in their adaptivities.

To illustrate the point that mode of operation or function can remain constant and yet the activity vary significantly in *quality* according to the differing input or 'material' of use, we can turn to examples of *lateral inhibition.*

In lateral inhibition, *what* is stimulated in one region inhibits reactiveness of neighboring regions, thereby enhancing its own effects. This mode of operation has enormously general application across different modalities, and the mode of operation can be present even in *nonconscious* neuronal interactions at the receptor level *only*, for instance, at the level of the skin itself (von Békèsy 1967).

The same mode of operation of use, namely lateral inhibition, can be found in three classic cases that are strikingly different only by virtue of qualitative differences in the 'material' or input of use: (1) the visual illusion of so-called Mach bands; (2) Aristotle's illusion of touch at two points felt as one; and (3) the Müller–Lyer, Helmholz, and Delboeuf illusions, which von Békèsy found occurred with touch as well as with sight when appropriate cut-outs were placed on the thigh. If nothing else, this ought to cast doubt on accounts of such illusions given in terms that are unique to sight.

**FIG. 9.1.** Mach Bands[1]

**FIG. 9.2.** Müller–Lyer Illusion[2]

Some inputs are used (reacted to) in intricate, highly complex nonmental autonomic nervous systems. Because not all neuronal signals are alike (although some theories, pure vector accounts, for instance, cannot explain why they are not), the *difference* between mental and nonmental directedness and use can be regarded, not solely in terms of quantitative complexity, but also, and without mystique, in respect to *qualitative* differences among the neuronal signals used. Such differences need not be *merely* functional to avoid sprinkling stardust. Qualities of what is used in a function can be allowed to count. Mother Nature is not purely functionalist any more than She is operationalist.

The way is open to see the obvious. The difference between *mental* and *non*mental directedness and between *agent* and *non*agent use is in the special *qualitative* difference between the *kinds* of neuronal sensory

---

[1] The image is made up of seven uniformly coloured bars. At the boundary of a lighter bar with a darker bar, however, the edge of the lighter bar appears darker than the rest of that bar, and the edge of the darker bar looks lighter than the rest of the darker bar.

[2] Despite being the same length, the top line appears shorter than the bottom line.

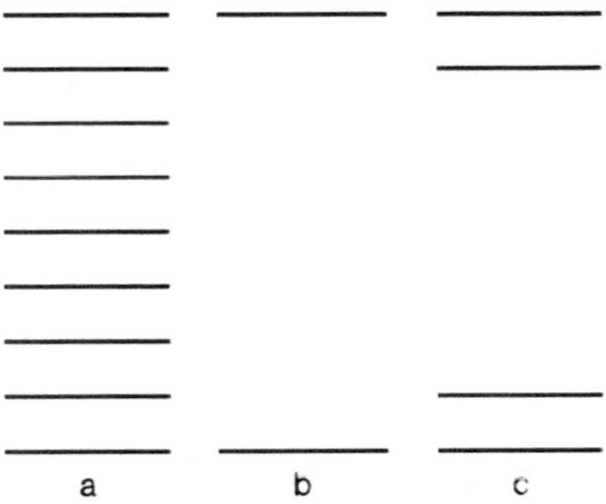

a          b          c

**FIG. 9.3.** Helmholtz and Delboeuf Illusions[3]

and sensory-like signals *used*—differences in the material of use—that we can detect or, given certain identificatory skills and linguistic skills, that we could identify or *characterize* as sensations, percepts, images, and feelings. If you wanted more than *that*, you would set your face against any naturalistic account.

(7) *Representational Use.* Requires a system of sufficient complexity and adaptive variability of response to be capable of integrative, adjustive, combinatorial, projective negative and positive feedback and feed*forward* reactivities to the system's input and output for which there is a *disposition base* involving *patterns* of interrelated dispositions for

(a) alternative kinds of potential processing reactivities to the reception of alternative kinds of potential input that provide a *capacity background* of capacities (largely unmanifested on the occasion, but still essential) of the system and that provide a degree of specificity and richness for the *actual* results (the system's parallel to *interpretation*) of the processing reactivities that determine the specific directedness and selectivities (content) of the actual input, that is, a *parallel* to interpretation; and for

(b) alternative kinds of potential directive and selective reactivity for potential formation and continuance or alteration of

---

[3] Compare the distance between the top and bottom lines in *a* and *b*. The distance appears greater in *a* (where the space between the two lines is filled) than in *b* (where the space is empty). This is the Helmholtz illusion. In contrast, the space between top and bottom lines appears greater in *b* than in *c*. This is the Delboeuf illusion.

potential kinds of output. These provide a capacity *background* within the system (largely unmanifested on the occasion but still essential) giving a degree of specificity and richness for the nature of the directive and selective reactivities (content) resulting in a preparation of readiness to go for the specific formation and continuance or alteration of actual output. This projective part is parallel to *affirmatory* activity: stating. (Such affirmatory activity could take nonlinguistic form, as one confirms something perceptually.)

(8) *Correlativity of manifestation and disposition base.* The particular manifestation of use of a particular input or output finds its full *point* and *specificity* only through the occasion of the particular use of the input or output. This is a use-*manifestation* arising from the depths of the capacities of the disposition base for *alternative* potential manifestations of uses of alternative potential inputs or outputs.

(9) *Representation.* Input or output as *given* representational use.

(10) *Content.* What the input and output are directive or selective *for*, given their representational uses.

These characterizations provide the groundwork for a detailed schema for an account of representational use applicable to mental or nonmental systems alike. I shall appeal to the nonconscious thermoregulatory system as an illustrative example. Later, we will be in a position to consider what *more* is needed for fully conscious representational use by mental agents.

## 9.2 REPRESENTATIONAL USE
## IN NONMENTAL SYSTEMS

Representational use requires a system of sufficient complexity and adaptive variabilities of response to be capable of integrative, adjustive, combinatorial projective negative and positive feedback and *feedforward* reactivities to the system's input and output for which there is a *disposition base* involving *patterns* of interrelated capacities for:

(1) Reactivities to *input*—alternative kinds of potential reactivities to (dispositions for)—the reception of kinds of input that provide a *capacity background* (largely unmanifested on the occasion but

still essential) of the system giving a degree of specificity and richness for the processing reactivities (the system's parallel to *interpretation*) that determine the specific readinesses, directedness, and selectivities (spatial–temporal content) of the input (*where* the input comes from and alternative targets for alternative outputs); and for

(2) Reactivities in formation and projectivities of output—kinds of potential directive and selective reactivities for potential formation and continuance or alteration of kinds of *output*. These provide a capacity *background* within the system (largely unmanifested on the occasion but still essential) giving a degree of specificity and richness for the nature of the directive and selective reactivities (content) resulting in a preparation of readiness to go for the specific formation and continuance or alteration of the actual output. This projective part is parallel to *affirmatory* activity. (Such affirmatory activity could take nonlinguistic form as one confirms something perceptually.)

There are interesting parallels to interpretation and representational projection in nonmental autonomic systems. The following is an attempt to schematize and provide an illustrative case of such representational use.

## 9.3 THE ABSTRACT MODEL

### I. Interpretive processing activity

An interpretation of an input is the result of an interpretive *kind* of processing activity. In particular, this processing activity involves a reactivity to—use of—input that is for the formation of projected preparation for output to various target areas.

(1) *Interpretation.* An interpretation of an input is the result of an interpretive *kind* of processing activity.

The reciprocal disposition partners are:

(A) the input (pre-processing stage), and
(B) other inputs and input traces of the fluctuating substrate of an integrative control centre (ICC), for the mutual manifestation of:

(i) the ICC's detection of that particular kind of input, including the receptor spatiotemporal *origin* of that input, and

(ii) the ICC, in response to the input, forms a preparedness for performing what it selects as appropriate output from what could be competing outputs. Such an output is typically for specific targets for certain kinds of effect. It is under feedback and feedforward ICC control. Finally, this preparedness is itself formed:

  (a) with comparison to and cooperation with some other preparedness for output, and

  (b) selectively against still other competing alternative spatiotemporally projective outputs.

Preparedness of the dispositional states of the ICC for the formation of projective output (through their own dispositionality and feedback and feedforward adaptivity) is *itself* projective. These states remain, even after the formation of particular output, to play roles in feedback and feedforward control. These states are the *sources* of projective *use* in the control and production of successive outputs. There can, of course, be hierarchies and parallel ICCs for higher and/or different integrative, etc., processes relevant to final related outputs.

## II. Representational projection

The reciprocal disposition partners are

(A) the input (post-processing stage),

(B) other inputs including any new inputs exclusive of inhibitory ones, and input traces including any new traces, and

(C) (i) and (ii) as acquired capacities of the fluctuating substrate for the mutual manifestation of:
The formation of the output signal by and from the ICC that is cooperative *with* some other output and selective *against* still other potential alternative competing outputs.

The output is temporally and spatially projected under feedback and feedforward control by the ICC to some distant effect of a particular sort, for instance, dilation of the blood vessels at the level of the skin rather than the core during thermoregulatory adjustments to exercise (Kenney and Johnson 1992). This output in such projective *use* is the representational projection in representational use.

The parallel is not with linguistic representation and misrepresentation, but instead with perceptual representation and misrepresentation. In particular, somatic sensorimotor representation has roughly the same 'physical environment' for its projective activity as autonomic systems—namely the inside (organs, tendons, muscles) and outside (skin) of the body itself.

## 9.4 THE WORKING MODEL

Part of the control of the cardiovascular system involves the constriction and dilation of blood vessels in the many different 'vascular beds' throughout the body (Dampney 1994). Vessels can be constricted or dilated to control temperature or blood pressure, or to coordinate with other autonomic responses (Spyer 1992).

Consider two thermal inputs, $A$ (from the left foot) and $B$ (from the left calf), that are fed to an integrative control centre (ICC) in the brainstem. Within the thermoregulatory processing stream, the ICC relates $A$ and $B$ to each other and to other inputs and also to *traces* of previous inputs for selective exclusion or inclusion in further processing. Input traces consist in the synaptic strengths, cell membrane properties, and internal cell properties affected by previous inputs. A new input will result in its own trace, even if minimal, which is part of the gaining of comparative and selective detection capacities for particular inputs associated with specific target areas.

When we move to the actual neurophysiological details of the workings of systems mediating conscious and nonconscious thermoregulation, each appears to be what Jeffrey Gray has called a 'comparator system,' a system having 'the general function of predicting, on a moment-to-moment basis, the next perceived state of the world, and determining whether the predicted and actual state match or do not match' (Gray 1995: 660).

All of this could be considered parallel to interpretation of input. It is also the gaining of capacities needed for the selective formation of particular outputs by the ICC. This will be explained in what follows.

The term 'map' is sometimes used to indicate dispositional structures within a system having a capacity for *comparative* and *selective* use of (reactivities to) input for the formation and continuance or discontinuance of output that is spatially and/or temporally projective to specific target areas through feedforward and feedback control. In order to spell out as clearly as possible some of the basic mechanisms, I shall here avoid the tempting but misleading terms 'map' and 'mapping.' These terms have unfortunate connotations, suggesting the need for an homuncular map *reader*.

Output reactivities of the ICC in the complex context of all its inputs and input traces are for the formation, continuance, or discontinuance of output directive for the constriction or dilation of blood vessels in the vicinity of *A*, or *B*, or both, or elsewhere, or for any combination of these targets. This formation of output is temporally and spatially projective and under feedforward and feedback control by the ICC. The ICC can also integrate nonthermal input with thermal input. An anticipated need for increased circulation in the gut due to food intake can result in the *absence* of a signal directed toward dilation in the calf, an output that would have proceeded otherwise. Such intermodal integration is a common feature of ICCs. It is not required for, but is an enrichment of, representational use.

ICCs exhibit countless adaptivities, individual-specific as well as species-general. Input traces have an effect on the use of subsequent similar and dissimilar inputs. The ICC is a 'fluctuating substrate' (Spector 1979). For change to be adaptive, an ICC must possess a certain amount of stability in a way that affects reactivities to future possible inputs.

An ICC exhibiting representational use possesses complex dispositional states for reactivities to inputs so that *differential* (comparative and contrastive with other intermodal inputs and input traces and selective between competing potential outputs) outputs obtain depending on the *context* of a particular input in relation to other inputs and input traces. Output is selective and projective with respect to its multiple targets under feedback and feedforward control by the ICC. Targets can be spatially or temporally distinct, or both. This is spatial and temporal projectivity to the immediate physical environment (target organs distant from the ICC). It is interactive manipulation of the immediate physical environment through *sensory* feedback and *parallel to perception*. The closest parallel would be the somatic sensory system, which shares its immediate physical environment—the muscles, organs, and skin of the body itself—with the nonconscious thermoregulatory system.

Contrast such systems with a bowl of water into which a pebble is dropped. At any time *t*, the dispositions of the water molecules and the bowl molecules form a complex net that is directed toward a particular output (ripples) given a particular input (the pebble dropping in the water). However, the bowl of water does not have an ICC that exhibits selective spatial and temporal projectivity under feedforward and feedback control. Nor do spinal reflexes display this kind of selective spatial and temporal projectivity. Such reflexes are for only one output from only one input.

The external signal is within the cortex as a relative *terminus* at the richest level of processing of what has been a vector path from the immediate environment to the sensory receptors. In most models, the *beginning* is the first and vital step at which 'information' is pumped in. Then, through resonating electrical connectivities, this 'information' has a directional flow through hierarchies of centers of more and more complex processing. Having what is informational in the pipeline, it is as if, once that bit of homuncularity is allowed at the start, one can manage with the 'path' of marvelously resonating and ever more complex connectivities. The 'information' part must be noted again as *what* about the internal (e.g. dreaming or hallucinating) that *makes* its origin in the cortex (a very different origin from that of the external signal) a *memory* circuit, so what makes the internal signal qualitatively similar to the external signal is not a *path*, but instead an 'information' content homuncularity.

What you put in the hat, you can take out again. This informational rabbit, however, appears illusory. It is difficult to envisage how vectorization, however resonant, is rich enough as a theoretical model. It is tempting, because it is an important *part* of what is happening and lends itself easily to comparatively simple mathematicization. If the story ends with this vectorization, however, it ends with *quantities* assessing complexes of neuronal tracks or paths and their resonating irradiations *qua* those paths—a Pythagoreanism of the brain.

This would be no less an error of exclusive emphasis than would be an exclusive emphasis on *qualities* of single-cell groups that ignored the cells' multiple complex interconnecting vectors. We need a model explicitly incorporating vectors (for the connectivities) and single-cell groups (for the *qualities* of *what* is being connected), with the different research emphases of each made necessary to the other.

A comment by Mircea Steriade is to the point (here, 'SF' refers to 'sleep factors as tonic and phasic events during dreaming sleep'):

Many electrophysiologists consider the 'wet' data to lack stringent method-ological criteria or they simply ignore these data. One the other hand, the fellows who manipulate SFs do not yet use the available tools to study the effects of SFs at the neuronal level in those areas that, from other types of experiments, proved to be critical for the full development of sleep. Indeed, sleep is ultimately the product of brain structures. Study of the actions of various hypothesized SFs at the level of single cells is needed urgently. (Steriade 1992: 10)

Llinás himself has done work on the intrinsic properties of single cells (Llinás 1988) as well as on the vector and tensor network approach (Pellionisz and Llinás 1979, 1982, 1985), each of equal and fundamental importance. A unitary model is evocatively and effectively suggested in the following quotation, despite the use of the overburdened and homuncular term 'information':

Although sensory nerve pathways deliver messages to the CNS that are quite invariant with respect to given sensory stimuli, the manner in which the CNS treats these messages depends on the functional state of each relay station. Thus, rather than a simple mirror of the external world, the CNS embodies a dialogue between the internal states generated by the intrinsic electrical activity of the nerve cells and their connectivity, which represents the internal context, and the information that reaches the brain from the senses. . . . Still more fundamental, however, is the possibility that the functional organization of the CNS, based in part on the intrinsic activity of neurons, may be key to understanding the nature of subjectivity. In principle one can see how the intrinsic activity of neurons, which reflect a closed reference system, may be the stage on which our image of the external world is ultimately generated. (Llinás 1988: 1663)

It is important to see that the central cortex is not the integrative, regulative command center for these complex vegetative functions. Such functions can exist in a nonconscious persistent vegetative state, whereas consciousness cannot exist without a functioning vegetative system.

The cerebral cortex can produce significant efferent signals to and receive afferent signals from the autonomic nervous system, but the cortex is not a prime integrative control system or command center for autonomic functions. It is important to see the difference.[4]

The function of such ingenious and complex integrative, regulatory processing centers—such as the solitary tract nucleus or the hypothalamus, which are characterized by negative and positive feedback and

---

[4] A difference that tends to be obfuscated in Bernard Engel's 'An essay on the circulation as behavior' and the ensuing discussion (Engel 1986).

forward-looping (individual-specific) adaptivities—is to input from the cerebral cortex *and* elsewhere for the most sophisticated control of the functions of the autonomic nervous system. The forebrain does not have the hook-ups to perform that complex task, although it can 'learn' to do *some* by biofeedback conditioning.

There is a great difference between (1) worrying about a wounded foot causing a nonvoluntary alteration of heart rate and (2) controlling heart rate voluntarily as in the case of at least halfway needing synchronous external stimuli (a metronome, for instance) for voluntary heart-rate adjustment, perhaps even attaining a 'sensation of control' (Cohn and Yellin 1984). All this requires the explicit detail provided in subsequent chapters.

Through all of this, a very large and still inadequately answered question for any neurophysiological account of the mind persists: 'How do we distinguish conscious or sentient activities (except by mere fiat of difference of location) from nonconscious, nonsentient activities of the marvellously complex activities of the vegetative autonomic systems?' This is the topic to which I shall turn in Chapter 10.

## 9.5 THE VEGETATIVE MIND

The quotations that follow are extracted from scientific work on nonmental, 'vegetative' systems found in the human body (and in the bodies of many nonhuman creatures). They are intended to illustrate my contention that philosophers have been naïve in imagining that minds can be given purely functional or structural characterizations. Such characterizations, as the quotations reveal, apply straightforwardly to nonmental, vegetative systems.

Even the lowly thermoregulatory system exhibits a range of capacities rivaling those of sophisticated computational simulations of human mental processes. More is needed if we are to make clear what distinguishes the mental from the nonmental.

On the basis of recent insights into the organization of the thermoregulatory system, and of evaluation of experimental evidence from electrophysiological, neuropharmacological, and neuroanatomical studies it can be concluded that these systems are involved in adaptive modifications. Receiving information from several sensory systems, they seem to deliver additional modulatory signals, which may interfere with the processing of specific thermal information at several sites. Theoretically, the central monoamines may participate in the control of thermal input, in the central integration of thermal signals, and in modification of output signals to thermoregulatory effectors. Best documented is their modulatory action on thermosensitive and thermointegrative hypothalamic neurons. There, the monoamines 5-hydrexytryptamine and noradrenaline act as antagonists, which enhance or diminish the effects of thermal efferents mediated by other transmitters. Moreover, the antagonistic monoaminergic systems are interconnected and can influence each other at the level of lower brain stem. The activity in central monoaminergic systems can also be modified by neurohumoral feedback mechanisms from the periphery. By means of these interrelations the vegetative responses of the organism can be corrected and optimized. These interrelations can explain also some cross-adaptive changes in the thermoregulatory threshold for shivering evoked by nonthermal factors such as food intake or long-distance running. (Brück and Zeisberger 1987: 205–6)

There is an anticipatory or forward-looking capacity in the functioning of the thermoregulatory system explained in K. Brück (1989).

In accounting for how there is coordination of separate respiratory and cardiovascular pumps, Feldman and Ellenberger refer to Koepchen *et al.*'s (1981) and Koepchen's (1983) postulation of three possible mechanisms for the coordination and integration of responses at the brainstem level to peripheral signals:

First, separate action on both of the control systems; second, an action on one control system which transmits the effect to the other by central connections; third, action on a substrate superposed on both systems. In addition, there are purely central interactions that suggest a unitary organization, with local interactions playing an important role. Whatever the mechanism, these systems are integrated in the brain stem in one or more of the regions described above. Given the nonlinearity of these systems and their state-dependent performance, as during the sleep–wake cycle or exercise, their linkage may be flexible, thus providing a further challenge to our understanding. (Feldman and Ellenberger 1988: 601)

Feldman and Ellenberger speak of assorted complex relationships between respiratory and cardiovascular neurons in ways that G. Edelman (1987) has spoken of neuronal interrelationships that were supposed to help us to see what is unique to the higher functions of the cerebral cortex and therefore special to the voluntary and conscious life of the mind. Command centers and coordinative, integrative, and regulatory centers can be found at the level of the nonvoluntary and nonconscious vegetative functions.

When respiratory and cardiovascular premotor control are considered separately, the locations of neurons assigned to each network (biased toward somatic location and presynaptic field distribution), by and large, are distinct. The local microcircuitry of each separate neuronal cluster is an important factor in their behavior. However, on a slightly larger scale . . . the locations of clusters assigned to each control system parallel each other. Their proximity and occasional commingling, with the likely overlapping of their dendritic fields, suggest that shared inputs and local processing, by collaterals or short axon interneurons, underlie cardiorespiratory coordination. Potent local interactions are suggested by the powerful cardiorespiratory effects of microinjection of subpicomole amounts of excitatory amino acid neurotransmitters in these brain stem regions. (Feldman and Ellenberger 1988: 598)

We can even find 'higher-order' states and processes in vegetative systems

Second or higher order neurons mainly in medial, commissural, intermediate, and dorsolateral NTS project to portions of the amygdale and hypothalamus, to the parabrachial nuclear region, and to the ventrolateral medulla. Inspiratory neurons in the ventrolateral region of NTS project to the ventrolateral medulla and are also a source of mono- and oligosynaptic drive to spinal inspiratory neurons [this region of cells is referred to as the dorsal respiratory group (DRG)]. (Feldman and Ellenberger 1988: 599)

Claus Jessen suggests a thermal control system with a *mapping* function that can 'discriminate between targets of the load' in the following:

In a recent study on the black Bedouin goat it was shown that the animal behaved differently in both situations; in the natural environment, generating a combination of high skin and lower core temperatures, sweating rate was high and respiratory frequency was relatively low, while an artificial environment of the same load resulted in a combination of higher core and lower skin temperatures, with more panting and less sweating (Borut *et al.* 1979; Dmi'el and Robertshaw 1983). Similar observations have been made in sheep (Hopkins and Knights 1984; Stephenson and Hopkins 1984). It must be concluded that skin and core temperature signals do not represent fully interchangeable components of an integrated afferent input which then generates a standardized efferent signal, graded to match the thermal load. Instead, the controlling system appears to discriminate between the targets of the load and to initiate those effector responses which are most suitable to counteract the dominant primary stimulus. (Jessen 1985: 13)

Jessen goes on to describe a temporal mapping involving 'anticipatory' or forward feedback.

The response of some thermoregulatory effectors to skin temperature does not depend entirely on its absolute level but also on the rate of change in skin temperature per unit of time. This becomes evident during a step exposure to cold which in man and animals is often followed by a transient burst of heat production occurring at constant core temperature and fading away gradually at constantly decreased skin temperature. . . . Concerning the effects of dynamic sensitivity to changing skin temperature on the stability of body temperature it is obvious that an overshooting 'anticipatory' response can permit temporary maintenance of core temperature even in the absence of a central error signal. A further effect of rate sensitivity is to smooth thresholds and discontinuities of the stimulus–response relationships (Brown and Brengelmann 1970). (Jessen 1985: 113).

Jessen then indicates a spatial mapping that 'is not just a function of the environment.'

Skin temperature at any site is determined by the interaction between the convection of heat to the surface by means of the blood stream and the removal of heat from the surface which is influenced by geometry, external insulation and ambient conditions. Therefore, surface temperature at those parts of the body of which the blood flow is controlled to modulate heat loss, is not just a function of the environment but simultaneously reflects the control action. During exposure to cold, skin temperature signals generated in these effector areas of the skin create a positive feedback loop (Gordon and Heath 1983). (Jessen 1985: 114)

Under the heading of 'viscerotopic pattern of organization in the nucleus tractus solitarius,' A. D. Loewry notes a pattern that suggests both degeneracy and mapping in the vegetative system:

The output of these NTS regions appears to be organized for two modes of responses. The 'organ-specific' NTS subnuclei project probably only to specific lower brain stem nuclei that control reflex adjustments of the end organ, but experimental evidence for this is still incomplete. Most, if not all, visceral afferents make connections with other NTS subnuclei besides their main 'organ-specific' receptive one. (Loewry 1990: 89)

Loewry's term 'pattern' seems preferable to 'map' because it seems a shade less homuncular, but the message is the same, and the passage nicely links the degeneracy and 'mapping' functions of the nucleus tractus solitarius.

There is recourse to the mapping vocabulary while referring to Strack *et al.* (1989) for noting that 'projections topographically organized as was demonstrated in the paraventricular hypothalamic nucleus' and even allows the luxury of the anthropomorphism 'coding' and 'decoding' (Loewry 1990: 100).

Loewry refers to a hierarchical interactive re-entering network of autonomic centers up and down.

Nerves carrying gustatory information project to the rostral part of the NTS. They synapse on NTS neurons that project to lower brain stem centers controlling chewing, swallowing, and salivation, and to other neurons in the same NTS region which project to higher neural centers involved in food sensation. Similarly, general visceral afferents project to specific NTS regions. Some project to NTS subnuclei that control lower brain stem neurons for reflex adjustment of the end organ. Others project to a common site in the NTS called the commissural-medial NTS, which acts as a relay center and projects to higher CNS regions. This connects to a central autonomic network that is made up of a collection of interrelated CNS nuclei, including the parabrachial nucleus, the central gray matter, the lateral and paraventricular hypothalamic nuclei, the central nucleus of the amygdala, and the bed nucleus of the stria terminalis. This central network probably functions like a microprocessor to integrate a wide range of autonomic afferent information and then causes output changes in the autonomic nervous system, the neuroendocrine system, and possibly behavioral activities. (Loewry 1990: 101).

Tetsuro Hori explicates the nonlinearity of the thermoregularity system:

On the basis of thermal sensitivity, the population and the shape of the thermal response curve, it is suggested that the former type of neurons are non-TS neurons and the latter type of neurons are warm-sensitive neurons. The non-linear shape of temperature vs. current response curves of the latter type of cells conforms well with the shape of the temperature vs. firing rate response curves. (Hori 1991: 2)

In claiming controller functions of thermoregulation from integrating mechanisms within and outside the preoptic and anterior hypothalamus (POA) that are organized hierarchically, Hori explains,

Instead of the classical negative feedback models of thermoregulation comprising a single integrator with multiple inputs and outputs, recent conceptual models assume a multiple thermostat system, in which warm and cold signals activate primarily separate sets of neural networks from TS neurons to thermoregulatory effectors. (Hori 1991: 11)

The 'degeneracy' of thermosensitive (TS) neurons is used in a hypothesis explaining the variability and adaptivity of the system:

In view of the survival values demonstrated by the two examples above, the modifications of thermoregulation by non-thermal events are not considered merely as the result of interfering actions of non-thermal homeostatic systems on the thermoregulation system. Rather, thermoregulatory changes may be understood as a part of adaptive responses of the organisms as a whole. The POA TS neurons having responsiveness to non-thermal homeostatic signals, together with their abundant neural connections with divergent areas of the brain (Hori 1984; Hori *et al.* 1982; Kiyohara *et al.* 1984; Shibata *et al.* 1988) may play a principal role in the coordination of different homeostatic functions to increase the probability of survival. . . . The findings that 40–70% of POA TS neurons respond to divergent types of non-thermal homeostatic signals and have abundant mutual connections with divergent areas of brain (limbic system and association cortices) indicate that TS neurons may be involved in the coordination of thermal and non-thermal homeostatic functions controlled in the hypothalamus. (Hori 1991: 18)

Gordon and Heath advance a model for thermal control that has, within the autonomic system, afferents and efferents for motor patterns of output of great complexity and flexibility:

Our understanding of the neural control of body temperature has been clarified by research over the past ten years. Overall, ascending thermal inputs are integrated with other thermal and nonthermal inputs, which results in efferent signals with the spatial and temporal characteristics necessary for driving effector organs involved in thermal homeostasis. There is substantial support for the hypothesis that the afferent component of the thermoregu-latory system integrates thermal stimuli into several neural patterns, the principal ones being a stepwise, switching response of neuron activity during scrotal thermal stimulation and a proportional response to other thermal inputs. Furthermore, some thermointegrative CNS neurons respond relatively rapidly or slowly during peripheral thermal stimulation, which may be critical in driving behavioral and autonomic motor outputs, respectively.

The control of thermoregulatory motor outputs is multifaceted and exhibits proportional, rate-sensitive, and/or on–off regulatory patterns during thermal stimulation. These complex motor patterns indicate the presence of extensive temporal and spatial integration of ascending thermal information. This is supported by the fact that the pattern of efferent nerve activity in various motor systems (e.g. vasomotor) is vastly different from that produced by recordings of primary thermoreceptor activity. (Gordon and Heath 1986: 609)

I leave it to the reader to compare these accounts of nonmental systems with familiar claims concerning the nature of mentality advanced in the cognitive sciences, especially by those theorists most influenced by functionalism. The passages speak for themselves.

# 10

# Emergence, Reduction, Mental Chauvinism

## 10.1 EMERGENCE

Take a complex whole. Let us try to talk and think about its simpler constituents and their relationships that constitute the whole as well as we can. Let us try to do this in the particular case of a complex *property*. In doing ontology, what we need to think about most is that concerning which we are largely ignorant. It is a good thing to recognize this fact and project to the constitution of things as responsibly as possible.

If the shape of a cloud is hazy and not sharp-edged, it is still dense enough in the middle, although less and less dense at the periphery, so that we can project degrees of density of elementary particle populations (or aspects of fields or superstrings or . . .) in a spatiotemporal region and with varying degrees of stability to constitute the shape of the cloud.[1] As Russell always saw, and before him Locke, observable physical wholes are *never* sharp-edged because of the penumbra of what Locke called 'fleeting particles.' As such, the 'sharp-edged' shape and size of a foot ruler is constituted without remainder by a density-cloud of elementary particle populations, or what have you. Reassuringly, this density-cloud has extensional properties and constitutes the extensionality of the macroscopic whole. This is consequently not a case of emergence *or* reduction. The extensional properties of the whole are found in density populations of elementary particles.

---

[1] To simplify the exposition, I will assume that reality comprises arrangements of particles. None of the philosophical points I want to make here, however, depend on this assumption. Reality could (and probably *does*) comprise overlapping fields, or a single substance (space–time, the One), or something stranger still. See Chapter 16 for the dénoument.

The case of fluidity is a clear case of the ontological reduction of what seemed to be simple and homogeneous (fluidity) to smoothly tumbling molecules.

We should stop looking for cases of emergent properties from one level of being to another, usually higher level—from the microphysical to the macrophysical, for instance, or from the macrophysical to the microphysical. Surely, by virtue of being complex, macro-properties are not *really* anything over and above complexes of simpler micro-properties. The causal work should *not* get done twice over, at the level of relationships among micro-properties and then again at the level of macro-properties that consist only in relationships among those simpler micro-properties.

The place to think about genuinely emergent properties is at subsequent stages or space–time segments at the *same* level, which is also the only and *basic* level: *uni*-level emergence rather than *higher*-level emergence. At this level, the question of reduction to some still more basic level cannot arise.

At the elementary particle level of physics, it seems excessive to demand that *every* intrinsic property produced in particular concatenations of particles must be in the concatenation that produced it. Somewhere in the New Mexico desert, very special and complex concatenations of particles might be produced by scientists operating a super-collider in hopes of the occurrence of both anticipated *and* unanticipated intrinsic properties that would occur only under the conditions of such specially complex elementary-particle concatenations. Emergence, it would appear, could occur at the most basic level of elementary-particle physics.

The medieval doctrine (or a twist on it) that all of the perfections (intrinsic properties) in the effect must be present in the cause is not self-evidently true. Were it true, the world would be not only dull, but *absolutely* and *evenly* dull. Emergence might not be a bad thing, not even a bad theoretical or explanatory thing. Emerging physical properties can be encompassed, with luck, in terms of general laws. This, however, makes them no less ontologically emergent.

Emergence might appear to be a metaphysically magical idea, but only so long as we do not look carefully at *non*-emergence. If there were no emergence of properties, then all simple and intrinsic properties of the effect have to be found in and extracted from the cause: the 'pipeline' conception of causality. The pipeline conception makes the world out to be a great deal more boring than it appears to be.

I say 'extracted from the cause' because that is the model that occurs to me to explain how the intrinsic properties in the effect *had* to be found in the cause—that is, they had to *come* from it somehow. Extraction is one, though very peculiar, possibility. The *non*-emergence metaphysicians must be able to suggest more intuitive alternatives. That would be their responsibility. The denial of emergence is a daring and exciting ontology that would require a careful, systematic defense and development to have any degree of plausibility whatsoever.

Group wholes such as armies, social clubs, or the year's weather can all be understood compositionally. Predicates such as 'winning the battle,' 'having a membership rally,' or 'having too much rainfall' are not translatable into statements about dynamic arrangements of ultimate constituents. There should be no attempt to find entailments between such predicates embedded in statements about these complexes and statements about the ultimate constituents.[2] What *fully* constitutes and *is* the whole complex object, group, event, state, process, property, or relation at any particular moment could vary across occasions. In some cases there might be inhibitory factors that require additional factors to cancel the inhibitory elements.

Let us suppose, then, that complex wholes *are* the simple constituents in their numerous relationships and connectivities with one another and with what is external to them and their potential (dispositions) for these with acceptable additions. It should be clear that if there *were* a simple, emergent property of a complex whole, it would be a simple property *among* the simple properties of the ultimate constituents. That is, it would be found only in the special, complex interrelations and interreactivities of all of the constituents with one another and whatever is external to them and their potentialities with their varying degrees of stability that together are just what the whole comes to or, if you like, boils *down* to. Such a simple emergent property undoubtedly would have enormously numerous interrelatednesses that we might never discover.

An apparent instance of property acquisition that fits the nonpipeline view in theoretical physics is the still conjectural case of neutrino oscillation, in which the neutrino oscillates from three forms: (1) electron neutrino, (2) muon neutrino, and (3) tau neutrino. This suggests intrinsic changes of property that can be regarded as not merely a

---

[2] John Wisdom spent much of his life trying to make this clear.

new combination of what it already had or something extracted from something else. If so, that would be emergence!

It does not count against a property or quality to say that it is emergent. A non-emergence view of the world does not seem to be obviously correct. What properties emerge from what remains uncertain.


## 10.2 REDUCTION

(1) *Explanatory reduction*. Different kinds of explanation are not 'reducible' (that is, by entailment or translation) to one kind of explanation, although the items and happenings mentioned in different kinds of explanation could be *ontologically* reducible, that is, come *down* to (be nothing over and above) the same items and happenings mentioned in that explanation. We could think of the occurrence of an event mentioned in *any* kind of explanation in an interest-relative way such that without that interest-circumscription the explanation would not be what it is. Explanations are mind-dependent, theory-laden, and interest-relative. None of this applies to objects or events *themselves* and how they are constituted—*they* are not interest-relative or language-relative. It should not take too much effort to see that this is just the obvious fact that the same object or event might figure in many different explanations, or might have figured in none because there were simply no explainers.

(2) *Ontological reduction*. Leaving aside the ontologically irrelevant matter of supervenience, ontological reduction concerns the question whether something, $a$, comes down to, reduces to, just consists in, is not anything over and above, something, $\beta$. It requires only the success of the disclaimer: 'nothing over and above.' There are two criteria for a plausible ontological reduction:

(A) What is being reduced must be complex to be reduced to its simpler constituents. Intuition is tricky, because we can err in our judgment of what is simple or what is complex. Beliefs and desires seem obviously complex, whereas the sensed aspect of a specific pitch of an auditory input seems simple.

(B) The reducing constituents should fit intuitively the nature of what is being reduced: it cannot be *ad hoc*, and it cannot be mere correlation, however exact.

The double helix had the right fit for DNA to the expert eye, and smoothly tumbling molecules have the right fit for fluidity. It is not evident that neuronal firings have that same kind of right fit for the features of experience, even for many expert eyes. This is why so many neuroscientists themselves keep coming back to 'the problem of sentience.' Arguments of the form, 'What *else* could it be, stupid?' or 'You'll get used to the idea' would not be considered conclusive in other areas of science.

If qualities of the experiential are simple and not evidently fit for reduction to familiar neuronal properties, then *unreduced* they find their way as *irreducible* properties among the elementary particles, fields, strings, or what have you, as the unreducible properties of extension are unreduced in the degrees of varying density populations of kinds of particle.

There is no flouting of laws of thermodynamics in this by bringing in causes from nowhere. It is simply a matter of not leaving out the intrinsic properties of what is involved in the work that is done.

The question is whether properties of immediate experience are unreduced, as in the case of the properties of extension, or reduced, as in the case of fluidity.

In Chapter 6, we saw how the quantitative is emphasized in our scientific representations of nature. A reasonable demand for measurable experimental results in science can easily lead to unreasonable restrictions to purely quantitative interpretations of such results. As I have observed, this pushes us in the direction of a Pythagoreanism of numbers in space–time with space–time itself perhaps collapsing into numbers.

I have argued that neither causality nor emergence can be thought of meaningfully as holding between different levels of being. Both are uni-level, both are found at the basic level of the simplest, most irreducible noncomposite, non*composable* elements of nature—the elementary particles or aspects of fields or strings or. . . . At *that* level it seems an absurd legislation to endorse the idea that properties of an effect must be found in its cause—the pipeline view. That would preclude the possibility of intrinsic irreducible nonrelational properties found in specific concatenations of particles that were explained by, but not also found in, some other concatenation of particles. There *do* seem to be cases of this within theoretical physics, as with neutrino oscillations. If that possibility is not an absurdity, then nature need not be a bore, and emergence can be considered normal, have a natural explanation, and not be considered inexplicable, anachronistic, or mystical.

Putting these results together shows how making room for the qualitative nature of experience need not be more strange, difficult, mystery-mongering, or in defiance of the laws of nature than would be making room for the qualitative nature of nonmental physical entities that might have been overlooked in giving exclusive priority to their quantitative, and perhaps dispositional, character.

## 10.3 QUALITIES AND FUNCTION

An infant has non-propositional perceiving long before perceiving *as*, non-propositional dreaming before dreaming *that* and non-propositional imagery before imagery *of*. In maturing, individuals come to perceive *as*, dream *that*, and have imagery *of*. Individuals have forms of reactivity to perceiving that are carried through to dreamings and to imagery. Individuals come to use kinds of imagery (that resesmble typical perceivings of objects, situations, properties, or processes) that are also representative of what they have perceived. It is natural for an individual to do this because of the qualitative similarity of imaging and perceiving. (Ryle was wrong about musical imagery. It was not his imaging his *own singing* of *Greensleeves* but imaging the hearing of *Greensleeves* by full orchestra. His deeply imaging could be as 'perfect' as his perceptual hearing of it.)

An individual's selective, projective, and abstractive capacities are formed in the individual's dealings with the immediate environment. Selectivity and abstraction are natural (acquired without being taught) processes. Selectivity and abstraction are required for the development of memory, because reminders and promptings are rarely replicas of what is being remembered. Selectivity and abstraction are required for quick response recognition as well. Just as, in perceiving, the tip of a leopard's tail should be enough, or the faint suggestion of part of the print of a paw, or what are sometimes called 'secondary cues.' A carcass in a tree is a secondary cue to the presence of a leopard, because only a leopard deposits its prey—a macaque monkey, for instance—in a tree. Some monkeys never catch on, but other non-human primates do. A mastery of secondary cues requires an abstract cognitive mediation process.

How is the qualitative fit for evolution? The quality display is a perfect internal model for external projections. It is the natural material for such projective use (rather than inference). There can be sensory and sensory-like griddings for percepts, dreaming, imagery, illusion, and hallucination with varying degrees and changes of qualitative occupancy.

Double or treble and hazy vision, pressures in the jaw muscles, a high whine in the ears, and feelings of unsteadiness on standing are all normal and familiar, although some of their causes might be cortical and hallucinatory.

Most of us develop defeasible but practical ways of determining whether what is going on is mostly a condition of ourselves or is a condition of our immediate environment causing qualitatively similar effects in us. Our grid or sensory field exhibits systematic changes of field occupancy. This is not the same as physical occupancy. Although one is natural material for projective use to the other, they need not be at all similar. Sand clocks and alarm clocks can be projective for time measures without similarity. An orange colour is between red and yellow. Three objects in a line can have a middle member that is between the other two.

Berkeley insisted that projection from sensation to the physical immediate environment is possible only for similars. That appears to be false.

Imagine viewing a painting from a considerable distance. You match your sighting of the edges of your two hands held before your eyes with the sighting of the edges of the painting. Now walk toward the painting. The painting itself remains unchanged in size. But your hands, in matching with changes in the results of the viewings of the painting, get farther and farther apart until the moment when they come in contact with the edges of the painting—a handsome cofunction of the visual with the tactile-motor-kinaesthetic! (See Chapter 13.)

What has changed so much on our walk has been the percept, the sensory fields and their relative field occupancies and betweenness. This is what makes us sensate.

The qualitative provides the *feel* of the feelings in our upsets and delights, our feelings of anticipation, unease at failure. The qualitative can be evoked in memory imagery for a *continuance* of actively dealing with what it is *used* to represent.[3] The qualitative is also *what* is apt for

---

[3] Damasio (1994) provides a neurophysiological modeling of this.

savouring—the qualities of sense experience and the qualities of the feel of feelings, negative as well as positive ones.

The argument has been that the nature of the physical world (which, by my reckoning, *includes* the mental) *cannot* be characterized fully in terms of only the quantitative and/or powers—dispositions that get turned into probabilifications that then push us in the direction of Pythagoreanism. The physical world requires the qualitative. The sparseness of a world without qualities, like the sparseness of phenomenalism, behaviorism and operationalism, appears attractive only because it is never spelled out in full, candid explanations. An explicit inclusion of the qualitative, whether in a mental case or a nonmental case, is not adding more 'work,' thereby breaching the laws of thermodynamics. It is only explicitly fulfilling the ontological requirements of the qualitative character of what *already* has quantity and the work potential of dispositionality. The need for qualitative character is the need to be complete as a property in the physical world.

## 10.4 VEGETATIVE CONTROL CENTERS

It can help to see how closely in its functioning a non-conscious system that is part of our body is like some other part of our body that is a conscious system. First, because, as we discovered in Chapter 9, functions that have been, and still are, thought to be unique to conscious systems are common among nonconscious systems. Second, because we will then be in a position to bring into sharp focus what functions are different and what can be learned from that difference.

Let us return briefly to the thermoregulatory system. Part of the function of the thermoregulatory system through the hypothalamus (HT) that is an integrative control center (ICC), constricting and dilating blood vessels in various regions of the body. Constriction and dilation control temperature, and blood pressure, and must be coordinated with other autonomic responses.

Earlier, we imagined a pair of thermal inputs, $A$ (from the left foot) and $B$ (from the left calf), reaching an integrative control centre (ICC) such as the hypothalamus (HT) in the brainstem. The HT relates $A$ and $B$ to each other and to other input traces for selective exclusion or inclusion in further processing. We have here a complex categorization response to input analogous to the interpretation of input by an intelligent agent. It is, in addition, the gaining of capacities for the selective formation of particular outputs by the HT.

Output reactivities of the HT in light of its inputs and input traces are for the formation, continuance, or discontinuance of outputs directive for the constriction or dilation of blood vessels in the vicinity of $A$, or $B$, or both, or elsewhere, or any combination of these targets. The formation of output is temporally and spatially projective and under feedforward and feedback control of the HT.

The formation of the output signal by and from the HT that is cooperative *with* some other output and selective *against* still other potential alternative competing outputs. Output is temporally and spatially projected under feedback and feedforward control by the HT to some distant effect of a particular sort, dilation of the blood vessels at the level of the skin rather than the core, for instance, or a potential is set for a particular reaction to occur if a particular input is not received after an interval of time has passed.

The HT can integrate nonthermal input with thermal input for *other* systems such as the respiratory or digestive system. Food intake could lead to an anticipated need for increased circulation in the gut, and this might result in a signal's *not* being directed to blood vessels in the calf, an output that would otherwise have occurred.

The formation of output for such projective *use* is representational projection in representational use. All of this is entirely literal and without ambiguity.

Again, it is important to recognize the parallel is not with *linguistic* representation, but with *perceptual* representation, especially somatic, sensorimotor representation. For my purposes here, the important point is that these complex capacities of the HT can be completely nonconscious. This was so in the case of Karen Ann Quinlan, who remained nonconscious for seven years without artificial aid from any life-supporting mechanism. At the same time, it should become clear that these capacities are adaptive in ways *specific* to the individual and not merely to the species generally, a function mistakenly thought to be unique to the cortex (Spector 1979).

Plainly, the nonconscious autonomic nervous system has more sophisticated capacities for spatial and temporal representations and 'has a complex neural organization in the brain, spinal chord, and periphery as the somatic nervous system' (the somatic system being a conscious system) (Bannister and Mathias 1992; Sharkey and Pittman

1995). So complexity of representational function cannot determine whether a system is conscious.

## 10.5 MENTAL CHAUVINISM

Let me return to a function found in most, probably all, mammalian mental cortical systems. Consideration of this function might enable us to see our way to a solution to otherwise perplexing problems in the philosophy of mind. We have seen in some detail how close to conscious cortical functioning the nonconscious vegetative system is. This detail is essential if we are to be clear about just what functions are lacking in these subtle and complex nonconscious systems.

The function I have in mind is that of *internal signaling*. An internal signal is a signal generated within a central integrative control center, primarily for use within that center, a signal that typically does not produce output to what is outside that center. The internal signal is *qualitatively* similar to an external signal that has its cause outside the center and that typically produces output to what is outside that center.

This function is noteworthy because it requires *qualitative* similarity: the qualitative is an essential ingredient of its operation. There is not and cannot be, however, any specification in terms of the function *itself* of what qualities are, in fact, similar. That is left entirely open to what kind of entity has such a function.

These points can be illustrated by three examples

(1) There is the mechanical chess player that has internal signals *vs.* external signals of registering the move of the opponent that are qualitatively similar to external signals that are given internal use and output inside the system *vs.* external use of what is registered that is external (move of opponent) and output (making the move) outside the system. The chess player had a problem hallucinating its opponent's moves on the board. A clever programmer corrected the problem.

(2) There seem not to be any internal signals (qualitatively similar to external signals) given *only* internal use in the job-oriented vegetative systems. With lesser or greater technical difficulty, however, it should be possible to induce such a functional capacity.

(3) Working out a problem in your head only for the satisfaction of making the attempt is a good (and pure) case of the mental, one I shall return to presently. When a tune as played by a string quartet is running through your head, you can 'turn up the volume,' you can make it 'sound' louder. There is no vegetative parallel.

Each of these cases requires *qualitative* similarity of its own internal and external signals and internal uses for internal function, yet there is *not* any qualitative similarity among all four.

I shall be a mental chauvinist (including at least my mammalian relations), holding in special regard (and reserving such terms as 'sentient' and 'consciousness' for) those qualities that make our internal (sensory-like) and external (sensory) signals similar—whether such qualities turn out to be simple and unreduced *or* complex and therefore reduced. They are the light of the world. They are *embedded* in the inner life of our minds. They are what we go over in our heads verbally and nonverbally, they embody the sensory richness of our dreaming and the very *feel* of our feelings.

# I I

# Dispositional Systems

## II.I DISPOSITIONS: A RECAPITULATION

Dispositionality has occupied centre stage during much of the preceding discussion, yet there is more to be said. Before moving on, however, it might be useful to pause briefly and recapitulate.

(1) *Actuality*. A disposition is actual even if its manifestations are *not* actual. An unmanifesting disposition is *not* 'potential being' or 'unactualized *possibilia*,' although that might be a way of characterizing a disposition's unmanifested manifestations. These manifestations are what a disposition could *do* under some, but not all, conditions. They are not what the disposition *is* or in what it *consists*. A disposition can come into existence and cease to exist quite apart from whether its manifestations exist during the disposition's existence.

(2) *Complexity*. States, processes, events, properties, situations, and objects can be complexes of simpler elements. Dispositions can be complexes of simpler dispositions.

(3) *Identity*. Spelling out the identity conditions for *anything* in terms of necessary and sufficient conditions is no better than a 'cheque's in the mail' gesture. But at least we can have a difference condition. That is, distinct kinds of disposition cannot have, under exactly the same conditions, exactly the same kinds of manifestation.

(4) *Exclusivity*. The manifestation of a disposition, under certain conditions, excludes or displaces other possible alternative manifestations under different conditions.

(5) *Properties*. A state of having a particular dispositionality need not have the properties of that disposition's manifestation. Here, several medieval principles should be distinguished.

(a) *The cause must be adequate for the effect.* This is true, although what is involved in the cause might be more than we can sum up.

Two other related principles are evidently false.

(b) *The effect is contained in the cause.* This falsely suggests that causality is an extraction or pipeline process: what is put into the pipeline at one end is extracted from the other end.

(c) *The cause must have at least as many perfections as the effect.* This falsely suggests that certain intrinsic or important properties of the effect must all be present in the cause. Considering the diversity of the causal conditions or 'disposition partners,' this is hard to envisage.

These ontologically primitive and false pipeline and containment principles led to certain theological views. More recently they have led, for example, to certain presentations of the Language of Thought theory, in which it is suggested that to explain the effect of acquiring a natural language, the causal factors *must* include another language-like Language of Thought.

(6) *Dispositional levels.*

(a) 'Muscular memory' is a case of this. The weightlifter $A$ who is out of practice and has muscular strength $S$ has lost the capacity to lift heavy weights, but when he starts lifting again he *has* the capacity to *develop* the capacity $S'$ to lift those heavy weights faster than someone $B$ who also has muscular strength $S$ but has never lifted weights before. This requires a higher or deeper level of dispositionality, no doubt in some dispositional structure base that $A$ has and $B$ lacks, that is, the capacity to acquire and strengthen the capacity $S'$.

(b) In mental cases of memory, there is a clear parallel. You might temporarily lose the capacity for remembering but retain the capacity to restructure or strengthen the lost or weakened capacity. In such cases you might be inclined to say, 'I can't *now*, but give me a few moments and I will be able to.'

## 11.2 ACQUIRING A FURTHER DISPOSITION

Amongst the manifestations that a particular dispositional state can produce, hard-wired or not hard-wired, can be the acquiring of a second, distinct, and future dispositional state. This second dispositional state can be fully *actual* without need of any actual manifestation. The whole point of a disposition, after all, is its *capacity* to do what it is *not* doing.

Amongst the manifestations of a dispositional state of molten glass that can be produced is the acquiring of a second, different, and further dispositional state of fragility under certain conditions. That second dispositional state of fragility is brought about and fully *actual* without need for the glass actually to break. Of course, in its first dispositional state, the molten glass was not in the least fragile (it was not just waiting for the right blow), although it had the capacity for the production, under certain conditions, of the fragility capacity. This gives us a general ontological model for capacities for the acquiring of further capacities for the acquiring of further capacities for. . . This is the basic model for the evolution of species, adaptivities of an individual, and for much else. The causes of a disposition are not what the disposition is for and cannot explain the content or *for*-ness of that disposition.

There is no need to think that the original dispositionality somehow contains within itself its myriad successors, or even that it is structurally similar to them. The 'original' is only a reciprocal disposition partner among many other reciprocal disposition partners for the *mutual* manifestation of the production of a successor dispositionality, which, in its turn, is only a reciprocal partner for. . . It would be difficult indeed to find the properties of what is found in their mutual manifestation among this indefinite number of interconnective partners. This should inhibit the drive to import a language-like *simulacrum* (Language of Thought) to explain the acquisition of a natural language capacity.

The capacity $C_1$ for the *acquiring* of the *further* capacity $C_2$ is clearly not the same capacity as $C_2$. Reciprocal disposition partners for the mutual manifestation of the acquiring of the disposition–capacity $C_2$ are *not* the reciprocal disposition partners of $C_2$ itself or of that *for* which $C_2$ has directedness and selectivity.

A capacity, $C_1$, of molten glass for the mutual manifestation of the *acquiring* of a capacity, $C_2$ (of having a particular kind of shattering pattern on being struck at a certain force by objects of a particular degree of hardness, etc.), for that mutual manifestation of the *acquiring* of $C_2$ are *not* the reciprocal disposition partners for different mutual manifestations of $C_2$ itself.

## 11.3 PERCEPTION AS DISPOSITIONAL

The *causes* of a disposition, then, are not *what* the disposition is a disposition *for* and *cannot* explain the content or *for*-ness of that disposition. As such, if beliefs and desires are in large part dispositional, their 'that-ness' and 'for-ness' should *not* be expected as coming from their *causes*. An explanation is needed for why, in this particular case at least, the directednesses and selectivities of the mental dispositional state *can*, very specially and as an understandable exception, be found in its cause. Similar kinds of event can be mutual manifestations of different kinds of reciprocal disposition partner. An order of stones brought about by an earthquake might be similar to an order of stones arranged to indicate a burial spot; an hallucination might be similar to a perceiving but differently produced. Externalism in the philosophy of mind has always had difficulty with the undeniable fact that similar effects can be brought about by very different causes.

These are some of the tools that can be used for the resolution of the 'narrow'–'broad' content, internalist–externalist debate. The particular reciprocal partner—perceiver or environment—is irrelevant with regard to the directedness of the disposition for the *mutual* manifestation of reference or perception, because the directedness is *all* in *each*, even if the other does not exist; it must be if it is (as it is) for the full *mutual* manifestation. The direction, subjective–objective, is from either, and the mutual manifestation is with both.

Details of the nature of the reciprocity of the disposition partners for some mental activities are far from clear because they would largely be internal to the organism and forbiddingly complex. What one does is treat the dispositional state from which one has started as somehow unique in the role of manifestation, yet this cannot be if the manifestation is (as it is) mutual *among* reciprocal partners. A reason for this relative priority, however, is that a particular dispositional state can have a degree of stability that its varying, fluctuating reciprocal partners lack. Less significantly, it might merely be chosen because of the interests of the describer.

Emphasis upon *mental* dispositional states that have a degree of stability bears upon the importance of establishing the temperament, personality, memories, beliefs, desires, motivations, and general states of mind, both cognitive and emotive, that accord a personal stamp to an individual. This does not in the least imply an ontologically second-rate status to the reciprocal disposition partners: the manifestation remains mutual.

Emphasis on the soundness of a bridge having a degree of stability stresses the importance of establishing tendencies for distortion and rupture that put the function of 'crossability' of the bridge on the *bridge*—the *functionality* of the bridge. *How* we view what we take to be most important about this physical object determines *what* is selected as the 'prior' disposition partner and should not imply a hierarchy among reciprocal disposition partners.

What we select as having 'priority' status in the order of being is only ever one among many reciprocal partners, but it provides an opportunity for singling out one disposition in order to apply the important criteria of dispositional *depth* and *breadth* (Chapter 6).

For almost *any* account—Burgeian, Davidsonian, Fodorian, Quinian, Chomskian, Putnamian, perhaps even Stichian, and others equally worthy—it must be admitted that understanding is not *all* 'outside the head' and that the nature, specific and general, of what is *inside* the head is important in explaining how understanding happens for only rather special beings with rather special neural structures. For a particular zapping from what is outside the head to be effective, the special being has to be in special neural states. Even for the most extreme externalist, not *everything* gets zapped, so there must be something significant about *us* that makes us zappable in the very special ways that we are.

Getting clear about the nature of properties and their dispositions can be of help. In particular, we should be able to see how an observer and the observer's immediate environment are *reciprocal* disposition partners for the mutual manifestation of the perception. As in all manifestations, it is the result of the reachings out of (the dispositions for) *each* partner to the other. This is obfuscated by clunky forms of information theory, which suggest that there is simply a vector path of information flowing that travels from the immediate environment of the cabbage patch and ends up in the cortex.

Perceptual activity is the most basic activity in which we engage. Sensory contact with the immediate physical environment is involved even with hearing the sounds and seeing the marks made by utterings of oneself and of others. This perception of utterings is just an ordinary case of perception; it cannot, of course, be used to validate perceptual credentials in general any more than can the perception of group activities involving making sounds, etc., of utterings or other physical signs of agreement. Before that can even begin to be a perception of something comfortingly *confirmatory*, a child must do a lot, mainly by himself, in acquiring the capacities of focusing, scrutinizing, discriminating, and identifying, and for determining object permanence and solidity—all of this by four or five months! This is well before the child can deal with noises of utterings and complex societal affirmations.

My task will be to try to describe the *part* that the observer plays as a reciprocal disposition partner in that mutual manifestation that constitutes perceiving. I shall do this by appealing to oddities in the partial, abstracted nature of *normal* perception, due largely to the contribution of perceivers, who can deal with only a small percentage of their perceiving in any fully aware and vividly focused way. Just as the immediate environment has a life of its own while not playing its part in being observed (by virtue of having unobservable states projected by physics), so observers have lives of their own while not playing their part in observing (by virtue of having internally caused states—dreaming and imaging—impervious to the immediate environment, but enjoyed by the subject and projected by neural-scanning neurology.)

We have complex interrelated structural dispositional neural states for constant and normal comparative, contrastive, projective, and anticipatory reactivities (uses) of such internal signals in dream, imagery, and hallucination. This forms the neural substrate for the inner life, which is the crucial function of mental activity *independent* of stimuli from the immediate physical environment. This is a function suited to creative use of rapid adaptivities. *Qualitative* similarity between internal and external signals encourages such adaptivities (paralleled in the use of reactivities and rapid adaptivities to *novel* external signals from the physical environment). Because of this qualitative similarity between internal and external signals, attention is centered on *qualities* of signals. Fortunately, not all cells are alike, and multitudes of their intrinsic differences are just beginning to be discovered. Pure functionalism and its behaviouristic cousins are left behind because they leave no room for irreducible qualitative differences, even on the assumption that there are no nonphysical *qualia*.

This discussion extends the argument of Chapter 6 against *purely* dispositional properties (having no implications for what is irreducibly qualitative) and against *purely* qualitative properties (having no implications for dispositionalities) and the argument for the Limit View of properties as qualitative–cum–dispositional.

## 11.4 NONMENTAL SYSTEMS

In what follows, attention will again be concentrated on the nonmental, vegetative, autonomic systems to discover what they so abundantly and surprisingly share and what they most importantly lack in comparison with mental systems of an organism. This provides a precision of focus for discussing the question, 'What is unique to a conscious, voluntary system?' Many answers that seem intuitive would unfortunately be applicable to subtle and complex but nonconscious and nonvoluntary vegetative systems.

Before setting off, let me sketch an account of such basic notions as 'system,' 'adaptivity,' 'use,' 'representation,' 'representational use,' and 'content,' showing how they apply, nonmetaphorically, to nonmental, as well as mental, cases. In Chapter 13, I will describe in detail a few of the subtleties of function of the nonmental vegetative, autonomic systems, with an eye toward providing a sharper understanding of what such wonderfully complex and adaptive and projective systems (outstripping most 'intelligent' computers) *lack* that is necessary for a conscious, voluntary system.

I shall use the term 'adaptive' very generally for any functional change of dispositional structure of a system.

(a) Sometimes it is used only for species, but I shall use the term for all levels, including the individual.
(b) Sometimes it is used only for a functional change that is selected, where 'selected' means 'environmentally caused' as opposed, for example, to being caused by a mutation internal to the organism, but I shall use the term more widely.

My use of 'adaptive' will be broad enough to embrace any functional change of structure, short-term or long-term, however caused. Limits upon this usage can be imposed later where it is thought useful for certain desired emphases.

A *system* is an organization of interconnective dispositional states optimally incorporating feedback and feedforward control of output with a degree of stability. This stability, of course, is entirely dependent on a constancy of particular sorts of reciprocal disposition partner. This applies to the most complex as well as the simplest systems. It applies, as well, to 'hard-wired' functional systems. Such systems require the constancy of particular sorts of reciprocal disposition partner for their unchanging continuance and patterned development. When those disposition partners change, then what was hard-wired becomes adaptive in function or extinct, whether in the species or in the individual. Trees will adapt dramatically in terms of 'hard-wired' features such as the number of branches under different altitudes.

The basic ontological model for adaptivities of a system, even of one that is 'hard-wired,' is that a system's dispositional structure with a difference of reciprocal disposition partners (it might just be a small difference that will tip the balance for change) will have a mutual manifestation of the system's acquiring a different dispositional structure. There is no such thing as a perfectly hard-wired system. Instead, it is *entirely* dependent for its apparent stability on an unreliable constancy of its reciprocal disposition partners, its causal environment.

In describing the important autonomic, nonconscious integrative center, the hypothalamus, N. H. Spector refers to:

the *theory of the fluctuating substrate* . . . which states that the internal environment, as well as the external environment, is *never* constant, indeed, that *all living organisms, from birth to death are in a state of non-equilibrium*. This is particularly true of the hypothalamus. (Spector 1979)

At the level of the higher functioning conscious and voluntary systems of the cortex, adaptivities are legion—some good, some bad. It is a place where adaptive responses to dramatically changing reciprocal partners, both internal and external to the organism, are made.

Brain lesions, Alzheimer's, and aphasia are only the most dramatic of adaptivities. If one lives in the real causal world of the myriads of alternating reciprocal disposition partners that are not only possible, but likely, and also uncountably many that are actual, then mental states (beliefs, hopes, desires, fears, hates, loves, etc.) are transient and, more importantly, *not* sharp at the edges. They are not at all like sharp-edged sentences in the head. They *cannot* be sharp at the edges, because they are dispositional states of the cortex that are ready to go, with all kinds of mischief-making alternative reciprocal partners ready to blur, block, obliterate, and alter out of shape those dispositional states—or more significantly, the dispositional states can, without being *altered*, produce with alternative reciprocal partners entirely different and contrary, even opposite, mutual manifestations (Chapter 6 and Morrison and Hof 1992).

From this position among the real causal interstices, the attempt to mathematize mental states via some form of computationalism is comic. Abstract idealizations of what is happening needed for the algorithms and computations are false and ultimately silly as a scientific account of the real capacities of the real systems of a real living brain and active mind with the warps and woofs of the causal network (where *small* differences can yield *big* differences) that cannot be *ceteris paribused* away.

Any activity, linguistic or nonlinguistic, overt or covert, mental or nonmental, that can be thought of as being representational is not simply a free-floating event, but has a neurologically systemic disposition base.

'Who denies this?' is not the question. The question is, 'Is there any theoretical context in which there is failure to make relevant and full use of what is not denied?' and the answer is, 'Yes.' Consider the following quotation:

> So far as anyone has ever proposed, images don't combine to produce logically complex images: What image represents that there are no green triangles, or that if there is someone who loves everyone then everyone is loved by someone? Sentences seem to be the only physically realizable objects that have this expressive potential. (Rey and Loewer 1991: xxi)

Sentence-tokens or thought-tokens themselves, even a lot of them, as we all know, do not have this expressive potential *in* them, as it were, and certainly sentence-types do not either, nor does any specific synaptic firing, whether in a conscious system or a nonconscious system.

## 11.5 FODOR'S CHALLENGE

Jerry Fodor advances two arguments against what he calls 'intentional causation' that need to be answered.

*Technical reason*: If thoughts have their causal roles in virtue of their contents per se, then two thoughts with identical contents ought to be identical in their causal roles. And we know that this is wrong; we know that causal roles *slice things thinner* than contents do. The thought that $\sim\sim P$, for example, has the same content as the thought that $P$ on any notion of content that

I can imagine defending; but the effects of entertaining these thoughts are nevertheless not guaranteed to be the same. Take a mental life in which the thought that $P \& (P \supset Q)$ immediately and spontaneously gives rise to the thought that Q; there is *no* guarantee that the thought that $\sim\sim P \& (P \supset Q)$ immediately and spontaneously gives rise to the thought that Q in that mental life.

*Metaphysical reason*: It looks as though intentional properties essentially involve relations between mental states and *merely possible* contingencies. For example, it's plausible that for a thought to have the content THAT SNOW IS BLACK is for that thought to be related, in a certain way, to the possible (but nonactual) state of affairs in which snow is black; viz., it's for the thought to be true just in case that state of affairs obtains. Correspondingly, what distinguishes the content of the thought that snow is black from the content of the thought that grass is blue is differences among the truth-values that these thoughts have in possible but nonactual worlds.

Now, the following metaphysical principle strikes me as plausible: the causal powers of a thing are not affected by its relations to merely possible entities; only relations to *actual* entities affect causal powers. It is, for example, a determinant of my causal powers that I am standing on the brink of a high cliff. But it is *not* a determinant of my causal powers that I am standing on the brink of a possible-but-nonactual high cliff; I can't throw myself off one of *those*, however hard I try.

Well, if this metaphysical principle is right, and if it's right that intentional properties essentially involve relations to nonactual objects, then it would follow that intentional properties are not per se determinants of causal powers, hence that there are no intentional mechanisms. I admit, however, that that is a fair number of ifs to hang an intuition on. (Fodor 1987: 140–1)

(1) In Fodor's 'Technical reason,' his claim that 'If thoughts have their causal roles in virtue of their contents per se, then two thoughts with identical contents ought to be identical in their causal roles' is confused. Real thoughts of real people are always thoughts-in-the-form-of a particular procedure, notation, idiolect, or language. There is a use of 'thought' that comes to that of 'proposition' that is not in-the-form-of any particular procedure, language, etc. But then thoughts in this sense could have no causal role.

Real thoughts have causal roles—not *just* 'in virtue of the contents per se,' but also in virtue of (at least) the form of procedure, notation, idiolect, or language they take. Someone may be capable of thinking-in-the-form $P \& (P \supset Q)$, but not thinking-in-the-form $\sim\sim P$, or may do so less competently, and obviously the 'causal roles' of each form can differ greatly.

(2) Fodor's 'Metaphysical reason' is equally confused. His argument is that:

the causal powers of a thing are not affected by its relations to merely possible entities; only relations to *actual* entities affect causal powers . . . and if it's right that intentional properties essentially involve relations to nonactual objects, then it would follow that intentional properties are not per se determinants of causal powers, hence that there are no intentional mechanisms. (Fodor 1987: 141)

Is Fodor arguing that a causal power in its relation to its object (manifestation circumstance) is like the cause in its relation to its object (effect) in that the relation cannot be to what is nonexistent?

This seems not to be what he has in mind. In a footnote he grants that 'relations to nonactual entities can perfectly well be *constitutive* of causal powers: the solubility of this salt consists in such facts as that if there *were* water here, the salt would dissolve in it' (1987: 166). What then does Fodor want? His answer is bewildering:

The point in the text, then, is that though relations to nonactual objects can figure in the analysis of a causal power, they can't be among its causal determinants. Nothing—causal powers included—can be an effect of a merely possible cause. (Fodor 1987: 166)

Allowing Fodor his claim that 'intentional properties essentially involve relations between mental states and *merely possible* contingencies,' it is obvious that these 'relations' are not those of the 'merely possible' *causing* the mental state. Why, then, should he demand that the relation between the causal power and its 'merely possible,' nonactual manifestation circumstance be that of the 'merely possible,' nonactual circumstance *causing* the causal power? Surely, that is as foolish as it would be to demand that the relation between a mental state and the 'merely possible' be that of the nonactual causing the mental state.

There is an essential and unnoticed difference between:

(a) all those many marks of intentionality, including, as Fodor admits, directedness to the nonactual found in the causal dispositions or powers (nonmental as well as mental) and through complex systems of such dispositional states manifesting complex forms of use of input (e.g. the autonomic nervous system) and

(b) having *significance* and point *for* an agent of the directedness, etc., of its activity.

We could save the word 'intentionality' for the latter, as I have tended to do, or use it more broadly to include the nonmental cases. It is important that the difference is observed, because the alternative is panpsychism.

Fodor repeatedly puts the intentionality problem in a particular way: 'How can anything manage to be *about* anything; and why is it that only thoughts and symbols succeed?' (1987: xi). Fodor sees clearly enough how odd it is that marks or sounds, even a series of them *or* a neural state or process, should have in themselves 'a propositional object.' Here, Fodor seems to have (b) in mind, the having of significance and point other than (a), but places this in the nature of certain kinds of particulars called 'thoughts' and 'symbols':

It's puzzling how a rock (or the state of having a rock in your intention box) could have a propositional object; but then, it's no less puzzling how a formula (or the state of having a formula in your intention box) could have a propositional object. It is, in fact, approximately equally puzzling how *anything* could have a propositional object, which is to say that it's puzzling how Intentional Realism could be true. (Fodor 1987: 137–8)

Locke's plagiarism of Wittgenstein can be a good corrective to Fodor and reminder to us all.

Universality belongs not to things themselves, which are all of them particular in their existence, even those words and ideas which are general . . . their general nature being nothing but the capacity they are put into by the understanding of signifying many particulars' (Locke 1690: III, iii, 2).

(1) If we extend this to significance in general, including signifying a particular as well as many particulars (as I think Locke went on to do in his discussion of our use of the term 'Aristotle'), then it is a downright mistake to look for significant about-ness in *any* particular object, property, state, or event. This holds even if the particular is a particular so-called mental state. Fodor is looking in the wrong place. We must take the lesson that intentionality and significance reside not in particulars themselves, but in their *uses*. They do not just have an intentionalistic halo. A beginning has been made characterizing the nature of use, and much remains to be done. It is a big job, but this will be a start.

(2) It is no help to look to entities of philosophical manufacture such as *propositions*. It is too obviously *ad hoc* to suppose that these propositions, which are in neither language nor idiom, are particulars

that (*pace* Locke) *essentially* have intentionalistic and semantic properties. As Fodor observes, 'it's not clear what the point would be of an explanation of the intentionality of the attitudes which presupposes objects (propositions) that are intentional intrinsically. Why not just say that the attitudes are?' (1987: 80).

Propositions are supposed to be essentially semantic and *somehow*, by their paralleling, invest some of our activities with contents. Real nonactual worlds (spatially, temporally, and causally disconnected from us) are thought to be of help through their paralleling. The thoughts of God would seem to do what propositions and real nonactual worlds can do and more. If we are going to go medieval, let us go the full route. It should be obvious that all such intellectual parallelism with made-to-order intellectual artifacts make good blackboard exercises and cannot be believed as realistic models for explanation.

(3) The Language of Thought is of no help in the problem of intentionality, as Fodor himself sees very clearly. To give inner states the 'systematic,' structural, and combinatorial complexities of a natural language might be a part of a causal explanation if, in excess of the need for the cause to be adequate for the effect, one felt the need for a further medieval injunction that 'there must be at least as must perfection in the cause as in the effect.' This gives us nothing, however, toward an explanation of the nature of the intentional. We will still need to know *how* those states and happenings that make up the Language of Thought are, themselves, intentional.

(4) Externalism also fails to help in the matter of intentionality. Those who claim that 'meaning ain't in the head' have hardly shown that it is *all* outside the head. To be relevant to the problem of intentionality, externalists must first give an account of what has to be the case *about us* for us to be significantly *got to* by what is 'outside.' After all, what is 'outside' has *many* causal dealings, but its intentionalistic deals are special to things like *us*.

I shall concentrate on our end of the matter, for which we can accept some responsibility. After getting clearer on that, we can better decide how much is left to what is 'outside' other than to provide the obvious—needing objects of reference for our *successful* referring attempts. We should then be better able to consider the Twin Earth range of cases.

Before moving on, let me briefly address the topic of 'rule-following,' a topic often seen as central to intentionality.

## 11.6 RULES AND DISPOSITIONS

In *Wittgenstein on Rules and Private Language*, Saul Kripke discusses an argument against 'meaning realism,' the view that some state of or fact about an agent constitutes the agent's meaning something by a particular utterance (Kripke 1982).[1] Kripke—or Kripke's Wittgenstein—dismisses the possibility that a dispositional account of rule-following could solve the problem. The argument depends on certain common misunderstandings of dispositionality, however. Chief among these is the idea that all there is to an object's possessing a disposition is for the object to answer to a particular conditional.

Consider a simple hand-held battery-powered calculator. The calculator is constructed so as to add numbers in a particular way: in accord with the familiar plus rule. Now, consider a different calculator. This calculator is constructed so as to add numbers in accord with a very different rule: Kripke's *quus* rule. Let us suppose that the plus and quus functions yield exactly the same answers for numbers up to a certain numerical threshold, and diverge thereafter. Thus 7 plus 5 and 7 quus 5, both yield 12. For very large numbers, however, $n_1$ plus $n_2$ and $n_1$ quus $n_2$ yield very different results.

Imagine that both calculators are deployed for several months by scientists recording data on tooth decay, and that both yield answers consistent with both the plus and quus functions. Neither calculator is used to compute values for the kinds of large number that would reveal a plus–quus difference.

In this case, can we sensibly ask whether there is some feature of the calculators in virtue of which it is true that one is operating in accord with the plus rule and the other is acting in accord with the quus rule? As the case has been described, there is every reason to think that the calculators do differ in some determinate way. It is merely an accident that scientists have not used the devices to compute values for numbers that would yield divergent results.

This might be thought to miss the point. The plus–quus difference takes hold when we imagine the two functions diverging at some point so far down the line that no terrestrial creature (or calculator) *could* produce results that would reveal—manifest—the divergence.

---

[1] The sections that follow summarize material addressed in Martin and Heil (1998).

The numbers might be so large that a creature would die, or, in the calculator case, the calculator would disintegrate before the computation could be completed. In such cases, can we say that there is nevertheless a fact of the matter that a given creature or calculator is computing the plus function or the quus function?

I believe there is. Consider a simple calculator designed to sum numbers in a conventional way: in accord with the plus function. Imagine that this calculator is powered by batteries that deteriorate rapidly. In particular, the battery will fail before the calculator could complete the following calculation: $68 + 57 = 125$. It will nevertheless be true that the calculator has the capacity to compute this sum. The envisaged failure stems not from the dispositional makeup of the calculator responsible for the computation, but from the battery, a disposition partner required for a particular kind of *manifestation* of this disposition. You could express this by saying that the calculator has the plus rule, but lacks the wherewithal to manifest the rule fully.

Notice that it would be false to say of the calculator that, were we to enter $68 + 57$, it would display $125$. The conditional is false. But, as we have seen, conditionals provide at best a rough, fallible guide to objects' dispositional makeup. The conditional is false, not because the calculator lacks the appropriate disposition, but because it lacks the battery power required for this disposition to be manifested.

The same point could be extended to ordinary human rule-followers. Agents could differ dispositionally, yet this difference never show up in anything they did, or could do, owing to a lack of appropriate disposition partners for the required manifestations. In that case, there would be a definite fact of the matter as to what rule had been mastered, and this fact would be embodied in the agents' respective dispositional constitutions.

An electric eye is disposed to open a door when a beam of light is interrupted. It is disposed to open the door in response to an infinite number of different kinds of interrupting stimuli, even though, unattended, it would certainly break down after a year or two of continuous use. Agents who have mastered rules with infinite consequences are in the same boat: they have a capacity that, like most capacities, could never be fully manifested.

All of this leaves open an epistemological difficulty. How could we *discover* what rule a given agent is following or whether distinct agents are in fact following the same rule—or, as I have put it, are identically disposed—if, owing to ordinary human frailty, the pertinent differences would be undetectable? There might be no in-principle barrier to determining that agents are differently disposed (something that might be ascertainable by examining their physical makeup), but this need not, by itself, entitle us to say what rule was being followed.

Epistemological fallibility, however, is just one consequence of realism. If there is something about you in virtue of which it is true that you are following a particular rule, then judgements as to which rule you are following are going to be defeasible. In any case, the question is not how might we *tell* what rule a given agent is following, but whether there was some feature of agents that *makes it the case* that they are following particular rules. Despite Kripke's Wittgenstein's scepticism on this score, dispositions make excellent candidates for the bases of rules in intelligent agents.

Let me now try to set all this out schematically.

## 11.7 A DISPOSITION FOR ADDITION

Imagine an agent, $A$, disposed to add in the conventional way: $A$ has a disposition, $P$, in virtue of which it is true that $A$ has mastered the rule for addition.

(1) $A$ is in dispositional state $P$ at $t_1$.

(2) $A$ acquires a capacity, $C$, for forming and grasping groups of very large numbers at $t_2$.

(3) In acquiring this new capacity $C$, we do not need to add disposi-tional state $P$, because $A$ already has it.

(4) $P$ is ready to go for plus-adding for the numbers that $A$ has acquired the capacity $C$ for forming and grasping.

(5) There would be a readiness for plus-adding groups of increasingly large numbers that are formed or grasped by any newly acquired capacities by virtue of $P$ without needing $P$ to be added or altered.

(6) $P$'s infinity is the being-there-ready without the need for addition or alteration of $P$ for *any* such numbers, whether $A$ gains the capacity to form and grasp them or not.

(7) Finitude comes only with the size of numbers $A$ is in fact capable of forming and grasping at any time. That limits the

*manifestations* of plus-adding of P only by limiting its reciprocal disposition partners for the capacities of forming and grasping large numbers.

(8) It does not limit the magnitudes of numbers for which P has its readiness for plus-adding. That dispositional readiness is for *any* magnitude and is, therefore, infinite. There is a parallel infinity of the quark's dispositional readinesses for reciprocal disposition partnerings with an infinite number of combinations of fellow quarks for an infinity of different manifestings.

## 11.8 READINESS FOR ALGORITHMIC COMPUTATION

There are always limitations in the number of a disposition's possible actual manifestations, because any actual manifestations exclude various other, simultaneous, manifestations.

Having disposition D for readiness for algorithmic computation according to rule R that is a rule without limit does not imply the manifestation of D without limit. It does imply that any manifestation failure, whether of omission or commission, is due, not to D, but instead to the lack of one or more needed disposition partners. Degrees of intelligence, speed of computation, memory, and physical capacities might all be necessary but, of course, not sufficient for acting on rule R. D will be a crucial factor for that.

Disposition D, which is a readiness for algorithmic computation according to R, a rule without limit, is distinct from disposition D', which is a readiness for having a knowing grasp of R (and its lack of limit) as the rule one is following. The latter is a cue-manifestation of D.

This projection without limit of the knowing grasp of R is a cue-manifestation of D (of being ready to 'go on' according to R that is a rule without limit). It is the dispositional readiness of D that explains and makes true the cue-manifestation representation of this cue-in grasp of following or being able to follow R rather than some other rule R'.

Projectivity without limit is natural to both mental and nonmental dispositionality as is shown even in a quark for its infinitely many kinds of directive, selective readinesses (although not just indiscriminately *any* kinds) for infinitely many combinations of fellow quarks. The dispositional readinesses could not, of course, all be manifested.

Importantly, what is allowed in a *system*—and a quark is not a system—is that a dispositional capacity or readiness, $D$, can be present even if something else about it is lacking that is needed as a disposition partner, or if there is something else about it that is a prohibitive and blocking partner to the manifestation of $D$.

# 12

# Two Jokes Explained

## 12.1 EXPERIENCES AND THE PRIVATE WORLD PROBLEM

A tendency toward experiential-blindness is occasioned by lapses into forms of verificationism, and by the conviction that it is only by embracing (usually unadmitted) aptness-physicalism, quasi-behaviourism, or anti-foundationalism that we can escape the private world of sense and sensation and enter into the shared, public domain of human interaction and language.

Judy, a behaviourist can be in a particular mental state without engaging in any actual relevant behaviour, so long as a host of counterfactuals or behavioural dispositions, no doubt cerebrally located, take the weight. They would need to take the weight anyway, *even* if there were some actual relevant behaviour, perhaps to countervail it! In the end, dispositional states have *decisive* weight. Judy's actual behaviour is only a defeasible indicator of her state of mind. We can hardly *compare* her behaviour with dispositional facts about her states, which can run counter to what her behaviour suggests.

Judy can hallucinate, too. But if she can hallucinate, she could hallucinate her own behaviour, including her *linguistic* behaviour. She should be able to manage this as well, and just as continuously as, the rest of us. Judy's mental states need not be behaviourally enacted, and when enacted at all, it could be in *hallucinated* behaviour that would be unknown to the agent and misleading to the observer.

If behaviourist Judy tries to make some quasi-necessary quasi-connections between the counterfactual facts or dispositional states and behaviour, then why would such connections not be possible for sensations and behaviour? It is more likely that they are not legitimate in *either* case. It is never just a matter of what inputs one has but of what the processing does with the inputs. The devil lies in the processing.

If you get rid of sensations, there is still a causal intermediary (that can act as a distorting medium full of possible epistemic mischief) between belief and the perceptual object of belief: the *processing* of sensory input. But sensory input is not belief, and processing is not belief.

There is no way belief can be directly 'zapped' by its object. On any model, there must be possibly distortive causal intermediaries between the object-cause and belief-effect, and these intermediaries will be internal to the agent.

The joke is that, sensations or no sensations, the spectre of the 'private world' arises equally—no more and no less—so sensations are not the problem if there is a 'private world problem.'

## 12.2 THE ANALOGICAL WAY OF THINKING ABOUT OTHER MINDS

The role of knowledge of behaviour (or what a sensation is 'apt to cause') and/or physical circumstances (or that by which the sensation is 'apt to be caused') needs better understanding. The rejection of analogical ways of thinking about the experiences of others and the complementary fixation on public, observable, shared behaviour and circumstances leads, when carried to its fair (but never drawn) conclusion, to a second joke.

Suppose that what you know about my behaviour and physical situation is sufficient to make it, beyond any question, reasonable for you to believe that I am having a particular kind of experience. Suppose further that I know the same things about my behaviour and physical situation that you do. Your knowing just those things is enough, is sufficient, for you to come to a reasonable belief that I am having a particular kind of experience. What about me? Is my knowing just those things enough, sufficient for *me* to come to a reasonable belief that I am having a particular kind of experience? If it is good enough for *you*, why is it not good enough for *me*? Am I in an unprivileged position here? Is the sufficiency for reasonable belief a personal variable—good enough for others but not good enough for me? *Why* is it even odd for me if it works out so well for others? The answer cannot be just that I have another or even better way of knowing, because we can have multiple sufficiencies. What I know by touch and by sight gives me double sufficiencies—why not?

The long-derided way of analogy works! Otherwise, why, when someone else is relishing a food we have not tried, is it reasonable for us to try it ourselves? My knowing the same as you does not work the same for me as it does for you, however. If I have another *way* of knowing about my experience, why should I need it when you do not? Why does *your* knowledge of my behaviour and physical circumstances work so well in giving you rational belief about my experience, while *my* knowledge of the same behaviour works so badly and inappropriately for my rational belief about my experience?

The only way out of this ludicrous situation is to embrace the obvious truth that we know about other minds by analogical thinking, reasoning *from our own case*. Of course, analogy from our own case ill fits our own case; what is ludicrous is *explained*.

I know about my own case introspectively and determine what *goes* with the experience I *already* recognize by (if I am not told) discovering what tends to cause it and what behaviour, if any, it tends to cause, and not the *other* way around.

A procedural-analogical way of thinking is part of our finding out just how it feels, smells or tastes to someone else. This is prior to and basic for learning and retaining the public language of perceiving and sensations. (An explanatory model for this was sketched in Chapter 8.)

## 12.3 INTROSPECTIVE ERRORS

If imagery and dreaming are qualitatively similar to perceiving—so that you could mistake the one for the other, as you could not mistake a tulip for a rainbow or a hippopotamus—then *just* as there could be hearing or seeing without hearing or seeing *as* or *that* something 'external,' so could there also be dreaming in various modalities without dreaming *as* or *that* something, and there could even be wakeful imagery that is not imagery *of* or *that* something external. The occurrence of REM in the infant in the womb and the newly born points to extensive multimodal dreaming. This could induce and strengthen various neural connections.

Inhibition of dreaming or imagery in infants (sensory-*like* deprivation) could, no less than sensory-deprivation itself, undermine development. Crick and Micheson (1983) suggest that the function of dreaming is 'de-learning.' This ignores the possible developmental benefits of dreaming, and ignores, as well, the usefulness of novel or even occasionally bizarre dream imagery (or, for that matter, wakeful daydream imagery). Such imagery involves combinations of elements that could facilitate connectivities for neurological readinesses that could prove useful—consciously useful—in unexpected circumstances. To regard the brain as built for tidiness is to sell creativity and adaptivity short. Creative thinkers are well aware that the unconstrained conscious mind can yield unforeseen treasures.

Now consider a case of introspective knowledge of some sensation, $S$. $S$ is the *object* of the belief that $S$ is occurring and $S$'s occurring is the immediate *cause* of the belief that $S$ is occurring. There are no intervening causal links that could be weak. There is nothing else *by* which or *from* which $S$ is known. This is what explains why, against the unlikely challenge '*Why* do you think you are in pain?', the only (polite) response would be the expostulation 'Because I *am*!'

We can grant that the neural–causal situation in the brain in the case of introspection is not quite as tidy as this model (inspired by Locke) would require, but it is at least about the nearest approximation to identity of cause of belief and object of belief that we have. Certainly, the cause–object gap is much narrower than even the most optimal perceptual cases.

This model explains why incorrigibility has been so tempting, but the model in no way implies incorrigibility. To establish incorrigibility, you need an extra premise. That premise is that there could be *no* other cause of the belief *other* than the object of the belief and that premise is *false*. It pays to remember, however, that sensations are complex and can share similarities and differences. Someone might have an expectancy set, $E$, for sensation, $S$, so that with a sensation, $S'$, that is in some respects similar to $S$, the combination of $E$ and $S'$ is enough to cause a belief that $S$.

Emphasis upon the inner life can be used to develop a physicalist, although not 'materialist,' account of conscious qualities.

# 13

# Tactile–Motor–Kinaesthetic Perception

## 13.1 HALLUCINATION, ILLUSION, AND AFTER-IMAGES

Implicitly in P. F. Strawson's *Individuals* (Strawson 1959) and explicitly in G. E. M. Anscombe's *Intention* (Anscombe 1957), and, typically amongst current authors (see, for instance, Heil 1983), there is a denial of the motor and kinaesthetic as genuine modes of perception.

The concept of a mode of perception surely has a place where the concepts of hallucination, illusion, and after-image have a place. Such concepts typically have a place in what can be said about our kinaesthetic and motor perception of our own bodily movement and position.

(1) *Tactile-motor-kinaesthetic hallucination*. A patient could, unknown to himself, have his legs amputated. Sometime after the operation the patient says, 'I'm wiggling my toes.' The patient's intention and his sincerity are evident, but the patient's toes are in another room and he is not wiggling them. The surgeon and nurses will not be persuaded, by the patient's making this claim, to think that he is wiggling his toes. But they *will* be persuaded, by his making this claim, that the local anesthetic must have worn off. The patient will not be persuaded that it does not feel as if his toes were moving. This, to all appearances, is a perfectly clear case of kinaesthetic and motor hallucination.

(2) *Tactile-motor-kinaesthetic illusion*. If your arm is bent in an uncomfortable position, the movement of your finger is felt to be greater than it is. This, to all appearances, is a perfectly clear case of kinaesthetic and motor illusion.

(3) *Tactile-motor-kinaesthetic after-images*. For a while, after getting off a boat, you can continue to feel your body 'roll,' even though it is strapped in a fixed position. This, to all appearances, is a perfectly clear case of a *positive* kinaesthetic and motor after-image.

If you have been spun around in one direction for some time and with some speed, and if the motion is stopped suddenly, you will feel your body spinning in the opposite direction, even though it is strapped in a fixed position. This, to all appearances, is a perfectly clear case of a *negative* kinaesthetic and motor after-image.

## 13.2 TACTILE-MOTOR-KINAESTHETIC PERCEIVING

If, as a result of accident or disease, a patient's brain does not receive nervous impulses from the muscles, joints, and tendons, the patient will lack kinaesthetic and motor experiences. In cases of this sort, if a doctor moves the patient's legs in such a way that the patient's other senses do not aid him, the patient will not know that his legs are moving. He and the doctor understand well enough that this new and unfortunate limitation on the range of his experience now gives him no way of knowing that his legs are moving. If he felt nothing and was nevertheless able to say that his legs were moving, if he suffered no impairment in what he could say and predict about his bodily movements, he would be dumfounded by this capacity 'just to know.' Putting it mildly, it would be a capacity unfamiliar to him and to us. If Strawson, Anscombe, Heil, and others were right, it *shouldn't* be.

Anscombe contends that an agent's kinaesthetic experiences are not used by the agent as a *datum* in judging the agent's bodily movements and position. Perhaps so. But we do not use our visual experience as a *datum* in judging what is before our eyes *either*. The *parallel* between kinaesthetic experience in perception and that of touch and sight still remains. (See Martin 1971 for a more detailed defense of the perceptual status of the kinaesthetic.)

Vision might or might not endow us with a capacity for more information (however that could be measured) than our tactile, motor, kinaesthetic senses as has commonly been thought, but it should be clear that vision is not as basic. Complex organisms, even human beings, can be blind, yet perfectly capable of making complex assessments of their environments. It is not at all clear that a creature could manage with sight but without tactile-motor-kinaesthetic perception.

Consider a famous experiment noted in every textbook on the psychology of perception. Infants are encouraged by their mothers to cross a solid but transparent glass surface through which the infants can see a drop of some distance to the floor below (Gibson and Walk 1960). The surface *feels* solid, but *looks* unsolid. Sometimes, though rarely (and to the probable annoyance of the experimenter), an infant crawls protestingly the whole way to its mother. Sometimes—more rarely—it will not crawl upon the glass at all. Most of the time, infants go part of the way and no further. The unthinking interpretation of psychologists and philosophers has been that the experiment demonstrates the dominance of the visual over other senses. The experiment establishes *no* such thing.

Suppose an infant were presented with a visually 'solid' holograph of a surface—but the tactile-motor-kinaesthetic sensory input were of lack of solidity, of falling. *Which* do you think would be dominant and *overwhelmingly* so?

It is through use of the tactile-motor-kinaesthetic sensory input and imagery that we learn the boundaries of self and not-self, and the geography of our own bodies and the three-dimensionality of things and of spaces between them.

## 13.3 FEELING AND FEELING BACK

Something, commonly unnoticed but of the greatest importance, that I have called the 'Feeling Once, Feeling Twice Phenomenon' is manifested when you place your hands on a surface and what you *feel* with your hands does not feel *back*; then, as you move your hands to come into contact with one another, *what* you feel does (even quite sensuously so) feel *back*. What feels back, and what is felt as continuous (for instance, ends of the hair) with that, forms the geography of your body and its limits against what is not your body, namely, what does *not* feel back.

Holding a solid object at either end in each of your hands and pulling and pushing against the object's resistance gives you the kinaesthetic 'feel' of the solidity of things. This is a clear and vivid case of projection from what is felt in each hand to what exists *between* them (see Locke 1690: II, iv).

As has been noticed often enough, we do not directly sense by vision the entire three-dimensional bounds, front–back–bottom–top, of anything. It is *easy* to sense directly by tactile-motor kinaesthetic means the entire three-dimensional bounds of something as you enclose, feelingly, the whole of something within your fist.

Space, in its emptiness between objects, is evident in your feeling *nothing* between felt things.

There is nothing like the weight of a heavy object crushing you down to the ground to give you a sense of the casual operativeness of things. *So* different from Hume's sight of billiard balls coming in contact, then moving away from one another—*just* one thing after another!

The image of the Mirror of Nature is just pointless concerning the tactile-motor-kinaesthetic senses. Modelling seems nearer the mark than mirroring.

An infant in the womb has a world to explore of tongue and thumb in and out of mouth, of feeling what feels back, and then, against the womb, what does not feel back.

I was amused when a cognitive psychologist spoke of research on newborn infants' reactiveness to voices as evidencing an innate propensity for verbalization. When I suggested that infants' reactions might have been conditioned by what was very familiar, the indignant response was, 'I *said* the infants were newborn.' I replied by noting recent technology allowing us to observe perceptual activity of the infant in the womb. The discussion ended.

# 14

# Verbal Imagery

## 14.1 KINDS OF IMAGERY

In this chapter I want to explore various innovative uses of sequential verbal and nonverbal imagery. For this use to have its measure of aboutness and full point and to take a 'propositional object,' it needs to be a manifestation from a holistic disposition base array. Previous chapters should be seen as attempts to clarify that theoretical framework.

The disjunction, 'pictorial or descriptive,' is awkward and misleading when applied to imagery, even if there is something right behind or underneath it. As Shepard, Kosslyn and others, including Locke and Hume, have often pointed out, imagery is not like what it is *of*, but it is instead like a *perceiving* of what it is of. 'Pictorial,' therefore, never fitted visual or auditory imagery and was ludicrous as a model for the classification of tactile, kinaesthetic, olfactory, or gustatory imagery.

Both 'pictorial' and 'descriptive' are misleading when applied to verbal imagery. The imagery in verbal imaging is like a perceiving of an utterance-tokening, either by oneself or someone else, and is given a meaningful use, usually derived from the uses of such types of utterance-tokening in a shared, public language.

Wittgenstein regards imagery with suspicion:

When we form an image of something we are not observing. The coming and going of the pictures is not something that happens to us. We are not surprised by these pictures, saying, 'Look!' (Wittgenstein 1967: §632)

But the 'coming and going' of images *is* 'something that happens' to *me*. I *am* sometimes surprised, even consternated, at the sudden appearance of a visual image, or an auditory image, and I am *always* surprised by certain features of the image—for instance, how much of the visual grid it occupies and its location within that grid. Most common kinds of imagery are under negative and positive feedback control. In that way, imagery is put to use by the imager.

As an alternative to the forced choice between pictorial and descriptive, we might try another account of verbal imagery.

(a) The imagery-tokening is in some sensory modality or a mixture of modalities and is a faint likeness to a *perceiving* (in the same modality or modality-mixture) of an utterance in speech, sign language, semaphoring with flags, or writing or reading, by sight or touch in Braille, by yourself or on the part of someone else.

(b) This covert imagery-tokening has the same declarative, descriptive uses your own overt speaking or signing, etc., would have had. Or, if the imagery-tokening is of someone else's uttering, then it has the same declarative, descriptive *interpretation* uses you would assign to the overt speaking, signing, or inscriptions by *another*.

Pure, imageless thought undoubtedly exists. Obvious cases are your sleeping on a problem without dreaming about it, then waking with the solution, or your pausing to collect your thoughts in a discussion and having your mind go blank just before you spontaneously give voice to an argument that had never occurred to you before. Imageless thought might be described as a *silent psychic hum*. A constantly occurring case, such as the higher processing going on behind any overt or covert vocalization and imaging, is a not-so-obvious instance of pure, imageless thought, and who could deny its existence?

Pure, imageless thinking, however, is boring and only indirectly retrievable; it is evidently not under voluntary feedback control as is the more sensuous, if impure, activity of going over something in your head.

Verbal imagery seems not to consist in an exclusively internal (that is, central) or external (that is, peripheral) signal. Pharyngeal, tongue, and lip muscles, as well as digital muscles for deaf users of sign language, show electrical activity above rest state with in-the-head verbal use. This is not just perception-like, but perception itself, largely unnoted, like peripheral vision. You can call attention to it yourself by trying to say 'Hermione' to yourself in your head without any sensation in the throat with the 'Her' and without any sensation toward the lips with the 'mi,' etc. These are feelings (percepts) that are, even when magnified in full vocalization, used largely without notice. Of course, an anaesthetized *lack* of feeling in the pharynx and tongue would be noticed, probably with alarm. It helps to think of the difference between not feeling the pressure of the seat of a chair and having *no* feeling of the pressure of the seat.

When the good and patient D. B., who was the subject of the classic study of 'blindsight' by Lawrence Weiskrantz, tried to describe how it was for him, he said, 'It is like when you close your eyes in a darkened room and then put your hands in front of your eyes' (Weiskrantz 1986). It is not for naught that our eyelids are translucent, enabling us to see light and alterations of light (serving us to detect or 'blind-guess' something lurking in the entrance to the cave) without awareness of, and even with denial of, seeing anything whatsoever.

Marcus Raichle observes that:

one caveat . . . should be mentioned about studies purporting to examine purely mental operations. It has been demonstrated . . . that internal language tasks induce pharyngeal muscle electrical activity (i.e., subvocalization) in hearing subjects, whereas similar tasks in the deaf induce digital muscle electrical activity. Similarly, visual imagination of objects is associated with eye movements. Thus to imagine walking down a street and looking at objects . . . involves motor planning and even motor execution in the form of eye movements and changes in somatic muscle tensions. Comparably, counting internally (i.e., mental arithmetic) involves subvocalization and thus motor planning and execution. Future studies designed to extend the observations of Roland and Friberg (1985: 220) must take into account these subtle but important considerations. (Raichle 1987: 666)

## 14.2 THE PHYSIOLOGY OF IMAGERY

Having done my inadequate best, with some tutelage, in considering recent relevant work, I have found no conclusive answers to the question, crudely phrased, 'Concerning verbal imagery (in normal-hearing people), to what degree are the signals internal or external or to what degree and mixture are they efferent or afferent?' It might help to introduce a classification of central neural effects brought about by a signal:

(1) *Magnification.* 'The monosynaptic recurrent excitation of secondary neurons . . . would provide a positive feedback that could strengthen the input signal' (Nicoll 1971).

(2) *Enhancement.* Properties of the signal are enhanced in such a way that they become discriminable within a single modality and their capacity to activate memory is amplified. Enhancement, however, remains within the modality of the signal:

Sensitivity in olfaction is enhanced by experience under reinforcement and is disenhanced without it. Most of us have a limited repertoire of about 16 odorants under absolute discrimination, but the number can be increased without limit by sustained practice (Cain and Engen, 1977). We can recognize some odors that were once important to us at intervals over many years in a flash flood of vivid associative memories that impel us to action. These are basic properties that olfaction shares with all other senses, far transcending in importance the decomposition of stimuli into lines, planes, and spectral peaks. (Freeman 1988)

(3) *Enrichment.* The signal triggers associated internal and cross-modal signals. This is a common kind of cross-modality reverberation. In certain rare clinical cases, it results in synesthesia (cf., Cytowic 1988).

The saying or sounding of something in your head is not simply a feeling of minuscule pharyngeal, tongue, mouth, and jaw movement. There occurs, as well, magnification, enhancement, and, more importantly, cross-modality auditory enrichment. Going over something in your head does not come to you as a making of, or a perceiving of a making of, these extraordinarily minute muscular movements that modern technology has allowed us to discover we make.

Exactly how best to represent verbal imagery *as* a case of perception or, perhaps, *not* as a case of perception is of interest for an examination of the nature of perception. It is evident that some of the signals (those involved in familiar goings-over-something-in-the-head) are *external*, that is, they are caused by muscular activity activating sensory receptors of the throat and mouth and are not *caused* only within the brain itself. It also seems evident that there is a great deal of *internally* caused magnification, enhancement, and enrichment of whatever signals are evoked by muscular proprioceptors. Except in cases of deafness, enrichment will be auditory and internally caused.

Muscular movement and electrical activity in proprioreceptors in the mouth and throat and their apparent informational input to higher functional systems are only a part, although they could be a necessary triggering part, of the full richness of the signals needed for feedback control involved in verbal tasks done for yourself in your head in, for instance, thinking through a problem. As such, the signals that will be providing feedback for in-the-head verbalizations will be a mix of the external and the internal, involving motor-kinaesthetic, tactile, and auditory modalities. Typically, as you can *hear*, you can also *sound* in the head more than you could mimic. The range of our imagery accords with how we *perceive*, not (*pace* Ryle) what we can mimic. It is easy to sound a voice too high, a group of voices, an orchestra, a birdcall, or an explosion in your head that you could not begin to voice aloud.

Musical imagery, as well as verbal imagery, is perhaps accompanied by proprioceptive, pharyngeal, etc., muscular activity, although musical *soundings* in the head are not at all as *of* those movements. Musical imagery is of *sounding*, and often not just of your own voice or any voice at all, but of one or more musical instrument, perhaps a full orchestra.

Glenn Gould is reported to have spent hours outdoors rehearsing without any piano and without observable movements of his fingers, hands, and arms, making innovative use of sequential imagery of the motor-kinaesthetic feel of his fingers, arms, and shoulders, plus enrichment of the *tactile* feel of the tips of his fingers on the keys of his own beloved Steinway *and* auditory enrichment—all of this in his head—for the inventing of *new* fingering techniques for some composition. There is not much hope of giving an account of this in terms of 'tacit knowledge.'

You can have static, nonsequential imagery, voluntary or involuntary, as when you see a face or hear or sound a name or word. (The latter is the most usual case in imagery experiments apart from the case of visual rotation.) You can also have running, sequential involuntary and often recurrent imagery such as a tune in your head, or seeing someone falling just beyond your reach. You can, as well, have different forms of recall imagery, either involuntary, such as 'flashbacks,' or voluntary, as you might have in sounding a whole tune or poem in full imagistic recall or, more interestingly, in *partial* imagistic recall in which the sounding in your head of two notes by a violin serve without the need of a full replay.

## 14.3 PARTIAL VERBAL IMAGERY

Let us look more closely at the inventive use of sequential verbal imagery as opposed to involuntary running-through-the-head or static imagery. There can be *full* sequential imagery of sounding-saying in complete sentences, making a fully completed thought-task intended to be repeated aloud or in writing for communication or *not to be repeated at all*. My interest, however, is in a still more common and central case: the *partial* use of (usually, but not always, sequential) 'shorthand' imagery of sound-saying involving ungrammatical, idiosyncratic, idiolectic, syntax-fractured sentences or sentence fragments, clauses, or even syllables that are *used* as the expression of a complete thought or argument that would take an hour in speech or a chapter in writing for full public enactment.

Abbreviations, shattered syntax, and idiosyncrasy of content for terms that do not carry that content, or perhaps *any* content in ordinary public use, have degrees of extremity according to the membership of the group. In a particular 'in' group, someone might expostulate 'Yeah, yeah' or even 'Fido-Fido!' and it would speak volumes to the initiated. Similarly, with close acquaintances, linguistic aberrations at odds with official uses of public language are common. If you were to read or overhear what I put in a diary or say aloud to myself, you would not necessarily understand me. What I sound in my head, in the theatre of my own mind, is my most frequent linguistic activity, and it is the extreme of fragmentary, shredded syntax, in a private, not-meant-for-communication idiolect. Add it all up, and such aberrant uses of language are common indeed. The need to treat these use episodes as manifestations *from* a rich disposition-base array is obvious.

Some philosophers will want to insist here that no matter how common such aberrances are, they still derive from a shared, public language with syntax in good order. I shall grant as much, but *solely* for the sake of the arguments at hand, acknowledging just the verbal point that aberrances need something from which to be aberrant, leaving aside the resolution of private language issues.

## 14.4 CUE MANIFESTATIONS

Idiosyncratic imagery and imagery use could be considered a personal idiolect. Here, a distinction must be drawn between *cue-manifestations* and *typifying-manifestations* of particular dispositional states.

The distinction can be made clear by first considering its application to mainly nonpsychological dispositional states. We sometimes wake in the morning with a particular sensation that *cues* us regarding the dispositional state of lameness-but-will-work-itself-out-during-the-day.

That is a cue-manifestation of the lameness dispositional state. It is, of course, fallible. It is obviously not a typifying-manifestation of lameness, as an awkward gait due to a muscular spasm would be. Athletes can be cued by particular *sensations* of 'body tone' as to whether they have full mastery of a complex set of capacities to perform. Such cue-manifestations are a gift of nature, and we vary in the sensitivity of our responses to them, sometimes to our peril.

Cue-manifestations are invaluable in the domain of the psychological. Here, too, they are fallible. These sometimes fleeting feelings of sureness or qualms concerning some unperformed (on the occasion) cognitive capacity are what James and Wittgenstein, too verbalistically, thought of as the 'Got it!', or 'I can go on' phenomenon, or its negation. These are fallible cue-manifestations *of* and *to* the infinite riches of our cognitive and linguistic dispositional states. They differ importantly from typifying-manifestations of such states. They allow us some signs for what we *can* and *cannot* get away with in our own fragmentary, shorthand, idiosyncratic, verbal and nonverbal, private, in-the-head uses of imagery. They can also serve us as signs of our understanding or failing to understand the verbal *and* nonverbal activities of others. They serve for much else, including the *reinforcement* of those states of which they are the cue-manifestations. They are not flotsam.

A. R. Luria held that a child's covert speech comes considerably later than does overt speech in language learning (Luria 1961). If the auditory is crucial (as I have been insisting it is) for the character of verbal imagery and, therefore, the nature of the feedback to the throat musculature, Luria's order of first language learning should be reversed. (Unfortunately, Luria *defined* inner speech as covert rehearsal for overt performance. We can just bypass this and point out that most verbal imagery is not inner speech in *this* sense.)

Children *hear* speech long before they speak, and we know children *understand* some speech before they can execute it themselves. Are we prepared to deny children a capacity to *dream*? Then why might they not dream the *hearing* of speech then awake with *sounding* imagery of speech they cannot mimic? Such covert sounding in the head could be of use in the development and activation of minute pharyngeal, tongue, jaw, and mouth movements. It should be remembered that there is some help in the development of mimicry from having *seen* the mouthing of the words as well as having heard them, and of course a developing child tries out a great many nonverbal vocalizations relevant to more general motor-muscular development in mouth and throat.

Imaging and dreaming, like perceiving, can be 'nonpropositional.' This might, without gestures to the innate, help account for the fact that, in so many cases, overt speech can lag behind obvious language-understanding, and account for why speech comes so suddenly when it comes.

## 14.5 IMAGERY OR TACIT KNOWLEDGE?

The importance of treating inventive dreaming or inventive verbal or musical imagery as central cases of the *imagistic* is twofold. First, such forms of imagery cannot possibly be accounted for in terms of 'tacit knowledge.' Second, this promises to free us for more productive study of the more basic nonverbal and nonmusical forms of imagery *uses*.

We do not have to run in the ruts of the dreary—and unimaginative!—analogue-versus-tacit-knowledge debate by limiting ourselves to unfortunate cases in which there is interference between imagery and perception in the same modality. In such cases, we should *expect* imagery to be impoverished or altogether absent. It is *not* a good idea to engage in a task of auditory imagery, such as bringing back the quality of timbre, etc., of someone else's voice, while the radio is blaring at peak volume. Imagine an auditory counterpart of a mental rotation task in which you attempt to sound in your head a familiar violin passage done backward in order to hear how it *would* sound or how it might work in the composition so played. Now, imagine trying to do this while actually hearing the passage being played (forward) in a recording by Heifetz! It would be natural to ask for the recording to be turned off to do the image rotation more easily. In the same way, the rotation of a visual image *ought not* to be the most natural and easy case of task use of visual imagery, or even of visual imagery rotation, while actually having the *interference* of a full visual field that includes the object you are supposed to be rotating imagistically. Perhaps you should close your eyes. Roland and Friberg's (1985) discussion of route-finding imagery is much less unnatural.

Whether cases of visual rotation are purely visual is another matter. Visual rotation almost certainly includes motor-kinaesthetic perception of eye movements, probably also head, hand, arm, neck, and shoulder movements, with the cross-modal chorus evidently providing the whole *feel* of the rotation. All of this is omitted from visual rotation studies and commentaries.

At the prelinguistic and language-impoverished stages of the race, it is important to implant, enrich, reinforce, and develop cognitive abilities by means of nonrandom perceptual and physically interactive procedures for all kinds of methods of reading nature and countless methods for the knowing manipulation of things and other people.

Although largely immobile, an infant can exercise a selective and partial way of considering things and situations *qua* some movement, color, shape, or distance relation rather than considering (perhaps before it is able to consider) these things as enduring objects or objects in relation to one another. This could be done and reinforced in dreaming and in imaging. Gradually, with increased mobility in its hands and other bodily parts, a child acquires a capacity for procedural exploration of the 'insides' and the 'behinds' of things, thereby coming to treat objects as observation-independent constituents of the world.

## 14.6 NONVERBAL IMAGERY

Let us have another quick look at the claim that only words combining into sentences have the 'expressive potential' or 'logical complexity' required for negative or general thought. An infant can make it clear through movement, gesture, and expressed feeling that the infant wants it *all* and not just *some*, that it wants *more* or *no more*, or that there is *none* left. A child can divide things into *equal* parts before the child has the words. At the other end of the spectrum, proficient language speakers can fail to manage 'If someone loves everyone, then everyone is loved by someone.' The same holds for negation. A fluent speaker can fail to appreciate the full at-no-time-at-no-place absolute generality of 'There are no green triangles.'

Not only can there be, there *are*, nonverbal negation movements. Think of a dismissive shake of the head, which treats what is present negationally, that is, as *not* being *something else*. Perhaps the only interest that the individual takes in what is present at that moment is its not being something else. (See Chapter 8 for more on the extent and richness of nonverbal procedural activity parallels to linguistic activity.)

Nonverbal procedural activities with associated movements, feelings, and their imagistic counterparts do not, of course, carry content in themselves, but neither does a sequence of vocalizations or inscriptions.

For verbal or nonverbal activity to have content, what is done has to come *from* a holistic network of dispositional states or readiness potentials that place those doings with an infinite number of alternative doings within limits of which such a network makes the individual capable.

This can result in a rich and deep holistic disposition-base-array of readiness potentials for the rule-governed shorthand uses of fragmentary, fleeting, idiosyncratic images having the representational force derived from and, in turn, enriching and reinforcing, these potentials for complex interrelated perceptual procedural activities of selective attention and innumerable procedural interactions with the agent's physical and social environment.

Prelinguistic individuals experience rich perceptual and physically interactive lives of meaningful doings. A young child, for instance, might not merely *do* these things, but *dream* or *imagine* doing them as well. A prelinguistic child or a prelinguistic humanoid could, on waking from dreams of its many activities, continue from the dream to *innovative* uses of imagery. (This is not to deny even more common, perhaps constant, uses of imagery.)

For the prelinguistic stage of the race and the individual, this would be nature's provision (*contra* Chomsky) for stimuli independent of the immediate physical environment. This kind of creative use of imagery as a procedure *from* a dream, which might also have been creative, is just what countless of the most inventive artists, composers, poets, mathematicians, and scientists attest to doing themselves. Such internal, central activities are an understudied and undervalued source and training ground for early *and* lifelong cognitive development and reinforcement.

Much goes on with various forms of processing in a system that is caused *within* the main control or processing centre of that system. This is so whether the processing takes place in the higher functioning of the cortex or in the vegetative, decorticalized functioning of the brain stem.

Despite that, there seems to be a real question of the greatest importance left unasked. Consider a particular class of centrally caused signals that are similar to specific kinds of signal (also *within* the central control or processing centre of the given system) that are typical of those normally generated by specific forms of peripheral activation. If the system is a sensory system, such centrally caused signals would form the class of dreams, imagery, and hallucination.

Consider next the fully functional thermoregulatory system of a fully comatose individual. Undoubtedly, the lower brain stem could be *artificially* stimulated directly to bring about specific kinds of signal similar to those that are typical of signals within the brain stem that are *normally* generated by specific forms of peripheral activation. This would be a vegetative parallel to the hallucinogenic.

My question is, 'Is any vegetative, nonsensory functioning system naturally, and without artificial direct stimulation, capable of such centrally caused hallucinogenic signals, or is this ability *only* found in a sensory functioning system?'

If the latter is the case, Mother Nature must be serious in making only the conscious systems capable of the origination of such centrally caused signals. Mother Nature is not a behaviourist, and she is certainly not an 'externalist.' Among centrally caused signals, imagery is meant to be *used* rather than noticed, and that might be a cause for its neglect.

# 15

# The Mind in Nature: A New View of the Mind

## 15.1 FROM NONMENTAL TO MENTAL

Mental phenomena have long seemed mysterious to philosophers. Jerry Fodor asks, 'How can anything manage to be about anything; and why is it that only thoughts and symbols succeed?' Fodor is not the first to find the intentionality or 'about-ness' of things like beliefs and desires extraordinary. We think of the world as being populated by all sorts of things—trees, chairs, quarks, volcanoes—that simply *are*. Most things, that is, seem to exist 'dumbly.' If someone were to suggest that this chair is about that plant, we would think we had misheard, or that the speaker was new to English, or perhaps that the speaker was not well in the head.

Things are not about each other, they just are, and yet mental things seem different. We can have beliefs that are *about* caterpillars or hydrogen atoms; we can have desires that are *for* steaks or freedom; we can have hopes that are for peace or a royal flush. How is it that mental things get outside themselves?

This volume amounts to an attempt to show that the 'mystery' of mental directedness is largely a consequence of bad metaphysics. The central purpose of this book is, in a way, twofold: first, to develop a wholly general ontological model of reality; second, to return to the 'problem' of the mental with a correct ontological foundation.

A number of traditional 'marks of intentionality,' including forms of *directedness*, have turned out to be intrinsic to causal dispositions as dispositions *to* or *for*. These are found throughout all of nature. Less obviously, *use* is intrinsic to systems of dispositional states capable of complex, directed, combinatorial, regulative, distal adjustments and control as well as negative and positive feedback. Such systems are to be found in nonpsychological, nonmental settings (e.g. the autonomic nervous system) and even in inorganic nature.

The way to break the intentionality logjam is straightforward. The directedness of dispositions and use can be found in systems of dispositions that are not essentially psychological. This means that we can appeal to directedness and use in giving an account of *mental* directedness and agent use without fear of circularity.[1]

A realist account of dispositions and manifestations as well as causal operativeness is needed, as is an account of the nature of use. The resulting picture is tripartite. It is, as well, gradualist. We want a model for the notion of use that can take us from semantic ooze to semantic light, and that does so in a way that makes these distinctions only a matter of *degree*.

We can begin by noting that use is best understood as incorporating three components:

(1) the nature of the *instrument* or agent/mechanism of use;
(2) the nature of the *mode of operation* of use;
(3) the nature of the *material* of use.

The first of these, the *instrument* or *mechanism* of use, can be made salient by reflecting on the way the composition and structure of an acid pistol might have to differ from the composition and structure of a water pistol. The cardiovascular system, with its complex regulative activity, should not have the composition and structure of a volume of hot air. Years ago, J. J. C. Smart (and more recently David Lewis) countenanced the possibility that something capable of complex cognitive performances *might* have to have something like the composition and structure of the human brain. The nature of the instrument or agent-mechanism of use should *not* be confused with the third part of the tripartite notion of use, namely, the nature of the *material* of use.

The second aspect of use, *mode of operation*, ought by now to be familiar.

The third, *material* of use, has remained largely unnoticed but is of great significance. The difference in material of use is an important element of the difference between the nature of use of a water pistol and an acid pistol.

---

[1] Such a basic notion should not be left to 'action theorists,' who typically neglect to discuss 83 per cent of all agent activity, namely, *mental*, in-the-head activity.

A better example might be a machine that manipulates material injected into it at one end, in the process heating the material to a certain temperature, then ejecting it at the other end. The device might be used for baking bread, making ceramics, or producing a fireworks display, according to differences in the nature, *not* of the *instrument* of use, or of the mode of *operation* of use, but of the *material* (or input) that is used. Another example might be a nonpsychological structure in which use is exemplified through the autonomic nervous system and its complex control and regulation of what occurs in the thermoregulatory, respiratory, and gastrointestinal systems.

If Locke and Wittgenstein are correct in thinking that particular entities or states ('whether word *or* idea,' as Locke puts it) do not *in themselves* have generality or significance, but 'only by use are made so,' we should look for something fit to *use*. Belief and desire states do not, as particular kinds of state, come equipped with intentionalistic halos. On the contrary, beliefs and desires are *not* well-suited for use, whereas sensory input and imagery is apt material, not for direct knowledge and inference, as empiricists wrongly thought, but instead for direct, noninferential externalizing and projective *use*.

Belief, desire, and other such mental states are best understood as dispositional state arrays whose nature is to be explained in terms of what such arrays are dispositions *for*, namely, those typifyingly appropriate *manifestations* that are the various modes of *use* of various forms of sensory input and sensory feedback and imagery. To make us knowing, Mother Nature must first make us sensate. Behaviour itself needs to be under sensory feedback control in order for us to know what we are doing. The kinaesthetic is a neglected sensory modality (Chapter 13).

We can find nonpsychological parallels to the 'opacity' that is thought to be distinctive of psychological states. The expression 'Cicero' designates the same individual as the expression 'Tully.' It does not follow from

(a)  Tom believes Cicero denounced Catiline,

that

(b)  Tom believes Tully denounced Catiline.

Now suppose the expression 'the only pink object at $L$' designates the same object as the expression 'the only object of mass $F$ at $L$,' it does *not* follow from

(a') acid *A* was able (was in a dispositional state) to turn litmus paper
   *P* into the only pink object at location *L*,

that

(b') acid *A* was able (was in a dispositional state) to turn litmus paper
   *P* into the only object of mass *M* at location *L*.

Nor is this all. We can identify nonpsychological parallels to negation
and assertion. In the realm of the nonmental, there are both negative
and positive types of feedback. These are corrective and reinforcing
uses of inputs and outputs. As I shall argue presently, what turns
use into *mental* agency is the input's being sensate. Its cognitive
*point* (if any) is located in interrelations of clouds ('systems') upon
clouds (other 'systems') of dispositional states *through* their typifying
*manifestations* in various modes of use of various kinds of (sensate)
input-sensory experience and forms of imagery. Our beliefs, thoughts,
hopes, and fears are found in deep and intermingling dispositional
states, and our takings-to-be, thinkings, wonderings, hopings, and
fearings are manifestations *based* in those dispositional states. These
manifestations take the form of varied uses of varied forms of sensory
and imagistic input.

   In addition to the directive, projective, discriminatory readinesses
of nonpsychological dispositional states of nonmental entities, such
entities can make *use* (nonmetaphorically) of input owing to the *systems*
of dispositional states constituting them. Systems of dispositional states
can provide nonmental entities with a capacity for complex, directed,
innovative and distal combinatorial negative and positive feedback
control and adjustments—in other words, *use*.

   At the (still nonmental) level of the autonomic nervous system *cum*
digestive system or cardiovascular system, there is evident directedness
and readiness and evident regulative control—or use—even in a
comatose individual.

   Imagine an organism endowed with a complex system of dispositional states that (1) are interrelated in such a way that these
interrelationships have biogenetic explanations concerning their evolution through their complex environmental sensitivities, and (2) have
positive and negative feedback and feedforward regulative control of
the movements of a complex set of (bodily) parts of the organism such
that *that* control of movement of (bodily) parts is regulative, functional
innovatively and distally adjustive, complex, and combinatorial. This

would undeniably count as use. The system is capable of the development of new movement sequences and even new movement types as *manifestations* of these developing dispositional states in their reactions to one another and, of course, to physical stimuli external to the system.

The autonomic nervous system is one such system. The autonomic nervous system comprises a multifaceted collection of dispositional states that (1) are interrelated in complex and systemic ways, etc., and (2) have positive and negative feedback regulative control of an array of alternative movement patterns of the many parts of the body involved in the cardiovascular and gastrointestinal systems. That movement of mostly internal bodily parts is regulative, adjustive *use*. Such a system can operate perfectly in a comatose individual. In any case, it is *clearly* not a mind, and so it is, I believe, a counterexample to current evolutionary-ecological accounts of the mind. A nonpsychological entity can be directive to and have *readiness* for things, and also *use* things in astonishingly complex and inventive ways, and yet not be psychological or mental.

## 15.2 DISPOSITIONS AND DISPOSITIONALITY

Partly as a result of my earliest reading of Locke, I reinvented the causal theory of perception (and *reference* in perception) wheel (Martin 1959: 108–9), the causal theory of remembering (and *reference* in remembering) wheel (Martin and Deutscher 1966), the causal theory of linguistic reference wheel, and that wheel of all wheels, the causal theory of natural kinds wheel. It then felt very daring to think that causal dispositions were essential and central in the characterization of almost every ontologically substantive concept.

It should be obvious to any decent ontological conscience that *if* dispositions have, as so many now grant, a central and essential role in the nature of ontologically substantive things, then dispositionality *itself* must be ontologically substantive. The only question left is what *kind* of realist account of dispositions is best. This can affect our account of those things that causal dispositions are supposed to explain in basic ways.

Most accounts of dispositionality have been either ludicrous anthropomorphisms, such as Ryle's or Hume's; mere ontic spatiotemporal geography, such as Quine's and, in the end, Mackie's; or logically pre-established harmonic parallelisms between entities that have nothing whatsoever to do with one another, not even sharing any real spatiotemporal relations, such as Lewis's. The latter account fails, as did its medieval predecessors, to provide any real model for explanation specific to the *location* of the things themselves that are to be explained.

Instead of thinking of causality in terms of the crudities of necessary and sufficient conditions or convoluted combinations of these, *à la* Mackie, or in terms of *the* cause, it is better to treat causality like the weather. Like the weather, causal dispositionality and operativeness is everywhere, even on Venus, but it is our decision how to divide it into spatiotemporal locale. That does not make either causal operativeness or the weather mind-dependent or anything else that would unnerve a good metaphysical realist by compromising objectivity. Causal operativeness in the world (wherever and whenever) and causal *explanation* remain as distinct as weather in the world (wherever and whenever) and weather explanation, *pace* Hilary Putnam.

As for counterfactuals, we do not need parallelisms with similar alternative worlds with minor miracles, *pace* David Lewis, when such counterfactuals can be treated as imperfect linguistic gestures to real causal powers *here*, on our own turf, in the *actual* world.

Dispositionality is utterly fundamental, but physical properties, states, and entities are not *exhausted* by their dispositionality. Operationalism is not true. Why, then, should *mental* properties, states, and entities be exhausted by *their* dispositionalities? Functionalism is not true. Even if knowledge of physical $x$ or mental $y$ necessarily involves the causal disposition of $x$ and $y$ to affect an agent's belief that $x$ or belief that $y$, that does not establish that *what* the agent knows is only the causal disposition or *function* to make that agent believe $x$ or believe $y$. We should not think *all* is disposition in *either* the nonpsychological or the psychological domains.

The lives of most honest dispositional states are spent largely in the presence of conditions that *prevent* those states from having any manifestations whatsoever. Any particular set of manifestation conditions for a kind of manifestation has to exclude *other* sets of manifestation conditions and consequently prevents the dispositional state from manifesting manifestations suited to the excluded conditions.

Causal operativeness is causal operativeness *for* or causal operativeness *against* (preventive of) the *reciprocal* manifestation of the causal powers to give of something $F$ and the causal powers to receive of something $G$. Water is causally operative for the manifestations (dissolution of salt) of the causal powers of the water to 'give' (dissolve the salt) and the causal powers to 'receive' of salt (be dissolved by water). The presence of air is causally operative for the prevention of such a dissolution manifestation for the salt. A manifestation of a dispositional state must be appreciated in depth as a component of a disposition or a power net at the time rather than necessarily spread out temporally.

It is difficult to give a fully adequate description of even the most ordinary cases of the manifestation of dispositions—salt's dissolving in water, for instance. It is not simply a matter of the dissolution of the salt in the water: God or something else could have caused the dissolution in the water before the water has had its chance to do the job. The character of a dispositional state derives from the pattern and complex variety of alternative manifestations (under a complex range of kinds of manifesting conditions) *to* or *for* which it is directed, and the manifestations are such only *from* that base.

## 15.3 PROPOSITIONS

Dispositions or readinesses are made by nature to be the only things that essentially have *directedness*, psychological or nonpsychological. *Nothing*, including dispositions, is *essentially* semantic or significance-bearing; significance depends rather on a particular kind of use.

Stronger stomachs stomach what I cannot, namely, propositions that, *pace* Locke, are entities essentially possessing semantic proportion (and satisfaction conditions); their semantic features are *built in*. As Fodor notes, 'it's not clear what the point would be of an explanation of the intentionality of the attitudes which presupposes the objects (propositions) that are intentional intrinsically. Why not just say that the attitudes are?' (1987: 80)

A philosopher friend of mine used to say when he was still a believer, 'I like to have all of my philosophical problems in one place, so I put them all in God.' Now, however, there is a tendency to put them in such entities as propositions, or alternative worlds, or even universals. In that case, semantic character is only given to a state or set of states of something as a kind of 'relational property.' The state, or set of states, is related—paralleled by—a set of propositions or a set of alternative worlds.

Propositions are supposed to be entities that are essentially semantic and *somehow*, by their paralleling, invest some of our thoughts with contents (objects of thought); alternative worlds are supposed to be entities that are at least numerous enough to fill out a *real* actual *or* possible Fido for every 'Fido.'

The thoughts of God would seem to do what the propositions and alternative worlds (that are not spatially, temporally, or causally connected to us) can do and *more*. It should be clear that all such intellectual parallelisms with made-to-order intellectual artefacts make good blackboard exercises but cannot be believed as realistic models for explanatory and genuine connections.


## 15.4 BOUNDS OF SENSE

Let us try to figure out what we are doing at our end of the semantic enterprise. The fact that belief and desire states are dispositional is both familiar and obvious. The nature of a disposition, what *makes* it one kind of disposition rather than another, is determined by the kinds of *manifestation* for which it is disposed. After all, that is what the disposition is *for*. As such, if the disposition is a belief sort of disposition, then what is *beliefish* about it comes to the kinds of *manifestations* for which it is a disposition. This, too, is obvious, if not quite so familiar.

There is the centuries-old idea that significance rests not in any happening or set of happenings, but in a dispositional state instead (with, no doubt, real causal powers if you are a candid ontologist), or perhaps an array of such dispositional states. Firmness of terminological resolution might seem to help here, at least if these dispositional states are only called 'belief–desire states.'

The significance of belief–desire dispositional states is not to be explained simply in terms of these states' complex interrelationships with other inner states, even when these interrelationships have their own biogenetic explanations concerning their evolution through their complex and systematic environmental sensitivities. That account works well enough for nonintentional states, such as states of the digestive system.

Various patterns of sounds and movements we make (which are not enough just in themselves to be significant) are given semantic explanation in terms of the dispositional states that are apt to produce the sounds and movements, and we have already, recall, *labeled* these states belief–desire states. In the end, the explanation of, or what is *significant* about, 'belief–desire' dispositional states is given in functionalistic terms as being apt to cause the various patterns of sounds and movements we make. This oddity remains, even if (in response to content problems created by believers in Earth water, $H_2O$, and Twin Earth water, XYZ) the functional role is limited to explaining *abouting* and not extended to explaining abouting *content*. How long it takes to make this circuit depends only on the ingenuity and candour of the philosopher making it.

Appeal to a Language of Thought does not help at this point. To give the inner state the 'systematic,' structured, and combinatorial complexities of the natural language might be part of a causal explanation if you hold a wholehearted belief in the medieval injunction, 'There must be at least as much perfection in the cause as in the effect.' That gives us nothing, however, toward an explanation of the nature of the intentional, for we will need an answer to the question, '*How* are those states and happenings that have been called the Language of Thought *intentional*?'

We are prevented from discerning simple answers to the questions, 'How is anything directed or projective to other things of one *kind* rather than another?' 'How is anything directed or projective to some other thing *in particular*?' and 'How does anything have a governing *use* of something?' by thinking that the questions apply only to mental psychological entities. It then appears that our only recourse is to some special mental magic.

Instead, the easy answers are to be given simply in terms of dispositions and positions in causal networks, whether these are for psychological *or* nonpsychological entities. We have seen briefly how states' being projective beyond themselves is just what dispositionality is *for* and how systems of dispositional states are capable of complex, directed, combinatorial, regulative adjustments and control reactivities—that is, *use*—even in instances of inorganic things.

Explaining how a projectedness, directedness, or use has *significance* or *import* for agents is a different matter. That will divide our knowing selves from the rocks and trees, and even from wonderfully complex and innovative things such as our own nonconscious autonomic nervous system.

Any event that is a manifestation-candidate for a particular disposition state is so defeasibly. That is the case even when the
manifestation-candidate is for a particular mental disposition state.
Talk of 'dispositional' and 'occurrent' beliefs is inapposite, gross, and
misleading. It suggests that one could, in some particular occurrence,
have a belief, whole and complete, actualized in its full totality. Anything that *happens*, however, somehow seems too thin for *all* of that.
This haunted James and Wittgenstein.

The *happening*—Wittgenstein's 'Aha,' Quine's assent-tokening
(these are more 'cues' to the belief than deep and typifying manifestations of it), or more typifyingly *sensory*-guided behaviour, enactive
of the disposition—can indeed be a manifestation of a particular
belief-that-*p* disposition array. If it is, then it is the tip of something
very large.[2]

Functionalist excess has been employed with no imagination in its
application to real cases. The nature of the material of use *matters*, and
the nature of the instrument of use is suited *to* this material as well as
to the mode of operation for the total character of the use.

The *difference* between what is used in the comatose case of the
autonomic nervous system *cum* cardiovascular system with the complex
*directedness* of its array of dispositional states *and* significances based in
the higher functioning of the central nervous system is to be found
in differences in the *material* of use in the two cases. For the making
of significance, the material of use must be *sensate*. To make the
mind knowing, it must first be made sensate through sensory input,
experience, and imagery.

In a passage anticipating Wittgenstein (and cited earlier, but worth
repeating here), Locke notes that:

> Universality belongs not to things themselves, which are all of them particular
> in their existence, even those words and ideas which are general . . . their
> general nature being nothing but the capacity they are put into by the
> understanding of signifying or representing many particulars. (Locke 1690:
> III, iii, 2)

The lesson is that intentionality and significance reside not in particulars themselves, but in their uses. Representations—representational
*entities*—do not merely have an intentionality halo.

---

[2] It is essential to remember that for behaviour to count as more than mere bodily
motion, it must be through the medium of *sensory* feedback, which is just the sensate
material for direct use (through no *further* medium).

Belief and desire states are particulars and, by virtue of their being dispositional states, are notably unamenable to any kind of direct *use* themselves. I have never used a belief in my life. Beliefs do not have traction or grip; they are not even candidates for the material of use we require for semantic or significant use. The great importance of beliefs and desires lies in their being the dispositional base for use-manifestations, the material of which *does* have traction and grip and, if we set our minds to it, can be introspectively scanned.

Belief and desire states cannot be invoked as semantic or psychological primitives, because they need to be dispositions *for* or *to* some typifying manifestation, so their nature *must* be characterizable in terms of those typifying manifestations.

As dispositional states themselves are *unamenable* to direct use, belief and desire states are intentional only through those typifying *use-manifestations* that they are dispositions *for* and *to*, and not the other way around (Locke). Manifestations that typify what belief–desire dispositional states are dispositions *for* will be vastly complex forms of direct *use* of what is directly usable by us, namely, our sensory input and feedback of verbal and nonverbal imagery. Without the discriminatory directedness and direct use of such sensate material involved in positive and negative *sensory* feedback, the motion of bodily parts would fail to be significant, intentional behaviour.

In each case, for verbal or nonverbal activity to have content, what is done has to come *from* a holistic network of dispositional states or readiness potentials that place those doings with an infinite number of alternative doings within limits, of which such a network makes the individual capable.

Wittgenstein's mistake, and the mistake of many others, was to treat the sensate (sensory input and imagery) only as, at best, an idle 'accompaniment' of behaviour—when it was grudgingly admitted to exist. It was considered to be 'a wheel that turns no wheel.' Instead, what is sensate is a gift of nature, the material of use needed for what is *semantic and significant*. It is not, as moles on the cheek may be, merely an evolutionary luxury. This failure to see the existence and role of the sensate in human cognition can be described as *the denial of sense*.

Sensory experience is not some dumb middleman, a trifling *byproduct* of physical stimulus and *cause* of belief and desire states. Its role is the right and necessary *material* for alternate forms of *use* as typifying manifestations of alternative arrays of dispositional and tendency states that are beliefs, desires, hopes, and fears, and all that makes up the cognitive life of the mind.

If various evolving disposition arrays are interrelated in sufficiently complex ways for interrelated alternative forms of reactiveness to alternative forms of *sensate* input, *then* such reactive manifestations may earn the name 'semantic or cognate use.' This, of course, is a matter of degree, as it should be. After all, we want an account that will take us from brute directedness and the use of mere physical governance to human significance.

## 15.5 INTROSPECTIVE PRIVILEGE

In the case of introspective knowledge, sensation, S, is the object of the belief that S and it is *also* the immediate cause of the belief that S. There are no causal links in between that could be weak. There is nothing else *by* which or *from* which S is known. It is this that explains why, against the unlikely challenge, '*Why* do you think you are in pain?', the only polite response would be the expostulation 'Because I *am!*'

(Perhaps the neural–causal situation in the brain in the case of introspection is not quite as tidy as the Lockean model would require, but it is at least about the nearest approximation to identity of cause of belief and object of belief that we have and still nearer even than the most optimal perceptual cases.)

As noted earlier (Section 12.3), this way of looking at things enables us to understand the perennial attraction of the doctrine of first-person authority or incorrigibility. In introspection, the gap between belief and the cause which is its object is narrow indeed. Narrowing the gap, however, does not amount to eliminating it. Incorrigibility requires that there could be no cause of our introspective beliefs other than their objects. But this is not so. Sensations can be complex and share similarities and differences. Imagine that you are expecting a sensation of a particular sort and experience, not that sensation, but a similar sensation, you could mistakenly believe that you had experienced the sensation you expected. If this seems implausible, think of the case in which you expect to feel a burning sensation as the result of being touched by a hot object on your back. Instead, you are touched by an ice cube.

Mistakes of this kind—akin to mistaking a vine for a snake in a jungle setting—are the chief source of introspective error.

## 15.6 SENSATE MATERIALS

It might help to say more about this sensate material and then to characterize some of the various uses having various forms of the experiential as material of use in order to answer the question, '*Why* is sensate material needed instead of some *other* material for use by anything that is a psychological, cognizing agent?' The challenge can then be issued, 'Now, what else *could* do what sensate material does as a material of use?' In any account of the mind, sensory input and imagery must be seen as a *product* or result of processing. It is this product that is, in turn, the *material* of use.

As a result of both past processing and uses of countless kinds of input, processing comes to result in greatly changed sensory and imagistic experience. Sensate material *itself* changes greatly and cannot be thought of as an unchanging constant. You open your eyes, and the processed result takes the form of sensory input of marks on a background in particular *groupings* because you have learned to read words in sentences.

A familiar technique of 'gridding' sensory fields can be employed to show voluminosities and bounds of occupancy, as well as variations of such occupancy, or 'movements,' native to fleeting sensory input or imagery material itself, but not to enduring external entities to which such sensate material might or might not come to be used as material for projection. Imagine grid lines crossing within your visual field and an internal and surface grid for your tactile and kinaesthetic field (and a grid even for your auditory field, although a description of that would require special care).

Voluminosities, bounds of occupancy, and changes in these, characterize our sensory states even if we have not yet achieved a degree of development in infancy whereby we are capable of using these for externalizing projections in perceivings *that* and perceivings *as*. Indeed, even with full percipient maturity, there are many kinds of sensory occurrence that are never used as material for perceptual projections—at any rate, they are not used *representationally*. (If you are a connectionist or some other kind of cognitive scientist, you might *call* them 'structured representations'; structured as they undoubtedly are, however, they are not used representationally. There is too much hustle and bustle in cognitive science to expect terminological responsibility.)

We all have countless bodily tweaks, twinges, tingles, and visual spots, flashes, blurrings, and less than total darkness with our eyes closed or open. These are mostly unnoticed, yet they can occasionally be objects of sensual regard or casual interest, or, when they intensify and become obtrusive, they can occasion special enjoyment or annoyance. They are, it would seem, entirely useless to us. Whatever 'systematic causes' they might have remain entirely beyond our ken. We have not the *least* idea of such sensate states as being *of, as, for, from,* or *that.* In some distant galaxy there might be humanoids who make use of such things, perhaps for the detection of the intensity of magnetic fields.

The following are just a few samples of different kinds of use requiring different sorts of sensate material:

(1) *Background use.* The sensate is unobtrusive and unnoticed; how-ever, its *ceasing* to be present would be strikingly noticeable. Here, use comes in the form of a stabilization use to *keep* such sensate material in the background. This is ecologically important for the development and survival of intelligent, mobile creatures. A sentient creature cannot be cognitively reactive to each and every sensory input, yet the background details of a sensory field might be the material for an enriched assessment of a particular kind of enormously complex whole.

(2) *Reverie use.* Such use is a matter of passively receiving, *keeping* to, and 'going with' varying input. Use of this kind is apparently important for the development of creativity, and has, for that reason, attracted the attention of researchers.

(3) *Phenomenological savouring use.* This is not a use of the sensate for externalizations, perceivings that something is $F$, internalizations, or takings of oneself to be in a particular state $S$. It is not a *classificatory* use of the sensate, but instead is something basic to classificatory use. Such use involves an agent's intense savouring attention focused on a variety of aspects of the agent's sensate state as they strike the agent. Not all sensual savouring is like discriminating, classificatory wine tasting. Simple savouring provides maximum diversity of connections with other input. Without being grooved into categorizing ruts, there is maximum flexibility of conditioning for a variety of uses with subsequent input. This can lead to maturation and a change in character of the sensory input itself. Processing of stimuli on later

occasions produces a different sensate material—some aspects are more dominant and others are more recessive, and aspects stand out in different relations.

(4) *Discriminatory and comparative, contrastive use* (with or without classificatory use). This kind of use can have the effects of the uses listed above and, like those uses, can be employed without classificatory embellishment. *With* classificatory use, however, an individual's recognitional capacities that depend on retention become fully manifested.

(5) *Direct noninferential projective use.* This is the standard use of sensory input, as Locke tells us, to '. . . pass through almost totally unregarded. . . as our inner constitution requires. . . and our condition needs' (1690: II, 19, iii). I return to this kind of use in the next section. It does not fit into either of the usual forms of foundationalism or antifoundationalism.

(6) *Inferential use.* In this use, for example, you might note a particular feeling and from that come to think that your leg is beginning to mend. This is a sophisticated and occasionally important use of the sensate. It is not common, however, and certainly not standard as empiricism has been understood (at least by its critics) to claim.

## 15.7 USING SENSATE MATERIALS

In seeking a form of inference from sensory input to object, theorists muddy the water by inserting 'information' into the nature of the sensory input or imagery that is not *there*. The mistake is compounded when, on recognizing that our perception and conception of things cannot work that way, they become sceptical that they work at all. Sides are taken pro-, anti-, or for 'modified' foundationalism. Berkeley counsels that 'only an idea is like an idea,' and Hume smirks about the nonrationality of any inference from ideas to objects. Their points are both right—but *irrelevant*! So are most current foundationalist, antifoundationalist, coherentist flutterings. My mentor in this, as in so much else, has been for many years Locke.

The following case of feeling at the end of a pole was discussed years ago in Cambridge as something odd and important. As I remember the surrounding debates, not much was accomplished.

A surgeon has been transplanting tissue to the ends of my fingers. He takes off the bandages and asks about my repaired fingertips: 'Now, try to feel with them.' I do, and it turns out all right. Then someone hands me a pole and says, 'Try to feel with *this*.' It must be some kind of joke. It is totally absurd! He seems to be asking me to treat this wooden pole as a sensitive, feeling extension of myself. I do not even try.

The next day, I am attempting to poke at something I cannot see and that I know is in a corner that I cannot reach to find out if it feels soft or not. Without hesitation, I feel at the end of the pole (where else?) how soft the thing in the corner is. I use the wooden pole as a sensitive, feeling extension of (what else?) myself. Perhaps if I am too much aware of the woodenness of the pole at the beginning, the feeling is in the hand, but as I become absorbed in the use of the pole in more and more delicate probings, the feeling 'transfers' to the end of it.

Just as we could not use the wooden, insensitive pole (so different from our feeling parts) in the subtle exploratory ways we do unless we were built to pass through the pole's nature to 'feel' (against its nature) *at* its end, so, more basically, we could not use sensory input and imagery in the projective and externalizing ways we do unless we were *built* to pass through *their* nature (whatever properties they have, they are not three-dimensional, solid, soft, or brittle, and they do not scratch or tear) to the perceivings of things that are three-dimensional and *do* scratch and tear.

We use the pole and our sensate material for projections of properties grossly inconsistent with the properties of the pole and the sensate material *themselves*. We do not do this by any inference from one set of properties to another set of incompatible properties.

Although sensory input and imagistic material can be directly (not incorrigibly) known, we, for excellent survival reasons, mostly 'pass through them almost totally unregarded,' as Locke observes.

Neither do we know about the nature of such input first and then *infer* objects, nor do we have the input *just in terms* of information about objects, nor are kinds of objects and their properties significant for us simply by virtue of some systematic cause of our sensory input.

The importance of sensory input and imagery is not that it is the material for direct knowledge, but instead that it is the material for direct *use*. There is nothing by *means* of which we use the sensate material. The sensate material is the direct means of use by which all *else* is used—including one's limbs or other moveable bodily parts by *sensory* feedback.

The human sensate organism comes to use its sensate material as projective of identities where there are *not* such identities in the material of use itself. Consider the following: a visual sensory input, S, followed by S's cessation (as when you blink your eyes or avert your gaze), followed by a somewhat similar sensory input, S' (as when you open your eyes or return your gaze to where it had been). These noncontinuous sensory inputs are used to project a single *continuant*. There is no need to make this 'perceptual permanence' a matter of *inference*, inductive or deductive. The array of causal dispositions that are the causal source of our externalizing uses of our sensory input (sensations, we used to call them) is noninferential (unless all cause and effect is inferential) and nonrelational. We do not make inferences *to* what we project. That is not to deny that we sometimes make inferences, deductions, and inductions in terms of what we have *already* projected. Of course we do.

The joke is on us. We were not built to be rational nor, of course, to be irrational. We were made instead to use our sensate material directly and projectively, *without* the need for or regard to knowledge of the details of its nature for inferences to properties of things that are *incompatible* with properties of the sensate material so used. This is Locke's point in noting that we 'pass through' sensory materials 'almost totally unregarded . . . as our condition demands.'

The human organism *is not*, not even remotely, a mental agent capable of understanding, feeling, and knowing *through* the uses under the governance of the autonomic nervous system. The human organism *is* such an agent *through* the uses under the governance only of the central nervous system. The distinction is not to be made in terms of degrees of complexity (the autonomic nervous system is evidently far more complex and flexible than some mental entities recognize), but rather in terms of the difference in the *material* of use, namely, sensory input, feedback, and imagery. Propositional attitudes of belief, desire, hope, fear, frustration, etc., are collections (or perhaps *clouds*) of dispositional state arrays whose typifying manifestations take the form of multifarious modes of use of various forms of sensation and imagery.

I have described the modes of use. What has impeded progress in the philosophy of mind has been poverty-stricken accounts of percepts and percept-like imagery, often enough due to the dead hands of Wittgenstein and Ryle. This volume is intended to provide a worked-out corrective.

# 16

# Warps and Woofs of Einstein

## 16.1 OBJECTS

The world is all that is the case. But *what* is the case? It is tempting to think that the world comprises objects arranged spatially (or spatiotemporally). An object is something that excludes other objects. Suppose $a$ is an object, a classical atom, for instance. There must be a sharp discontinuity between the being of $a$ and the non-being of $a$. Objects are *mutual exclusions*.

On reflection, however, the coherence of a world of mutually excluding objects proves surprisingly elusive. To see why, first consider causality. The basic concepts of the account of causality given in this volume are not of a simple off or on, but of various degrees. Similarly, readinesses or dispositionalities themselves have continuous degrees of strength.

The spatiotemporal concepts of proximity and distance are not absolutes, but of varying degrees of relativity.

Field properties in spatiotemporal segments have no sharp edges. Fields have varying degrees of intensity. Different fields occupy the *same* volume of space–time. Fields are made-to-order 'blurry' entities—more misty than mist.

All of this helps somewhat toward making the fit between the very large (relativity) and the very small (quantum physics), so long as we avoid the disastrous conflation of the ontic and the epistemic that bedevils so much of the philosophy of science.

I wish to try to establish ontologically some of what Einstein established in physics. Einstein was himself driven by ontological forms of argument. Seeing what might have been underneath and behind some of Einstein's most basic thoughts should teach us something valuable.

A point of space has no size; an instant of time is supposed to have no duration, and as the mathematician warns us, 'no nearest neighbour' to other points or instants. In even the smallest space–time segments, there is always room for any number of points and instants.

In Chapter 5, I pointed out that 'no nearest neighbour' problems beset traditional accounts of causation framed in terms of successive spatially contiguous events. My suggestion there was that we replace this conception of causation with a conception of causation as mutual partnerings and manifestings of dispositions.

The two-event cause-and-effect view is easily avoided and replaced by the view of mutual manifestation of reciprocal disposition partners, suggesting a natural contemporaneity. This is not surprising in the least because the reciprocal dispositional *partnering* and their mutually *manifesting* are *identical*. No temporal gap or spatial gap is needed—not one happening before another. It is not a matter of two events, but of one and the same event—a reciprocal dispositional partnering as a *mutual* manifesting. This surprising identity of what we had dimly thought of as the two-event cause and effect loses its surprise in the clear light of day.

This identity of partnering-manifesting becomes clear at the atomic level of bindings for molecular formings. The dispositional partners of key and lock, in their hardnesses, shapes, kinetic, and resistance forces, etc., *are* the manifestings of the locking, jamming, or unlocking. The more closely a cause-and-effect is examined, the more natural the replacement view—of seeing the event of partnering as an activity identical with the event of mutual manifesting—becomes.

The model being developed here is not limited to particle-objects-in-space-time; it also fits well for explanations in terms of warps and woofs *of* space–time as infinitesimal energy loops or superstrings. I have insisted that space–time *has* properties, yet it is not itself had as a property or even a set of properties, and it could not exist without properties. A propertied space–time is a one-object universe and space–time satisfies the correct definitions of 'substratum.'

## 16.2 THE ARGUMENT

The lack of sharp edges of objects (as in the case of clouds or mist) suggests that distinctions between

(a) the being of an object, $x$, at $l$ (a definite location in space–time) and

(b) the not-being of an object, $x$, at $l$

is also not sharp. This suggests the 'blurring' in the case of clouds, but not in most cases of objects where (a) and (b) are supposed to be mutually exclusive. But the combining of the contradictories (a) and (b) simply results in a contradiction and no new logical category, 'blurring.' It appears that our notion of objects generates a contradiction. That is a serious fault.

The notion of an infinite series and of a mathematical point or instant are the province of the mathematician. So let us ask whether the mathematician helps. I think not.

Consider the following infinite series:

$$1/2 + 1/4 + 1/8 + 1/16 + 1/32 \ldots$$
$$(3/4) \quad (7/8) \quad (15/16) \quad (31/32) \ldots$$

In following the rule for forming such an infinite series, the *limit* is the least figure such that no member along this series results in this figure as product. The limit is 1.


## 16.3 THE RULE

The figure to be added to the series is determined by adding one half the previous figure along the series. The sum of all figures at every point in the series is in brackets, only one half of the number that is needed to achieve the product in summation of the limit 1. So it is an error to think of the limit as a member—'the last member'—of the series. The rule for forming the series is enough to forbid this. Adding an infinite number of members also breaks the rule and gives no rule for determining the *individual* numbers to be added to the series. This is still needed even if their totality is infinite. *How* is this possible? I haven't any idea. Talk of adding infinity is purely gestural and does *not* make clear the rule for doing so. Without these emendations, the mathematician is of no help in the discussion.

We began with space coming down to relations among objects. Then we changed to objects coming down to propertied spatial segments. Thinking of objects as propertied spatiotemporal regions is to make motion something in which motion is not *of any* entity. But wait! What happens to $E = MC^2$, where C is acceleration? The answer: motion is apparent and not real, as the lighting of bulbs in a succession in an electric sign is an apparent and not a real motion. So there would be a successive 'lighting up' of properties in different spatiotemporal regions giving only apparent, not real, motion.

The question remains, 'How can such a fundamental concept in physics be given an account in terms that come down to appearance and not reality?'

We have uncovered fundamental objections to conceiving of objects in space–time and conceiving of properties as spatiotemporal lightings-up sequentially to replace the motion of objects. There appears to be a crisis in our most sophisticated thought about the material order of the world. New and basic ways of thinking are needed.

Thinking of motion, for instance, as something (change of spatial-temporal properties) happening to objects has been replaced by an ontological critique of objects and by their replacement with spatio-temporal propertied segments concerning which motion makes no sense.

We could try acceptance: 'I suppose that's all motion comes down to then.' We can have equivalents to velocity, acceleration, deceleration, and directions. Is that not enough for us?[1] (Does this assume an absoluteness of space? No more than is necessary.)

But remember: objects are not to be taken to be fundamental or basic. They are replaced by spatiotemporal trajectories of successive lightings-up of properties of spatiotemporal regions. You cannot have both this *and* objects. Propertied spatiotemporal regions and their warps and woofs are what there really are, as Einstein told us.

Objects, whether large (observers) or small (electrons), are gone from any fundamental basic picture of the world. They are gone from the ultimate and basic physics.

John Wisdom reported to Moore that Wittgenstein once commented, in criticism of Moore, 'The idealist doesn't deny that under my trousers I wear pants.' Moore replied, 'Is that so?', and took down a volume of McTaggart and read: 'So now we see that physical objects are in the same position as the gorgons and the harpies.'

There is a *huge* ontological shift here: *from* having objects with their properties and relations as basic and explaining spatiotemporal regions in terms of relations among objects *to* having regions explaining

---

[1] John Heil suggested this reply; see Heil (2003: 41–2).

and replacing relations of objects by field properties and relations of spatiotemporal regions. Their properties and regional warps and woofs are basic and explain and replace objects.

The account I am endorsing makes no mention of objects but only of spatiotemporal segments *instead*.

Saying that the replacement of objects moving by sequential lightings-up of field properties of the warps and woofs of space–time regions is 'just what objects moving comes down to' is like saying that Einstein's relativity is just what the all-pervasive ether comes down to. This flattens the ontological novelty of scientific discovery.

Einstein declared that he wanted to know the mind of God. Someone asked, 'What kind of God?' Einstein replied, 'Spinoza's God.' This expresses Einstein's ontology.

# References

Anscombe, G. E. M. (1957) *Intention*. Oxford: Blackwell.

Armstrong, D. M. (1968) *A Materialist Theory of the Mind*. London: Routledge and Kegan Paul.

Armstrong, D. M. (1983) *What is a Law of Nature?* Cambridge: Cambridge University Press.

Armstrong, D. M., Martin, C. B., and Place, U. T. (1996) *Dispositions: A Debate*, ed. Tim Crane. London: Routledge.

Bacon, J. (1995) *Universals and Property Instances: The Alphabet of Being*. Oxford: Basil Blackwell.

Bacon, J., Campbell, K., and Reinhardt, L. (eds) (1992) *Ontology, Causality, and Mind*. Cambridge: Cambridge University Press.

Bannister, R., and Mathias, E. J. (eds) (1992) *Autonomic Failure: A Textbook of Clinical Disorders of the Autonomic Nervous System*. Oxford: Oxford University Press.

Basar, E. (ed.) (1988) *Dynamics of Sensory and Cognitive Processing by the Brain*. Berlin: Springer-Verlag.

Bennett, J. (1976) *Linguistic Behaviour*. Cambridge: Cambridge University Press.

Bird, A. (1998) 'Dispositions and antidotes', *The Philosophical Quarterly* 48: 227–34.

Bisiach, E. (1988) 'Language without thought', in L. Weiskrantz, *Thought Without Language*. Oxford: Clarendon Press, pp. 478–81.

Black, M. (1952) 'The identity of indiscernibles', *Mind* 61: 153–64. Reprinted in M. Black, *Problems of Analysis*. Ithaca: Cornell University Press, pp. 80–92.

Black, M. (1954) *Problems of Analysis*. Ithaca: Cornell University Press.

Blackburn, S. (1990) 'Filling in space', *Analysis* 50: 62–5.

Borut, A., Dmi'el, R., and Shkolnik, A. (1979) 'Heat balance of resting and walking goats: Comparison of climatic chamber and exposure in the desert', *Physiological Zoology* 52: 105–12.

Brown, A. C., and Brengelmann, G. L. (1970) 'The interaction of peripheral and central inputs in the temperature regulation system', in J. D. Hardy, A. P. Gagge, and J. A. J. Stolwijk (eds), *Physiological and Behavioral Temperature Regulation*. Springfield, IL: Thomas, pp. 684–702.

Brück, K. (1989) 'Thermal balance and the regulation of body temperature', in R. F. Schmidt and G. Thews (eds), *Human Physiology* (2nd edn). Berlin: Springer-Verlag, pp. 636–7.

Brück K., and Zeisberger, E. (1987). 'Adaptive changes in thermoregulation and their pharmacological basis'. *Pharmacology and Therapeutics* 35: 163–215.

200                          The Mind in Nature

Cain, W. S., and Engen, T. (1977) 'Olfactory adaptation and the scaling of olfactory intensity', in C. Pfaffman (ed.), *Olfaction and Taste* III. New York: Rockefeller University Press, pp. 127–41.

Campbell, K. (1981) 'The metaphysics of abstract particulars', *Midwest Studies in Philosophy* 6: 477–88.

Campbell, K. (1990) *Abstract Particulars*. Oxford: Blackwell.

Carruthers, P. (1989) 'Brute experience', *Journal of Philosophy* 86: 258–69.

Cartwright, N. (1983) *How the Laws of Physics Lie*. Oxford: Clarendon Press.

Cohn, J. N., and Yellin, A. M. (1984) 'Learned precise cardiovascular control through graded central sympathetic stimulation', *Journal of Hypertension* (Suppl.) 2: 577–9.

Colodny, R. G. (ed.) (1962) *Frontiers of Science and Philosophy*. Pittsburgh: University of Pittsburgh Press.

Crick, F., and Micheson, G. (1983) 'The function of dream sleep', *Nature* 304: 111–14.

Cytowic, R. E. (1988) 'Tasting colors, smelling sounds', *The Sciences* 28: 32–7.

Damasio, A. R. (1994) *Descartes' Error: Emotion, Reason, and the Human Brain*. New York: G. P. Putnam's Sons.

Dampney, R. A. L. (1994) 'Functional organization of central pathways regulating the cardiovascular system', *Physiological Review* 74: 323–64.

Dennett, D. C. (1981) 'True believers: The intentional strategy and why it works', in A. E. Heath (ed.), *Scientific Explanation: Papers Based on Herbert Spencer Lectures Given in the University of Oxford*. Oxford: Clarendon Press, pp. 312–31. Reprinted in D. C. Dennett, *The Intentional Stance*. Cambridge, MA: MIT Press, pp. 13–35.

Dennett, D. C. (1987) *The Intentional Stance*. Cambridge, MA: MIT Press.

Dmi'el, R. and Robertshaw, D. (1983). 'The control of panting and sweating in the black bedouin goat: A comparison of two modes of imposing heat load'. *Physiological Zoology* 56: 404–11.

Dummett, M. A. E. (1979) 'Common sense and physics', in G. F. Macdonald (ed.), *Perception and Identity: Essays Presented to A. J. Ayer With His Replies*. Ithaca: Cornell University Press, pp. 1–40.

Edelman, G. (1987) *Neural Darwinism*. New York: Basic Books.

Einstein, A. (1949) 'Remarks concerning the essays brought together in this co-operative volume'. In P. A. Schilpp (ed.), *Albert Einstein: Philosopher–Scientist*. Chicago: University of Chicago Press, pp. 663–88.

Engel, B. T. (1986) 'An essay on the circulation as behavior', *The Behavioral and Brain Sciences* 9: 285–318.

Feldman, J. L., and Ellenberger, H. H. (1988) 'Central coordination of respiratory and cardiovascular control in mammals', *Annual Review of Physiology* 50: 593–606.

Fetzer, J. (1981) *Scientific Knowledge*. Dordrecht: Reidel.

Feynman, R. P., Leighton, R. B., and Sands, M. (1963) *The Feynman Lectures on Physics* vol 1. Reading, MA: Addison-Wesley Publishing Co.

Fine, A. (1986) *The Shaky Game: Einstein, Realism, and the Quantum Theory.* Chicago: University of Chicago Press.

Fodor, J. (1987) *Psychosemantics: The Problem of Meaning in the Philosophy of Mind.* Cambridge, MA: MIT Press.

Freeman, W. J. (1988) 'Nonlinear neural dynamics of olfaction as a model for cognition', in E. Basar (ed.), *Dynamics of Sensory and Cognitive Processing by the Brain.* Berlin: Springer-Verlag, pp. 19–29.

Gerger, R., Koepahen, H. P., Monormaerts, W., and Windhorst, U. (eds) (1995) *Autonomic Failure: A Textbook of Clinical Disoprders of the Autonomic Nervous System.* Oxford: Oxford University Press.

Getting, P. A. (1989) 'Emerging principles governing the operation of neural networks', *Annual Review of Neuroscience* 12: 185–204.

Gibson, E. J., and Walk, R. D. (1960) 'The visual cliff', *Scientific American* 202: 64–71.

Goodman, N. (1965) *Fact, Fiction, and Forecast* (2nd edn). Indianapolis: Bobbs-Merrill.

Gordon, C. J., and Heath, J. E. (1983) 'Reassessment of the neural control of body temperature: Importance of oscillating neural and motor components', *Comparative Biochemical Physiology* 74A: 479–89.

Gordon, C. J., and Heath, J. E. (1986) 'Integration and central processing in temperature regulation', *Annual Review of Physiology* 48: 595–612.

Gray, J. (1995) 'The contents of consciousness: A neuropsychological conjecture', *Behavioral and Brain Sciences* 18: 659–722.

Hales, J. R. S. (ed.) (1984) *Thermal Physiology.* New York: Raven Press.

Hardy, J. D., Gagge, A. P., and Stolwijk, J. A. J. (eds) (1970) *Physiological and Behavioral Temperature Regulation.* Springfield, IL: Thomas.

Heath, A. E., ed. (1981) *Scientific Explanation: Papers Based on Herbert Spencer Lectures Given in the University of Oxford.* Oxford. Clarendon Press.

Heil, J. (1983) *Perception and Cognition.* Berkeley: University of California Press.

Heil, J. (2003) *From an Ontological Point of View.* Oxford: Clarendon Press.

Hopkins, P. S., and Knights, G. (1984) 'Sweating can be a significant route of evaporative loss in sheep'. In J. R. S. Hales (ed.), *Thermal Physiology.* New York: Raven Press, pp. 275–78.

Hori, T. (1984) 'Capsaicin and central control of thermoregulation', *Pharmacology and Therapeutics* 206: 389–416.

Hori, T. (1991) 'An update on thermosensitive neurons in the brain: From cellular biology to thermal and non-thermal homeostatic functions', *Japanese Journal of Physiology* 41: 1–22.

Hori, T., Kiyohara, T., Nakashima, T., and Shibata, M. (1982) 'Responses of preoptic thermosensitive neurons to medial forebrain bundle stimulation,'. *Brain Research Bulletin* 8: 667–675.

Jackson, F. C. (1996) 'The primary quality view of colour'. *Philosophical Perspectives* 10: 199–219.

Jessen, C. (1985) 'Thermal afferents in the control of body temperature'. *Pharmacology and Therapeutics* 28: 107–34.

Kenney, W. L., and Johnson, J. M. (1992) 'Control of skin blood flow during exercise', *Medicine and Science in Sports and Exercise* 24: 303–12.

Kiyohara, T., Hori, T., Shibata, M., and Nakashima, T. (1984) 'Effects of Angiotensin II on preoptic thermosensitive neurones in the rat'. In J. R. S. Hales (ed.), *Thermal Physiology*. New York: Raven Press, pp. 141–4.

Kirk, R. (1967) 'Rationality without language', *Mind* 76: 369–86.

Koepchen, H. P. (1983) 'Respiratory and cardiovascular 'centres': Functional entirety or separate structures?' In: M. E. Schläfk, H. P. Koepchen, and W. R. See (eds), *Central Neurone Environment and the Control Systems of Breathing and Circulation*. Berlin: Springer-Verlag, pp. 221–37.

Koepchen, H. P., Klüssendorph, D., and Sommer, D. (1981) 'Neurophysiological background of central neural cardiovascular-respiratory coordination: Basic remarks and experimental approach. *Journal of the Autonomic Nervous System* 3: 335–68.

Kripke, S. (1982) *Wittgenstein on Rules and Private Language: An Elementary Exposition*. Cambridge, MA: Harvard University Press.

Lewis, D. K. (1997) 'Finkish dispositions', *The Philosophical Quarterly* 47: 143–58.

Lewis, D. (2001) 'Truthmaking and difference making', *Noûs* 35: 602–15.

Llinás, R. (1988) 'The intrinsic electrophysiological properties of mammalian neurons: Insights into central nervous system function', *Science* 242: 1654–63.

Llinás, R., and Paré, D. (1992) 'Of dreaming and wakefulness', *Neuroscience* 44: 521–35.

Locke, J. (1690/1978) *An Essay Concerning Human Understanding*, ed. P. H. Nidditch, Oxford: Clarendon Press.

Loewry, A. D. (1990) 'Central autonomic pathways'. In A. D. Loewy and K. M. Spyer (eds), *Central Regulation of Autonomic Functions*. Oxford: Oxford University Press, pp. 88–103.

Loewry, A. D., and Spyer, K. M. (eds) (1990) *Central Regulation of Autonomic Functions*. Oxford: Oxford University Press.

Luria, A. R. (1961) *The Role of Speech in the Regulation of Normal and Abnormal Behavior*. Oxford: Pergamon Press.

Macdonald, G. F. (ed.) (1979) *Perception and Identity: Essays Presented to A. J. Ayer With His Replies*. Ithaca: Cornell University Press.

Martin, C. B. (1959) *Religious Belief*. Ithaca: Cornell University Press.

Martin, C. B. (1971) 'Knowledge without observation', *Canadian Journal of Philosophy* 1: 15–24.

Martin, C. B. (1980) 'Substance substantiated', *Australasian Journal of Philosophy* 58: 3–10.

Martin, C. B. (1984a) 'Anti-realism and the world's undoing', *Pacific Philosophical Quarterly* 65: 3–20.

Martin, C. B. (1984b) 'The new Cartesianism', *Pacific Philosophical Quarterly* 65: 236–58.

Martin, C. B. (1987) 'Proto-language', *Australasian Journal of Philosophy* 65: 277–89.

Martin, C. B. (1992) 'Power for realists', in J. Bacon, K. Campbell, and L. Reinhardt (eds), *Ontology, Causality, and Mind*. Cambridge: Cambridge University Press, pp. 175–86.

Martin, C. B. (1993) 'The need for ontology: Some choices', *Philosophy* 68: 505–22.

Martin, C. B. (1994) 'Dispositions and conditionals', *The Philosophical Quarterly* 44: 1–8.

Martin, C. B. (1996) 'How it is: Entities, absences, and voids', *Australasian Journal of Philosophy* 74: 57–65.

Martin, C. B. (1997) 'On the need for properties: The road to Pythagoreanism and back', *Synthese* 112: 193–231.

Martin, C. B. (2000) 'On Lewis and then some', *Logic et Analyse* (169–70): 43–8.

Martin, C. B., and Deutscher, M. (1966) 'Remembering', *Philosophical Review* 75: 161–96.

Martin, C. B., and Heil, J. (1998) 'Rules and powers', *Philosophical Perspectives* 12: 283–312.

Martin, C. B., and Pfeifer, K. (1986) 'Intentionality and the non–psychological', *Philosophy and Phenomenological Research* 46: 531–54.

Mellor, D. H. (1974) 'In defense of dispositions', *Philosophical Review* 83: 157–81. Reprinted in D. H. Mellor, *Matters of Metaphysics*. Cambridge: Cambridge University Press, pp. 104–22.

Mellor, D. H. (1991) *Matters of Metaphysics*. Cambridge: Cambridge University Press.

Molnar, G. (1999) 'Are dispositions reducible?' *The Philosophical Quarterly* 49: 1–17.

Molnar, G. (2003) *Powers: A Study in Metaphysics*, ed. S. Mumford. Oxford: Oxford University Press.

Morgane, P. J., and Panksepp, J. (eds) (1979) *Handbook of the Hypothalamus: Vol. 2, Physiology of the Hypothalamus*. New York: Marcel Deker.

Morrison, J. H., and Hof, P. R. (1992) 'The organization of the cerebral cortex: From molecules to circuits'. *Discussions in Neuroscience* 11: 1–80.

Nicoll, R. A. (1971) 'Recurrent excitation of secondary olfactory neurons: A possible mechanism for signal amplification', *Science* 171: 824–6.

Pellionisz, A. J., and Llinás, R. (1979) 'Brain modeling by tensor network theory and computer simulation. The cerebellum: Distributed processor for predictive coordination', *Neuroscience* 4: 323–48.

Pellionisz, A. J., and Llinás, R. (1982) 'Space–time representation in the brain. The cerebellum as a predictive space–time metric tensor', *Neuroscience* 7: 2949–70.

Pellionisz, A. J., and Llinás, R. (1985) 'Tensor network theory of the metaorganization of functional geometries in the CNS', *Neuroscience* 16: 245–73.

Pfaffman, C. (ed.) (1977) *Olfaction and Taste* III. New York: Rockefeller University Press.

Prior, E. W., Pargetter, R., and Jackson, F. C. (1982) 'Three theses about dispositions', *American Philosophical Quarterly* 19: 251–7.

Plum, F., and Mountcastle, V. (eds) (1987) *Handbook of Physiology*, vol. 5. Bethesda, MD: American Physiological Association.

Quine, W. V. O. (1948) 'On what there is', *Review of Metaphysics* 2: 21–38. Reprinted in W. V. O. Quine, *From a Logical Point of View* (2nd edn). Cambridge, MA: Harvard University Press, pp. 1–19.

Quine, W. V. O. (1960) *Word and Object*. Cambridge, MA: MIT Press.

Quine, W. V. O. (1961) *From a Logical Point of View* (2nd edn). Cambridge, MA: Harvard University Press.

Quine, W. V. O. (1976) 'Whither material objects?' *Boston Studies in the Philosophy of Science* 39: 497–504.

Raichle, M. (1987) 'Circulatory and metabolic correlates of brain function in normal humans', in F. Plum and V. Mountcastle (eds), *Handbook of Physiology*, vol. 5. Bethesda, MD: American Physiological Association, pp. 643–74.

Rey, G., and Lower, B. (eds) (1991) *Meaning in Mind: Fodor and His Critics*. Oxford: Basil Blackwell.

Robb, D. M. (2005) 'Qualitative unity and the bundle theory', *The Monist* 88: 466–92.

Roberts, A., and Roberts, B. L. (eds) (1983) *Neural Origin of Rhythmic Movements*. London: Cambridge University Press.

Roland, P. E., and Friberg, L. (1985) 'Localization of cortical areas activated by thinking', *Journal of Neurophysiology* 53: 1219–43.

Schilpp. P. A. (ed.) (1949) *Albert Einstein: Philosopher–Scientist*. Chicago: University of Chicago Press.

Schläfke, M. E., Koepchen, H. P., and See, W. R. (eds) (1983) *Central Neurone Environment and the Control Systems of Breathing and Circulation*. Berlin: Springer-Verlag.

Schmidt, R. F., and Thews, G. (eds) (1989) *Human Physiology* (2nd edn), Berlin: Springer-Verlag.

Searle, J. R. (1992) *The Rediscovery of the Mind*. Cambridge, MA: MIT Press.

Sellars, W. (1962) 'Philosophy and the scientific image of man'. In R. G. Colodny (ed.), *Frontiers of Science and Philosophy*. Pittsburgh: University of Pittsburgh Press, pp. 35–78. Reprinted in W. Sellars (1963) *Science, Perception, and Reality*. London: Routledge and Kegan Paul, pp. 1–40.

Sellars, W. (1963) *Science, Perception, and Reality*. London: Routledge and Kegan Paul.

Selverston, A. I., Miller, J. P., and Wadepuhl, M. (1983) 'Cooperative mechanisms for the production of rhythmic movements', In A. Roberts and B. L. Roberts (eds), *Neural Origin of Rhythmic Movements*. London: Cambridge University Press, pp. 55–88.

Sharkey, K. A. and Pittman, Q. J. (1995) 'The autonomic nervous system: Peripheral and central integrative aspects'. In R. Gerger, H. P. Koepahen, W. Monormaerts, and U. Windhorst (eds), *Autonomic Failure: A Textbook of Clinical Disoprders of the Autonomic Nervous System*. Oxford: Oxford University Press.

Shibata, M., Hori, T., Kiyohara, T., and Nakashima, T., (1988) 'Convergence of skin and hypothalamic temperature signals on the sulcal prefrontal cortex in the rat', *Brain Research* 443: 37–46.

Shoemaker, S. (1980) 'Causality and properties'. In P. van Inwagen (ed.) *Time and Cause*. Dordrecht: Reidel, pp. 109–35. Reprinted in S. Shoemaker, *Identity, Cause, and Mind: Philosophical Essays*, Cambridge: Cambridge University Press, pp. 206–33.

Shoemaker, S. (1984) *Identity, Cause, and Mind: Philosophical Essays*, Cambridge: Cambridge University Press.

Simons, P. (1994) 'Particulars in particular clothing: Three trope theories of substance', *Philosophy and Phenomenological Research* 54: 553–75.

Sinclair, N. R., and Challis, J. R. (1993) 'Tentativeness and fervor in cell biology require negative and positive feedforward control', *Life Sciences* 52 (25): 1985–93.

Smith, A. D. (1977) 'Dispositional properties', *Mind* 86: 439–45.

Spector, N. H. (1979) 'The central state of the hypothalamus in health and disease: Old and new concepts'. In P. J. Morgane and J. Panksepp (eds), *Handbook of the Hypothalamus: Vol. 2, Physiology of the Hypothalamus*. New York: Marcel Deker, pp. 453–517.

Spyer, K. M. (1992) 'Central nervous control of the cardiovascular system', in R. Bannister and E. J. Mathias (eds), *Autonomic Failure: A Textbook of Clinical Disorders of the Autonomic Nervous System*. Oxford: Oxford University Press, pp. 54–77.

Stephenson, R., and Hopkins, P. (1984) 'Comparative environmental physiology of sheep and goats during exposure to ambient heat stress'. In J. R. S. Hales (ed.), *Thermal Physiology*. New York: Raven Press, pp. 289–94.

Steriade, M. (1992) 'Basic mechanisms of sleep generation', *Neurology* 42 (7 Suppl 6): 9–17.

Strack, A. M., Sawyer, W. B., Hughes, J. H., Platt, K. B., and Loewy, A. D. (1989) 'A general pattern of CNS innervation of the sympathetic outflow demonstrated by transneuronal pseudorabies viral infections', *Brain Research* 491: 156–62.

Strawson, P. F. (1959) *Individuals: An Essay in Descriptive Metaphysics*. London: Methuen.

van Fraassen, B. C. (1980) *The Scientific Image*. Oxford: Clarendon Press.

van Inwagen, P. (ed.) (1980) *Time and Cause*. Dordrecht: Reidel.

von Békèsy, G. (1967). *Sensory Inhibition*. Princeton: Princeton University Press.

Weiskrantz, L. (1986) *Blindsight: A Case Study and its Implications*. Oxford: Clarendon Press.

Weiskrantz, L. (ed.) (1988) *Thought Without Language*. Oxford: Clarendon Press.

Williams, D. C. (1953) 'On the Elements of Being', *Review of Metaphysics* 7: 3–18, 171–92. Reprinted as 'The Elements of Being' in D. C. Williams (1966) *Principles of Empirical Realism*. Springfield: Charles C. Thomas, pp. 74–109.

Williams, D. C. (1966) *Principles of Empirical Realism*. Springfield: Charles C. Thomas.

Wittgenstein, L. (1953/1968) *Philosophical Investigations*, trans. G. E. M. Anscombe, Oxford: Basil Blackwell.

Wittgenstein, L. (1967) *Zettel*. G. E. M. Anscombe and G. H. von Wricht, eds. Translated by G. E. M, Anscombe. Oxford: Basil Blackwell.

# Index

about-ness; *see* intentionality
absence 3, 6, 32
*abstracta* 1, 29, 31, 47
abstraction 134, 145; *see also* partial
    consideration
acceleration 196–7
act, pure 54, 55, 68, 91
action 9
    mental 100, 148, 178, 180
    non-mental 122, 148
'action theory' 178
actuality 38, 47, 57, 60, 85, 140, 142,
    149
after-images 162–3
    negative 163
    positive 162
    tactile-motor-kinaesthetic 162–3
agency, 7, 185
    mental 180
ambiguous figure 54, 66, 67–9
analogy 159–60
Anscombe, G. E. M. 162, 163
Aristotle 151
anti-realism 83
*aqua regia* 51
Armstrong, D. M., 1, 5, 12, 20, 22,
    44, 64, 68, 72, 91, 111
artificial intelligence 111
attention, selective 81–3, 99
autonomic system 6, 119, 121, 122,
    146, 147, 178–81, 185, 193; *see
    also* vegetative systems;
    thermoregulatory system

background condition 50
Bacon, J. 43
Bannister, R. 137
behaviour xvi, 122, 158–60
    communicative 102, 104
    experientially loaded 97, 100
    intentional 187
    linguistic 158
    mental xvi
    sensory-guided 186
behaviourism 62, 67, 136, 158–60,
    176

belief, 8, 58, 99–100, 103, 106, 132,
    143, 147, 177, 179, 180, 182, 184,
    187, 188, 193
    as dispositional 58, 184, 186
    'occurrent' 58, 186
Bennett, J. 93, 101–2
Berkeley, G. 77, 135, 191
Bigelow, J, 28
Bird, A. 20
Bisiach, E. 9
Black, M. 27, 29
Blackburn, S. 67, 77
'blindsight' 168
Born, M. 71
Borut, A. 125
boundedness 41, 58
Bradley, M. C. 16
Brerngelmann, G. L. 126
Broad, C. D. vii, 21
Brown, A. C. 126
Brück, K. 124
bundle theory 44
Burge, T 144

Cain, W. S. 169
Campbell, K. 43
capacities 84–8; see also dispositions;
    properties, dispositional
    for capacities 84
capacity background 115–17
Carnap, R. 76
Cartwright, N. 40
categorization; *see* classification
causal explanation 182
causal network 5, 6, 21, 29, 47, 50, 52,
    87, 148, 183, 185
causal powers 149, 150, 182, 184; *see
    also* dispositions
causal role 148–9
causally operative 63, 80, 87, 165, 182
causation xv, 2, 3, 22, 35–6, 46–53,
    54–6, 64, 74, 86–7, 91, 107, 141,
    143, 161, 182, 188, 194, 195
    bottom-up 35–6, 37
    intentional 148–52
    local 23

causation (*cont.*)
  macro- 35, 74
  micro- 35, 74
  ontology of 48–53, 74, 91–2
  pipeline conception of 37, 130–1,
    133, 141
  singular 22
  top-down 35–6, 37
  two-event model, 46–7
*ceteris paribus* 16–18
Challis, J. R. 112
chance, pure 18, 22
change 54
charity 106
chauvinism, mental 138–9
Chomsky, N. 144, 175
class 42
classification 37, 82–4, 137
cognitive science 189–90
communication; *see* behaviour,
    communicative
compositional model 1, 36–42, 83–4,
    130–1
computationalism 148
concepts 41
conditionals, counterfactual xv, 1, 25,
    26, 31, 48–9, 67, 85, 107
  causal 19, 48
consciousness xv–xvi, 3, 6, 78–9, 136,
    146; *see also* experience,
    conscious
constitution 39
content 59, 112, 116, 143, 148, 175,
    184, 185, 187
  broad 4–5, 59, 60, 143
  narrow 4, 59, 60, 143
context 106, 120
contingency 3, 31, 63, 64, 74, 76
contradiction 33–4
corpuscles 65, 71, 77
  insensible 39
cortex 6, 7, 122, 124, 138, 147, 175
counterpart 29
covariation, property 63, 69, 74
creativity 32, 102, 161, 173, 175
Crick, B. 10, 160
Crusoe 102
Cytowic, R. E. 169

Damasio, A. R. 135
Dami'el, R. 125
Dampney, R. A. 119

Davidson, D. 84, 144
Dennett, D. C. 5
deontologizing 76–7, 85
Descartes, R. 43, 69
desire 99–100, 132, 143, 147, 177,
    179, 184, 186, 188, 193
  as dispositional 184
determinateness 32
Deutscher, M. 181
difference-making 27
directedness 2, 3, 5, 7, 9, 28, 29–33,
    57, 59, 83, 88, 105, 111, 112, 115,
    117, 142, 143, 177–8, 183, 187
  for any of a kind, 53, 59, 106, 118,
    185
  for an individual 9, 53, 59, 106, 185
  mental 177, 178
  nonmental 111, 114, 115, 177–8
discernability and indiscernibility, 27
discrimination, perceptual 80–3, 100,
    102, 145
  nonmental 180
disjunctive state, irreducibly 72–3
disposition base array 3, 5, 55–6, 57,
    58, 91–2, 115, 116, 148, 171, 175,
    177, 180, 183, 184, 186, 187
disposition breadth 3, 56–8, 60, 91–2,
    143
disposition depth 3, 55, 56–8, 60,
    91–2, 116, 143, 183
disposition flutter 72–3
disposition line 24–34
dispositionality; *see* dispositions
dispositions xv, 1–6, 12–23, 33,
    36–9, 54–6, 84–8, 111, 112,
    14–57, 136, 158, 181–3, 193; *see
    also* capacities; properties,
    dispositional; readinesses
  activating conditions 15–16
  causes of 143
  conditional analysis of 2, 12–23, 67,
    153–4
  for addition 155–6
  for dispositions 141–2
  forms of 20
  inhibitory 20, 29, 58, 60, 89, 118,
    157, 182
  reformed conditional analysis
    (RCA) 19–21
  as relations, 12–13
  Rylean 19
DNA 133

dreaming, 7, 9, 10, 121, 134, 145, 160–1, 173, 175
    inventive 173
Dummett, M. 57

Eddington, A. S. 41
Edelman, G. 124
Einstein, A. 23, 70, 71, 194, 198
electro-fink 14, 15, 17
Ellenberger, H. H. 124–5
    emergence 36, 129–32
uni-level 130–1
Engel, B. 122
Engen, T. 169
entailment 31, 62
epiphenomena 35
epistemic priority 26
epistemological fallibility 154–5, 159, 160
evolution 32, 135, 142, 181, 187
existentials, negative 1, 6
experience, conscious 63, 133, 134–6, 158–60, 187
    tactile motor kinaesthetic 163
explanation 132
    as mind-dependent 132
externalism 5, 53, 59, 143, 144, 152, 176

fact, counterfactual 19, 21–3
    non-localized 19
    second-order 19
falsehood 24, 25
feedback 115, 116, 118, 120, 121, 137, 145
    positive and negative 32, 112, 122, 126, 167, 177, 180, 187
    sensory xvi, 8, 62, 97, 120, 179, 191–3
feedforward 33, 112, 115, 116, 118, 121, 122–3, 125, 137, 146
feeling back 164
Feldman, J. L. 124–5
Fetzer, J. 61, 62
Feynman, R. 74–5
field, 2, 3, 39, 41
Fine, A. 69, 70
'finer interstices of nature' 40, 55, 65, 74, 78, 79
Fodor, J. A. 33, 144, 148–52, 177, 183
for-ness; 47–8, 57–61; 84; *see also* intentionality

Freeman, W. J. 169
Friberg, L. 168, 173
functional role 185
functionalism 66, 78, 114, 123, 128, 182, 185, 186

gap; *see also* introspection, causal gap in metaphysical 72–3
    spatial 46, 195
    temporal 46, 195
Georgopolous, A. 9
Getting, P. A. 78
Gibson, E. J. 163–4
God 64, 68, 91, 152, 183, 184, 198
Goodman, N. 16
Gordon, C. J. 126, 128
Gould, G. 62, 170
gradualism 29, 51–2, 178
    linguistic 93, 109–10
Gray, J. 119
grid; *see also* visual field
    sensory 189
    visual 166
group wholes 131

hallucination 7, 9, 121, 135, 138, 143, 158, 162, 175
    tactile-motor-kinaesthetic 162
    vegetative 176
Heath, J. E. 126, 128
Heil, J. vii, 6, 28, 31, 34, 153, 162, 163, 197
higher cognitive function 7
Hof, P. R. 148
holism 6, 59
*holus bolus* view 80
Hopkins, P. S. 125
Hori, T. 127–8
Hoskins, Z., vii
Hume, D. 48, 63, 74, 77, 165, 166, 181, 191
hypothalamus xv, 7, 32, 122, 124, 125, 136–7, 147

Ideal Observer 67
idealism 197
identity 37–8, 67–9
    conditions 47, 140
    surprising 67–9, 195
    causing and affecting 22
illusion 9, 113–15, 135, 162
    Aristotle's 113

illusion (*cont.*)
  Delboeuf 113, 115
  Helmholtz 113, 115
  Mach bands 113–14
  Müller–Lyer 113–14
  tactile-motor-kinaesthetic 162
image, manifest 40
image, scientific 40
imagery 7, 8–11, 24, 53, 134, 145,
    148, 160–1, 175, 186, 189, 191,
    193
  auditory 9
  'descriptive' 166, 167
  episodic 10
  hypnogogic 9
  hypnopompic 9
  interference with 173–4
  inventive 173, 175
  multimodal 9
  musical 170
  nonlinguistic 9
  non-propositional 134, 173
  nonverbal 166, 174–6
  partial 170–1
  physiology of 168–70
  'pictorial' 166, 167
  prelinguistic 9
  sensory 186
  tactile-motor-kinaesthetic 9
  verbal 9, 166–76
  visual rotation 173–4
implicature, linguistic and
    procedural 107
incorrigibility 161, 188, 192
indeterminacy 69, 72–3
indiscernibility; *see* discernibility and
    indiscernibility
infant 8, 102, 163, 174
infinity 3, 28, 30, 88–9, 154, 156,
    196–7
  bounded 30, 58
'information' 99, 100, 121, 127, 191
  theory 144
innateness 103
instant, temporal 46
integrated control center (ICC) 32,
    117–21, 136–7, 147, 175, 193
'intentionalistic halo' 151, 178, 186
intentionality xv, 33, 99, 148–52, 177,
    178, 185, 186
  broad 5
  narrow 5
  resides in use 186

interpretation 115, 117–18, 119, 167
introspection 160–1, 188–9
  causal gap in 187
introspective error 160–1

Jackson, F. C. 12, 44
Jessen, C. 125, 126
Johnson, J. M. 118

Kenney, W. L. 118
Kirk, R. 93
Kiyohara, T. 128
Knights, G. 125
knowledge, tacit; *see* tacit knowledge
Koepchen, H. P. 124
Kosslyn, S. M. 166
Kripke, S. 6, 153–5

Language of Thought 141, 142, 152,
    185
language, 24, 93–110
  learning 172–3
  private 103–4, 171
  proto-; *see* protolanguage
  social 103–4
  unshared 102
  verbal 103
lateral inhibition 113
law, causal 21, 223
level 36, 37
  of being 38, 130
  of description 38
  of explanation 37
  macro- 35–6, 46, 64, 77, 86, 130
  micro- 35–6, 64, 77, 86,
      90, 130
Lewis, D. K. xv, 1, 19–21, 22, 24,
    26–9, 31, 178, 182
Limit View 63, 65, 146
linguisticism 80–92
linguistic–nonlinguistic parallels 94–8
Llinás, R. 9, 122
Locke, J. vii, 1, 22, 39, 40, 43, 47, 64,
    65, 69, 74, 79, 87, 99, 100, 129,
    151, 152, 161, 164, 166,
    179, 181, 183, 186, 187, 188, 191,
    192, 193
Loewer, B. 148
Loewry, A. D. 126–6
logic 30, 31
Luria, A. R. 172
lying 108–9

Mackie, J. L. 181, 182
McLaughlin, B. P. 108
McTaggart, J. M. E. 197
manifestation 1, 29–33, 54–6
  as dispositional 91–2
  alternative 51–2, 55–6, 89, 183
  cue 7, 156, 171–3, 186
  mutual 3, 5, 6, 22–3, 29–30,
    46–53, 55–6, 60, 87, 88,
    89–91, 116, 117–18, 143–4,
    195
  typifying 60, 171, 172, 180, 187
  unmanifested 2, 5, 140, 142
map xv, 32, 119–20, 126
Marcel, A. 9
Margenau, H. 71
Martin, C. B., vii, 4, 5, 6, 12, 24, 28,
  31,29, 34, 44, 47, 54, 64, 80, 83,
  93, 98, 100, 153, 163, 181
materialism 11, 161
mathematics 25, 28, 30, 31, 33–4, 54,
  69, 72, 74–6, 78–9, 175
Mathias, E. J. 137
meaning; *see also* semantic point
  agent 105
  procedure 105
  public 105
  sentence 105
  speaker 105
  vehicles of 101–2
  iconic and noniconic 101–2
measurement 67–72, 73, 74, 75, 77,
  83, 133
Mellor, D. H. 22, 44, 61, 62, 68
memory 32, 121, 134, 137, 141, 143
  causal theory of 181
  muscular 141
mental chauvinism; *see* chauvinism,
  mental
mentality 51, 52–3
  nature of 138–9, 177–93
Micheson, G. 10, 160
mimicry 172–3; *see also* language
  learning
mind dependence 70, 82–3, 87, 132
miracle 26–7
modality 6, 25, 31, 65
mode; *see* trope
moleculo-fink 16
Molnar, G. 12, 19
Moore, G. E. 197
Morrison, J. H. 148

motion 196–8
motor system xv–xvi

natural kinds 181
necessity 1, 2, 18, 31, 63, 64, 69, 74, 76
nervous system
  autonomic 113, 117
  cerebral 113
neural network 78–9
neuropsycology 8
neuroscience 33, 78–9, 119–28
Nicoll, R. A. 168
'no nearest neighbour' 46, 194, 195
nonconscious systems, *see* nonmental
  systems; *see also* vegetative
  systems
nonexistence; *see* absence
nonmental systems xv–xvi, 3, 56, 58,
  59–61, 111–28, 146–8, 151,
  175–81; *see also* vegetative
  systems; *see also* motor system
number 54, 72–9

object 80, 81–2, 194–8
  as properties regions of
    space–time 195–8
  complex 36–40, 83–4, 129, 132
  not sharp-edged 129, 194–6
observer dependence; *see* mind
  dependence
ontology, basic xv, 1, 3, 33, 44, 48, 51,
  54, 60, 61–2, 69–72, 76, 79, 80,
  82, 89, 129, 136, 141, 177, 181,
  194, 197, 198
  ontological candour 26, 27, 61–2,
    184
  commitment 61
  ontological ground 20, 60, 71–2,
    73, 141
  ontological priority 26; *see also*
    epistemic priority, 70–1
'opacity' 179–80
operationalism 1, 66, 67, 77, 114, 136,
  182
other minds 159–60
'over and above' 37, 38, 131, 132
overdetermination 36

Pargetter, R. 12, 44
partial consideration 74–6, 77, 100; *see*
  *also* abstraction

particle, elementary 2, 3, 29–33, 37, 39, 41, 49–50, 52, 54, 55, 59, 60, 63, 64, 72–3, 74–76, 79, 83, 86, 89, 112, 129, 130, 133, 156, 157, 195
particularity 99–100
parts and wholes xv, 1, 35–45, 83–4, 129, 140; *see also* compositional model; group wholes
parts, *see* parts and wholes
Pauli, W. 71
Pellionisz, A. J. 122
perception 8–11, 60, 81–3, 115, 119, 120, 137, 160–1, 169–70, 191
   as dispositional 143–6
   causal theory of 181
   non-propositional 134, 173
   proprioceptive 169, 170
   reference in 181
   tactile-motor-kinaesthetic, xvi, 135, 162–5, 169, 179
   three-dimensional 164
   visual 163–4
Peré, D. 9
Pfeifer, K. 4, 100
phenomenalism 62, 67, 77, 136
physicalism 11, 161
physics 31, 33, 39, 40, 41, 44, 47–8, 54, 130, 133, 194–8
Pittman, Q. J. 137
Place, U. T., 5, 111
plenum 33, 40, 41
point, spatial 46
*possibilia* 12, 32, 140, 149, 150
possibility 38, 48, 50
power net; *see* causal network
powers; *see* dispositions active and passive 87, 182–3
predicate 80
Prior, E. W. 12, 44
private world problem 158–9
probabilities, 67–72
   irreducible 67–72
   higher-order 72
procedure 94–104
   communicative 104
   higher-order 104–6
   interrelated 99
   learned 103
   nonlinguistic 93–4, 174–6
   observational 99, 104
   semantic 94–104, 105, 109–10

shared 103
projectability; *see* directedness; for-ness; intentionality
properties xv, 1, 31, 35, 36, 38, 42–5, 54–79, 85, 111, 112, 136, 140, 144
   as particulars; *see* tropes
   as respects 42, 80, 81
   as tropes; *see* tropes
   as universals; *see* universals
   as ways 42, 64–5, 80
   categorical 44, 49
   complex 2, 89, 129
   dispositional 42, 44, 49, 58, 61–3, 64, 74, 77, 78–9, 145
   emergent 131
   extensional 129
   field 195–8
   inert 66
   intentional 149–50, 152
   intrinsic 2, 4, 61, 63, 64, 74, 77, 85, 113, 112, 130, 133
   irreducible 133
   macroscopic 129, 130
   mental 51–3, 182, 192
   microscopic 130
   nonmental 51–3, 58, 59–61
   nonqualitative 63
   occurrent 58
   semantic 3, 152
   simple 2, 49, 55
   qualitative 1, 2, 7, 33, 42, 44, 60, 63–7, 74, 77, 78–9, 85, 113, 121, 133, 134–6, 138–9, 145, 161
propositional attitudes 57, 193; *see also* belief; desire
propositions xv, 25, 98, 149, 151–2, 183–4
protolanguage 93–110
psychology
   cognitive 165
   developmental 8, 81, 175
Putnam, H. 144, 182
Pythagoreanism 1, 50, 54–79, 80–92
   neurological 78–9, 121, 133, 136

*qualia* 77, 145
   physical 77, 78–9; *see also* property, qualitative
qualities; *see* properties, qualitative
quality, secondary 77, 83

quantum theory xv, 69–73, 194
Quine, W. V. O. 20, 54, 55, 68, 76,
    80, 83, 86, 144, 181, 186
Quinlan, K. A. 137

Raichle, M. 168
readinesses 2, 4–6, 10, 23, 29–33,
    46–53, 58, 60, 71, 111, 175, 180,
    187; *see also* dispositions
anticipatory 32
realism 1, 26, 30, 41, 48, 60, 63, 66,
    79, 83–4, 85, 98, 181, 182
meaning 153
receptors 78, 90
reciprocal disposition partners 3,
    29–33, 46–53, 54–6, 57–8, 87,
    88, 89–92, 117, 118, 143–4,
    146–7, 154
recursive function 30
reduction 49, 51–2, 129, 132–4
explanatory 132
linguistic 131
ontological 130, 132
reference 59
causal theory of 181
Reisberg, D. 9
relations 35, 36, 38, 45, 82, 84, 149–50
relativity, general xv, 194, 198
REM 10
representation xv, 24, 25, 28, 96–100,
    116
nonlinguistic 29, 96–8, 116
perceptual 99
representational use; *see* use,
    representational
representationalism 8
resemblance; *see* similarity
respects; *see* properties as respects
Rey, G. 148
Robb, D. M. 43
Robertshaw, D. 125
Roland, P. E. 168, 173
rule 29, 94, 95, 104, 153–7, 196–7
rule following 6, 33–4, 94, 95, 104,
    105, 152, 153–7
Russell, B. 22, 79, 129
Ryder, J. D., vii
Ryle, G. 19, 56, 95, 134, 170, 181, 193

Sachtung, Wal 12
satisfaction 96

Sauvé, K. vii, 90
Schrödinger, E. 69–71
Searle, J. 35
secondary cue 134
secondary quality; *see* quality,
    secondary
Sellars, W. 40
Selverston, A. I. 78
semantic evolution 94
semantic ooze 93, 178
semantic point 93–4, 95, 96, 100,
    103–4
semantics 96–8
prelinguistic 93–4, 96–8
sensory feedback; *see* feedback,
    sensory
sentence 94–6, 103–5, 148, 174
sentience 122
Sharkey, K. A. 137
Shepard, R. 166
Shibata, M. 128
Shoemaker, S. 44, 61, 62, 63
signal
afferent 122, 125, 127, 128, 168
centrally caused 175, 176
efferent 122, 125, 128, 168
enhancement 168–9
enrichment 169
external 138, 145, 167, 168, 169
internal 138, 145, 167, 168
magnification 168, 169
similarity 42–4, 80, 81–3, 89, 101
qualitative 27, 114, 134, 135,
    138–9, 145, 160–1, 176, 188
relational 27
Sinclair, N. R. 111
sleep 122, 124
Smart, J. J. C. 12, 178
Smith, A. D. 12
Snowdon, P. 100
socialization 102
solidity 41
space 165
space–time 1, 29, 31, 38, 75, 82–3,
    86, 194–8
as substratum 195
regions 44, 47, 129
segment 54, 83, 195, 198
warps and woofs 47
Spector, N. H. 120, 137, 147
Spinoza, B. 43, 69, 198
Spyer, K. M. 119

St. Thomas Aquinas 68
stage, temporal 54, 85
Stebbing, S. 41
Stephenson, R. 125
Steriade, M. 121–2
Stich, S. P. 144
Strack, A. M. 126
Strawson, P. F. 162, 163
structure, 2, 49–50, 54, 55, 86, 123
subject–predicate 96–7
substance 31
substratum 1, 44, 47, 195; *see also*
    space–time as substratum
supervenience 1, 35, 36, 64,
    86, 132
symbol, 24
syntax 95

tacit knowledge 173–4
tactile-motor-kinaesthetic imagery; *see*
    imagery,
    tactile-motor-kinaesthetic
perception; *see* perception,
    tactile-motor-kinaesthetic
thermodynamics 77, 79, 133, 136
thermoregulatory system 111, 116,
    119, 120, 123–4, 126–8, 136,
    176, 179
thinking 58, 180
    counterfactual 107
    general 174, 179, 186
    imageless 167
    mathematical 101
    negative 174
    operational 101
    procedural 101
Thomas Aquinas, Saint 68
thought; *see* thinking
tropes 43, 81–3
    non-transfeerable 44
    transferable 44
truth 24–34, 97, 98–99, 104
truth bearers 24, 28, 29, 33
truthmakers 24–34, 63
Truthmaker Principle 24, 25
truthmaking xv, 24–34
Twain, M. 21
Twin Earth 152, 185

universality 99, 110, 151, 186
universals 1, 31, 43, 80, 81–3, 98, 183

universe, null 31
use 6–10, 32–3, 111–28, 177–81
    of imagery 166–76
use, representational 32, 33, 98–100,
    111–12, 118, 135–8, 148, 151–2,
    183–4, 189
    agent of; *see* use, instrument of
    background 190
    conscious 33, 116, 138
    discriminatory and comparative, and
        contrastive 191
    inferential 191, 193
    instrument of 178–9, 186
    internal 138
    linguistic 119, 137
    material of 113, 115, 135, 178–9,
        186, 187, 189–93
    mechanism of; *see* use, instrument of
    mental 10, 33, 111–16, 123,
        148
    mode of operation of 178–9, 186
    nonlinguistic 112, 119
    nonmental 6–7, 111–17, 118, 123,
        137, 148, 179–81
    'passing through' material of 191–3
    phenomenological savouring 190–1
    projective 179
    reverie 190
    sensate material of 186, 187, 189–93

van Fraassen, B. 40
vegetative mind 123–8, 138–9, 175
vegetative state 121
    higher-order 125
vegetative systems xv–xvi, 6–7, 111,
    123, 124, 125, 126, 136–8, 146
verification 89
verificationism 27, 66–7, 76
    strong 66
    weak 66
verification-transcendent 66–7
visual cliff 163–4
visual field 8, 135; *see also* grid
von Békèsy, G. 113

word, 94–5, 98
Walk, R. D. 163–4
wave function 67, 71, 73
ways; *see* properties as ways
web, disposition; *see* causal network
Weiskrantz, L. 9, 168

wholes, *see* parts and wholes
Williams, D. C. 43
Wisdom, J. 131, 197
Wittgenstein, L. vii, 151, 153–5, 166, 172, 179, 186, 187, 193, 197

worlds, alternative 1, 20, 22, 23, 25–33, 48, 98, 149, 182, 183, 184
worlds, possible; *see* worlds, alternative

Zeisberger, E. 124

# Index of Names

Anscombe, G. E. M. 162, 163
Aristotle 151
Armstrong, D. M., 1, 5, 12, 20, 22,
    44, 64, 68, 72, 91, 111

Bacon, J. 43
Bannister, R. 137
Bennett, J. 93, 101–2
Berkeley, G. 77, 135, 191
Bigelow, J. 28
Bird, A. 20
Bisiach, E. 9
Black, M. 27, 29
Blackburn, S. 67, 77
Born, M. 71
Borut, A. 125
Bradley, M. C. 16
Broad, C. D. vii, 21
Brown, A. C. 126
Brerngelmann, G. L. 126
Brück, K. 124
Burge, T 144

Cain, W. S. 169
Campbell, K. 43
Carnap, R. 76
Cartwright, N. 40
Challis, J. R. 112
Chomsky, N. 144, 175
Crick, B. 10, 160
Cytowic, R. E. 169

Damasio, A. R. 135
Dami'el, R. 125
Dampney, R. A. 119
Davidson, D. 84, 144
Dennett, D. C. 5
Descartes, R. 43, 69
Deutscher, M. 181
Dummett, M. 57

Eddington, A. S. 41
Edelman, G. 124
Einstein, A. 23, 70, 71, 194, 198
Ellenberger, H. H. 124–5

Engel, B. 122
Engen, T. 169

Feldman, J. L. 124–5
Fetzer, J. 61, 62
Feynman, R. 74–5
Fine, A. 69, 70
Fodor, J. A. 33, 144, 148–52, 177, 183
Freeman, W. J. 169
Friberg, L. 168, 173

Georgopolous, A. 9
Getting, P. A. 78
Gibson, E. J. 163–4
Goodman, N. 16
Gordon, C. J. 126, 128
Gould, G. 62, 170
Gray, J. 119

Heath, J. E. 126, 128
Heil, J. vii, 6, 28, 31, 34, 153, 162,
    163, 197
Hof, P. R. 148
Hopkins, P. S. 125
Hori, T. 127–8
Hoskins, Z., vii
Hume, D. 48, 63, 74, 77, 165, 166,
    181, 191

Jackson, F. C. 12, 44
Jessen, C. 125, 126
Johnson, J. M. 118

Kenney, W. L. 118
Kirk, R. 93
Kiyohara, T. 128
Knights, G. 125
Koepchen, H. P. 124
Kosslyn, S. M. 166
Kripke, S. 6, 153–5

Lewis, D. K. xv, 1, 19–21, 22, 24,
    26–9, 31, 178, 182
Llinás, R. 9, 122

Locke, J. vii, 1, 22, 39, 40, 43, 47, 64,
     65, 69, 74, 79, 87, 99, 100, 129,
     151, 152, 161, 164, 166, 179, 181,
     183, 186, 187, 188, 191, 192, 193
Loewer, B. 148
Loewry, A. D. 126–6
Luria, A. R. 172

Mackie, J. L. 181, 182
McLaughlin, B. P. 108
McTaggart, J. M. E. 197
Marcel, A. 9
Margenau, H. 71
Martin, C. B., vii, 4, 5, 6, 12, 24, 28,
     31,29, 34, 44, 47, 54, 64, 80, 83,
     93, 98, 100, 153, 163, 181
Mathias, E. J. 137
Mellor, D. H. 22, 44, 61, 62, 68
Micheson, G. 10, 160
Molnar, G. 12, 19
Moore, G. E. 197
Morrison, J. H. 148

Nicoll, R. A. 168

Pargetter, R. 12, 44
Pauli, W. 71
Pellionisz, A. J. 122
Peré, D. 9
Pfeifer, K. 4, 100
Pittman, Q. J. 137
Place, U. T., 5, 111
Prior, E. W. 12, 44
Putnam, H. 144, 182

Quine, W. V. O. 20, 54, 55, 68, 76,
     80, 83, 86, 144, 181, 186
Quinlan, K. A. 137

Raichle, M. 168
Reisberg, D. 9
Rey, G. 148
Robb, D. M. 43
Robertshaw, D. 125

Roland, P. E. 168, 173
Russell, B. 22, 79, 129
Ryder, J. D., vii
Ryle, G. 19, 56, 95, 134, 170,
     181, 193

Sachtung, Wal 12
Sauvé, K. vii, 90
Schrödinger, E. 69–71
Searle, J. 35
Sellars, W. 40
Selverston, A. I. 78
Sharkey, K. A. 137
Shepard, R. 166
Shibata, M. 128
Shoemaker, S. 44, 61, 62, 63
Sinclair, N. R. 112
Smart, J. J. C. 12, 178
Smith, A. D. 12
Snowdon, P. 100
Spector, N. H. 120, 137, 147
Spinoza, B. 43, 69, 198
Spyer, K. M. 119
Stebbing, S. 41
Steriade, M. 121–2
Stephenson, R. 125
Stich, S. P. 144
Strack, A. M. 126
Strawson, P. F. 162, 163
St. Thomas Aquinas 68

Twain, M. 21

van Fraassen, B. 40
von Békésy, G. 113

Walk, R. D. 163–4
Weiskrantz, L. 9, 168
Williams, D. C. 43
Wisdom, J. 131, 197
Wittgenstein, L. vii, 151, 153–5, 166,
     172, 179, 186, 187, 193, 197

Zeisberger, E. 124

# Index of Topics

about-ness; *see* intentionality
absence 3, 6, 32
*abstracta* 1, 29, 31, 47
abstraction 134, 145; *see also* partial
    consideration
acceleration 196–7
act, pure 54, 55, 68, 91
action 9
    mental 100, 148, 178, 180
    nonmental 122, 148
'action theory' 178
actuality 38, 47, 57, 60, 85, 140, 142,
    149
after-images 162–3
    negative 163
    positive 162
    tactile-motor-kinaesthetic 162–3
agency, 7, 185
    mental 180
ambiguous figure 54, 66, 67–9
analogy 159–60
anti-realism 83
*aqua regia* 51
artificial intelligence 111
attention, selective 81–3, 99
autonomic system 6, 119, 121, 122,
    146, 147, 178–81, 185, 193; *see
    also* vegetative systems;
    thermoregulatory system

background condition 50
behaviour xvi, 122, 158–60
    communicative 102, 104
    experientially loaded 97, 100
    intentional 187
    linguistic 158
    mental xvi
    sensory-guided 186
behaviourism 62, 67, 136, 158–60,
    176
belief, 8, 58, 99–100, 103, 106, 132,
    143, 147, 177, 179, 180, 182, 184,
    187, 188, 193
    as dispositional 58, 184, 186
    'occurrent' 58, 186
'blindsight' 168

boundedness 41, 58
bundle theory 44

capacities 84–8; see also dispositions;
    properties, dispositional for
    capacities 84
capacity background 115–17
categorization; *see* classification
causal explanation 182
causal network 5, 6, 21, 29, 47, 50, 52,
    87, 148, 183, 185
causal powers 149, 150, 182, 184; *see
    also* dispositions
causal role 148–9
causally operative 63, 80, 87, 165, 182
causation xv, 2, 3, 22, 35–6, 46–53,
    54–6, 64, 74, 86–7, 91, 107, 141,
    143, 161, 182, 188, 194, 195
    bottom-up 35–6, 37
    intentional 148–52
    local 23
    macro- 35, 74
    micro- 35, 74
    ontology of 48–53, 74, 91–2
    pipeline conception of 37, 130–1,
    133, 141
    singular 22
    top-down 35–6, 37
    two-event model, 46–7
*ceteris paribus* 16–18
chance, pure 18, 22
change 54
charity 106
chauvinism, mental 138–9
class 42
classification 37, 82–4, 137
cognitive science 189–90
communication; *see* behaviour,
    communicative
compositional model 1, 36–42, 83–4,
    130–1
computationalism 148
concepts 41
conditionals, counterfactual xv, 1, 25,
    26, 31, 48–9, 67, 85, 107
    causal 19, 48

consciousness xv–xvi, 3, 6, 78–9, 136,
    146; *see also* experience, conscious
constitution 39
content 59, 112, 116, 143, 148, 175,
    184, 185, 187
  broad 4–5, 59, 60, 143
  narrow 4, 59, 60, 143
context 106, 120
contingency 3, 31, 63, 64, 74, 76
contradiction 33–4
corpuscles 65, 71, 77
  insensible 39
cortex 6, 7, 122, 124, 138, 147, 175
counterpart 29
covariation, property 63, 69, 74
creativity 32, 102, 161, 173, 175
Crusoe 102

deontologizing 76–7, 85
desire 99–100, 132, 143, 147, 177,
    179, 184, 186, 188, 193
  as dispositional 184
determinateness 32
difference-making 27
directedness 2, 3, 5, 7, 9, 28, 29–33,
    57, 59, 83, 88, 105, 111, 112, 115,
    117, 142, 143, 177–8, 183, 187
  for any of a kind, 53, 59, 106, 118,
    185
  for an individual 9, 53, 59, 106, 185
  mental 177, 178
  nonmental 111, 114, 115, 177–8
discernability and indiscernibility, 27
discrimination, perceptual 80–3, 100,
    102, 145
  nonmental 180
disjunctive state, irreducibly 72–3
disposition base array 3, 5, 55–6, 57,
    58, 91–2, 115, 116, 148, 171, 175,
    177, 180, 183, 184, 186, 187
disposition breadth 3, 56–8, 60, 91–2,
    143
disposition depth 3, 55, 56–8, 60,
    91–2, 116, 143, 183
disposition flutter 72–3
disposition line 24–34
dispositionality; *see* dispositions
dispositions xv, 1–6, 12–23, 33,
    36–9, 54–6, 84–8, 111, 112,
    14–57, 136, 158, 181–3, 193; *see
    also* capacities; properties,

dispositional; readinesses
  activating conditions 15–16
  causes of 143
  conditional analysis of 2, 12–23, 67,
    153–4
  for addition 155–6
  for dispositions 141–2
  forms of 20
  inhibitory 20, 29, 58, 60, 89, 118,
    157, 182
  reformed conditional analysis
    (RCA) 19–21
  as relations, 12–13
  Rylean 19
DNA 133
dreaming, 7, 9, 10, 121, 134, 145,
    160–1, 173, 175
  inventive 173

electro-fink 14, 15, 17
emergence 36, 129–32
  uni-level 130–1
entailment 31, 62
epiphenomena 35
epistemic priority 26
epistemological fallibility 154–5, 159,
    160
evolution 32, 135, 142, 181, 187
existentials, negative 1, 6
experience, conscious 63, 133, 134–6,
    158–60, 187
  tactile-motor-kinaesthetic 163
explanation 132
  as mind-dependent 132
externalism 5, 53, 59, 143, 144, 152,
    170

fact, counterfactual 19, 21–3
  non-localized 19
  second-order 19
falsehood 24, 25
feedback 115, 116, 118, 120, 121, 137,
    145
  positive and negative 32, 112, 122,
    126, 167, 177, 180, 187
  sensory xvi, 8, 62, 97, 120, 179,
    191–3
feedforward 33, 112, 115, 116, 118,
    121, 122–3, 125, 137, 146
feeling back 164
field, 2, 3, 39, 41

'finer interstices of nature' 40, 55, 65,
    74, 78, 79
for-ness; 47–8, 57–61; 84; *see also*
    intentionality
functional role 185
functionalism 66, 78, 114, 123, 128,
    182, 185, 186

gap; *see also* introspection, causal gap in
    metaphysical 72–3
    spatial 46, 195
    temporal 46, 195
God 64, 68, 91, 152, 183, 184, 198
gradualism 29, 51–2, 178
    linguistic 93, 109–10
grid; *see also* visual field
    sensory 189
    visual 166
group wholes 131

hallucination 7, 9, 121, 135, 138, 143,
    158, 162, 175
    tactile-motor-kinaesthetic 162
    vegetative 176
higher cognitive function 7
holism 6, 59
*holus bolus* view 80
hypothalamus xv, 7, 32, 122, 124, 125,
    136–7, 147

Ideal Observer 67
idealism 197
identity 37–8, 67–9
    conditions 47, 140
    surprising 67–9, 195
    causing and affecting 22
illusion 9, 113–15, 135, 162
    Aristotle's 113
    Delboeuf 113, 115
    Helmholtz 113, 115
    Mach bands 113–14
    Müller–Lyer 113–14
    tactile-motor-kinaesthetic 162
image, manifest 40
image, scientific 40
imagery 7, 8–11, 24, 53, 134, 145,
    148, 160–1, 175, 186, 189, 191,
    193
    auditory 9
    'descriptive' 166, 167
    episodic 10
    hypnogogic 9

hypnopompic 9
    interference with 173–4
    inventive 173, 175
    multimodal 9
    musical 170
    nonlinguistic 9
    non-propositional 134, 173
    nonverbal 166, 174–6
    partial 170–1
    physiology of 168–70
    'pictorial' 166, 167
    prelinguistic 9
    sensory 186
    tactile-motor-kinaesthetic 9
    verbal 9, 166–76
    visual rotation 173–4
implicature, linguistic and
    procedural 107
incorrigibility 161, 188, 192
indeterminacy 69, 72–3
indiscernibility; *see* discernibility and
    indiscernibility
infant 8, 102, 163, 174
infinity 3, 28, 30, 88–9, 154, 156,
    196–7
    bounded 30, 58
'information' 99, 100, 121,
    127, 191
    theory 144
innateness 103
instant, temporal 46
integrated control center (ICC) 32,
    117–21, 136–7, 147, 175, 193
'intentionalistic halo' 151, 178, 186
intentionality xv, 33, 99, 148–52, 177,
    178, 185, 186
    broad 5
    narrow 5
    resides in use 186
interpretation 115, 117–18, 119, 167
introspection 160–1, 188–9
    causal gap in 187
introspective error 160–1

knowledge, tacit; *see* tacit knowledge

Language of Thought 141, 142, 152,
    185
language, 24, 93–110
    learning 172–3
    private 103–4, 171
    proto-; *see* protolanguage

social 103–4
unshared 102
verbal 103
lateral inhibition 113
law, causal 21, 223
level 36, 37
of being 38, 130
of description 38
of explanation 37
macro- 35–6, 46, 64, 77, 86, 130
micro- 35–6, 64, 77, 86, 90, 130
Limit View 63, 65, 146
linguisticism 80–92
linguistic–nonlinguistic parallels 94–8
logic 30, 31
lying 108–9

manifestation 1, 29–33, 54–6
as dispositional 91–2
alternative 51–2, 55–6, 89, 183
cue 7, 156, 171–3, 186
mutual 3, 5, 6, 22–3, 29–30,
46–53, 55–6, 60, 87, 88,
89–91, 116, 117–18, 143–4,
195
typifying 60, 171, 172, 180, 187
unmanifested 2, 5, 140, 142
map xv, 32, 119–20, 126
materialism 11, 161
mathematics 25, 28, 30, 31, 33–4, 54,
69, 72, 74–6, 78–9, 175
meaning; *see also* semantic point
agent 105
procedure 105
public 105
sentence 105
speaker 105
vehicles of 101–2
iconic and noniconic 101–2
measurement 67–72, 73, 74, 75, 77,
83, 133
memory 32, 121, 134, 137, 141, 143
causal theory of 181
muscular 141
mental chauvinism; *see* chauvinism,
mental
mentality 51, 52–3
nature of 138–9, 177–93
mimicry 172–3; *see also* language
learning
mind dependence 70, 82–3, 87, 132
miracle 26–7

modality 6, 25, 31, 65
mode; *see* trope
moleculo-fink 16
motion 196–8
motor system xv–xvi

natural kinds 181
necessity 1, 2, 18, 31, 63, 64, 69, 74, 76
nervous system
autonomic 113, 117
cerebral 113
neural network 78–9
neuropsycology 8
neuroscience 33, 78–9, 119–28
'no nearest neighbour' 46, 194, 195
nonconscious systems, *see* nonmental
systems; *see also* vegetative
systems
nonexistence; *see* absence
nonmental systems xv–xvi, 3, 56, 58,
59–61, 111–28, 146–8, 151,
175–81; *see also* vegetative
systems; *see also* motor system
number 54, 72–9

object 80, 81–2, 194–8
as properties regions of
space–time 195–8
complex 36–40, 83–4, 129, 132
not sharp-edged 129, 194–6
observer dependence; *see* mind
dependence
ontology, basic xv, 1, 3, 33, 44, 48, 51,
54, 60, 61–2, 69–72, 76, 79, 80,
82, 89, 129, 136, 141, 177, 181,
194, 197, 198
ontological candour 26, 27, 61–2,
184
commitment 61
ontological ground 20, 60, 71–2,
73, 141
ontological priority 26; *see also*
epistemic priority, 70–1
'opacity' 179–80
operationalism 1, 66, 67, 77, 114, 136,
182
other minds 159–60
over and above 37, 38, 131, 132
overdetermination 36

partial consideration 74–6, 77, 100; *see
also* abstraction

particle, elementary 2, 3, 29–33, 37,
    39, 41, 49–50, 52, 54, 55, 59, 60,
    63, 64, 72–3, 74–76, 79, 83, 86,
    89, 112, 129, 130, 133, 156, 157,
    195
particularity 99–100
parts and wholes xv, 1, 35–45, 83–4,
    129, 140; *see also* compositional
    model; group wholes
parts, *see* parts and wholes
perception 8–11, 60, 81–3, 115, 119,
    120, 137, 160–1, 169–70, 191
    as dispositional 143–6
    causal theory of 181
    non-propositional 134, 173
    proprioceptive 169, 170
    reference in 181
    tactile-motor-kinaesthetic, xvi, 135,
        162–5, 169, 179
    three-dimensional 164
    visual 163–4
phenomenalism 62, 67, 77, 136
physicalism 11, 161
physics 31, 33, 39, 40, 41, 44, 47–8,
    54, 130, 133, 194–8
plenum 33, 40, 41
point, spatial 46
*possibilia* 12, 32, 140, 149, 150
possibility 38, 48, 50
power net; *see* causal network
powers; *see* dispositions active and
    passive 87, 182–3
predicate 80
private world problem 158–9
probabilities, 67–72
    irreducible 67–72
    higher-order 72
procedure 94–104
    communicative 104
    higher-order 104–6
    interrelated 99
    learned 103
    nonlinguistic 93–4, 174–6
    observational 99, 104
    semantic 94–104, 105, 109–10
    shared 103
projectability; *see* directedness;
    for-ness; intentionality
properties xv, 1, 31, 35, 36, 38, 42–5,
    54–79, 85, 111, 112, 136, 140,
    144
    as particulars; *see* tropes
    as respects 42, 80, 81
    as tropes; *see* tropes
    as universals; *see* universals
    as ways 42, 64–5, 80
    categorical 44, 49
    complex 2, 89, 129
    dispositional 42, 44, 49, 58, 61–3,
        64, 74, 77, 78–9, 145
    emergent 131
    extensional 129
    field 195–8
    inert 66
    intentional 149–50, 152
    intrinsic 2, 4, 61, 63, 64, 74, 77, 85,
        113, 112, 130, 133
    irreducible 133
    macroscopic 129, 130
    mental 51–3, 182, 192
    microscopic 130
    nonmental 51–3, 58, 59–61
    nonqualitative 63
    occurrent 58
    semantic 3, 152
    simple 2, 49, 55
    qualitative 1, 2, 7, 33, 42, 44, 60,
        63–7, 74, 77, 78–9, 85, 113,
        121, 133, 134–6, 138–9, 145,
        161
propositional attitudes 57, 193; *see also*
    belief; desire
propositions xv, 25, 98, 149, 151–2,
    183–4
protolanguage 93–110
psychology
    cognitive 165
    developmental 8, 81, 175
Pythagoreanism 1, 50, 54–79, 80–92
    neurological 78–9, 121, 133, 136

*qualia* 77, 145
    physical 77, 78–9; *see also* property,
        qualitative
qualities; *see* properties, qualitative
quality, secondary 77, 83
quantum theory xv, 69–73, 194

readinesses 2, 4–6, 10, 23, 29–33,
    46–53, 58, 60, 71, 111, 175, 180,
    187; *see also* dispositions
    anticipatory 32
realism 1, 26, 30, 41, 48, 60, 63, 66,
    79, 83–4, 85, 98, 181, 182
    meaning 153

receptors 78, 90
reciprocal disposition partners 3,
    29–33, 46–53, 54–6, 57–8, 87,
    88, 89–92, 117, 118, 143–4,
    146–7, 154
recursive function 30
reduction 49, 51–2, 129, 132–4
    explanatory 132
    linguistic 131
    ontological 130, 132
reference 59
    causal theory of 181
relations 35, 36, 38, 45, 82, 84, 149–50
relativity, general xv, 194, 198
REM 10
representation xv, 24, 25, 28, 96–100,
    116
    nonlinguistic 29, 96–8, 116
    perceptual 99
representational use; *see* use,
    representational
representationalism 8
resemblance; *see* similarity
respects; *see* properties as respects
rule 29, 94, 95, 104, 153–7, 196–7
rule following 6, 33–4, 94, 95, 104,
    105, 152, 153–7

satisfaction 96
secondary cue 134
secondary quality; *see* quality,
    secondary
semantic evolution 94
semantic ooze 93, 178
semantic point 93–4, 95, 96, 100,
    103–4
semantics 96–8
    prelinguistic 93–4, 96–8
sensory feedback; *see* feedback,
    sensory
sentence 94–6, 103–5, 148, 174
sentience 122
signal
    afferent 122, 125, 127, 128, 168
    centrally caused 175, 176
    efferent 122, 125, 128, 168
    enhancement 168–9
    enrichment 169
    external 138, 145, 167, 168, 169
    internal 138, 145, 167, 168
    magnification 168, 169
similarity 42–4, 80, 81–3, 89, 101

qualitative 27, 114, 134, 135,
    138–9, 145, 160–1, 176, 188
    relational 27
sleep 122, 124
socialization 102
solidity 41
space 165
space–time 1, 29, 31, 38, 75, 82–3,
    86, 194–8
    as substratum 195
    regions 44, 47, 129
    segment 54, 83, 195, 198
    warps and woofs 47
stage, temporal 54, 85
structure, 2, 49–50, 54, 55, 86, 123
subject-predicate 96–7
substance 31
substratum 1, 44, 47, 195; *see also*
    space–time as substratum
supervenience 1, 35, 36, 64, 86, 132
symbol, 24
syntax 95

tacit knowledge 173–4
tactile-motor-kinaesthetic imagery; *see*
    imagery,
    tactile-motor-kinaesthetic
    perception; *see* perception,
    tactile-motor-kinaesthetic
thermodynamics 77, 79, 133, 136
thermoregulatory system 111, 116,
    119, 120, 123–4, 126–8, 136,
    176, 179
thinking 58, 180
    counterfactual 107
    general 174, 179, 186
    imageless 167
    mathematical 101
    negative 174
    operational 101
    procedural 101
Thomas Aquinas, Saint 68
thought; *see* thinking
tropes 43, 81–3
    non-transferable 44
    transferable 44
truth 24–34, 97, 98–99, 104
truth bearer 24, 28, 29, 33
truthmaker 24–34, 63
Truthmaker Principle 24, 25
truthmaking xv, 24–34
Twin Earth 152, 185

universality 99, 110, 151, 186
universals 1, 31, 43, 80, 81–3, 98, 183
universe, null 31
use 6–10, 32–3, 111–28, 177–81
    of imagery 166–76
use, representational 32, 33, 98–100,
    111–12, 118, 135–8, 148, 151–2,
    183–4, 189
  agent of; *see* use, instrument of
    background 190
  conscious 33, 116, 138
  discriminatory and comparative, and
    contrastive 191
  inferential 191, 193
  instrument of 178–9, 186
  internal 138
  linguistic 119, 137
  material of 113, 115, 135, 178–9,
    186, 187, 189–93
  mechanism of; *see* use, instrument
    of
  mental 10, 33, 111–16, 123, 148
  mode of operation of 178–9, 186
  nonlinguistic 112, 119
  nonmental 6–7, 111–17, 118, 123,
    137, 148, 179–81
  'passing through' material of 191–3
  phenomenological savouring 190–1

projective 179
reverie 190
sensate material of 186, 187, 189–93

vegetative mind 123–8, 138–9, 175
vegetative state 121
  higher-order 125
vegetative systems xv–xvi, 6–7, 111,
    123, 124, 125, 126, 136–8, 146
verification 89
verificationism 27, 66–7, 76
  strong 66
  weak 66
verification-transcendent 66–7
visual cliff 163–4
visual field 8, 135; *see also* grid

word, 94–5, 98
wave function 67, 71, 73
ways; *see* properties as ways
web, disposition; *see* causal network
wholes, *see* parts and wholes
worlds, alternative 1, 20, 22, 23,
    25–33, 48, 98, 149, 182,
    183, 184
worlds, possible; *see* worlds,
    alternative